Eliminate Your Competition

A Trapper's Guide to Increasing Your Commission

Sean O'Shaughnessey

ISBN: 0692111921
ISBN-13: 978-0692111925

Dedication

To Ryan, Erin and Connor

My 3 wonderful children that have taught me more about life than anyone else

To my wife Sharon

You have been the love of my life as I have learned to master my craft and create the content of this book. Thank you for your patience, support, and love.

CONTENTS

Acknowledgments

This book is the accumulation of decades of working with sales managers, fellow salespeople, pre-sales technical support people, and most notably, customers. I have learned from all of you in some way, and this book is a reflection on that learning. This book would not have been written if it was not for your interactions over the years.

I am also appreciative of all of the authors of the dozens of sales process books and sales classes that I have taken over the many years. This book is an improvement on those many tools, but I could not have written this book if I hadn't learned the basics over the years.

Chapter 1 – Introduction To Trapping

"Winning is not a sometime thing. You don't win once in a while; you don't do things right once in a while; you do them right all the time. Winning is a habit. Unfortunately, so is losing."

- Vince Lombardi

Most salespeople lose the deal before they ever get started! It isn't uncommon for the customer to have already made a decision before most salespeople even learn of the opportunity. Most salespeople have to beat the preferred competitor by a significant margin just to be considered equivalent. Don't you wish that you could be the preferred vendor in all of your opportunities?

Selling is a difficult career in which to make a living; it is not uncommon to have the commission check denied before the salesperson even gets a chance to win. Analysis of thousands of sales situations has made it phenomenally obvious that most salespeople begin their sales campaign so late in the decision-making process that they are virtually guaranteed to lose the order. To make matters worse, when they do start the campaign early enough, most salespeople do not know how to control the prospect adequately so that they can guarantee their victory.

Typical turnover for a sales department is 10-20%. Many companies see turnover that approaches 40-60%! This turnover costs them 50%

1

of their revenue-generating capability. In any organization that exceeds 25% turnover, the loss of trust with the customer can be astounding as the new salesperson tries to rebuild the entire relationship. Further, a salesperson who is making quota is probably not going to leave the company. Excessive turnover means that for six to eighteen months before leaving, the territory was not performing well and then the salesperson left. To make matters worse, this lack of performance is followed by weeks (and maybe months) of no coverage (or little coverage) as a replacement is found, trained, and starts to become productive.

Other organizations such as accounting or manufacturing in the company see a turnover that is under 10%. Why is selling so difficult that two to ten times as many people fail in the profession compared to any other profession? This book is designed to reduce or eliminate this problem by explaining how to be successful in the sales profession.

In any given quarter dozens or hundreds of companies do not make their forecasted numbers and are dramatically punished by Wall Street. This book will provide the management of a company with a framework to teach their salespeople how to attain their quotas with higher profits. It will also allow salespeople to rise to the top of their organization and be the super-achievers who win awards, trips, bonuses, and respect.

Most sales strategies on the market do an excellent job of trying to teach the salesperson how to align the vision between the vendor and the customer. The overall problem with this is that just because your 'vision' aligns with the prospect does not necessitate that you will win the order; after all, your competitors know how to align vision as well. Hence, we must take the process to the next step; we must learn how to eliminate our competition so that the customer has little choice but to buy our solution. This strategy results in higher win rates and higher levels of profitability.

The most successful salespeople are Trappers by nature. The salesperson may not completely understand the techniques that make a successful Trapper. Instead, the successful salesperson simply became a Trapper due to necessity and paying attention to techniques that have historically worked.

Trappers understand that each sale is a negative-gain endeavor. For one salesperson to win, many competitors need to lose. For every order, there is one winner and many losers. The goal of the Trapper is to make all of the competitors lose so that he can win. There is no second place in sales - only winners and losers.

You may have heard that you need to build a moat around your business. Warren Buffett, the famed investor, popularized the idea of building a moat. As a salesperson, you don't want just to build a moat - you want to lead your competition to a fake bridge over the moat, where they will fall into the water. You want your competitor to be one of those salespeople who becomes frustrated and changes jobs.

Most of the sales methods available today were written twenty years ago or longer (perhaps the 70s or 80s). In general, these books may be helpful in orchestrating an individual sales call or sales conversation. Without diminishing the work required in the 20th century, it is important to understand:

- Many companies had budgets so flush with cash that they bought millions of dollars of product based on quick demos and slideshows (this is especially true of technology companies).
- Most of the processes and systems proposed by other books on the market do a poor job of taking advantage of today's tools. Some of them have been revised to include software or the Internet, but they are not endemic to their philosophy.

This book is different in that I will show you how to eliminate your competition and maximize your commission.

What Is A Product?

Throughout this book, the term "product" ubiquitously applies to whatever you are selling to the prospect. You may sell a physical thing shipped to the prospect, you may sell a service provided to the prospect, you may sell a license for software that runs within the company's data center or on the cloud, or you may sell a combination of all of these things. The term 'product' applies to all of these types of things. It is anything that requires a selling process in which the prospect will give you something in value in return for it.

Who Should Read This Book?

You should not read this book if you are new to sales. This is not a 'basics' book or a book for dummies. In fact, if you have not been in sales for at least five selling periods then you probably do not have enough experience to take the leap to being a Trapper. You are ready to be a Trapper when you have personally experienced all of the following:

- You lost an opportunity that was a perfect fit for your service or product.
- You had to take out a significant portion of what you were offering to make the sale, or you had to offer steep discounting.
- You have experienced a selling period where you did extremely well against your goals and expectations.
- You have experienced a selling period where you did extremely poorly against your goals and expectations.
- You acknowledge that 'there must be a better way' to regularly sell at the top of your plan, with fewer losses, bigger orders, and fewer selling periods with poor revenue.

This book is for people involved in complex sales with a variety of selling and buying influences

Companies that have an insignificant presence (under 1%) in a vast market will not need most of these techniques. The reality is their sales force is populated by "cherry picker" salespeople. Cherry pickers are more attuned to the hunter methodology and stealing orders from others. I will spend more time later explaining Hunters, but Hunters are more activity-based than strategy-based salespeople.

Companies with low penetration in their target markets will find that when their salespeople begin to string successes together as Hunters the revenue stream will start to flatten. These companies must evolve their sales skills or they will always be relegated to an insignificant status. Interestingly, if the company has been under 1% for longer than three to five years, it has already reached the point where it no longer can afford to compete solely with Hunters and must begin to start controlling the entire sales process.

This book is for people involved in corporate sales and not consumer sales.

Some "consumer" salespeople will derive some value from this book, but it is primarily focused on business-to-business corporate salespeople. Successful consumer salespeople may find that they use some of the conversation elements in the book, especially setting Traps.

Just because you sell "business-to-business" (or B2B) doesn't mean that you are not involved in consumer-based sales. Corporate sales have the following characteristics:

- Many decision makers with different roles and agendas
- Many buying influences
- Relatively long decision cycles
- Buyer rarely visits the seller (in other words, the seller visits the buyer's place of business)

Let's examine these with a bit more explanation.

A Corporate Sale Has Many Decision Makers

The single biggest differentiator between consumer and corporate sales is the number of decision makers. A consumer sale has fewer decision makers, typically three or less, while a corporate sale has more decision makers. For this reason, many products may be sold business-to-business (B2B) but still be called a consumer sale because of the low number of decision makers.

Conversely, a product that is sold in a corporate sales model will have multiple decision makers that are typically in different departments with different goals. Many times the company will form a committee to evaluate the options.

A Corporate Sale Has Many Buying Influences

Most people envision the consumer sale as being handled by a clerk in the store. This is not sales; this is order-taking, and we won't discuss improving the order-taking process in this book. Order-taking has more to do with marketing than salesmanship. The common technique is for marketing campaigns to drive customers to the store, then suggestive marketing techniques are used to increase the chance of a sales transaction and increase the quantity of the order.

There are some techniques that the consumer salesperson can learn from this book. The consumer sale is where a clerk or customer care agent helps the customer make a decision by suggesting features about the product that might appeal to the buyer and offering reasons the customer should buy one product over another. They also are quite concerned that the client doesn't buy the same product down the street at another store, so they frequently bring up positives about their organization such as service, hotlines, return policy, etc. in the hopes that the customer will not leave. Trapping is incredibly important and many of those techniques are valid in this situation.

A Corporate Sale Doesn't Have A Short Sales Cycle Or A Short Decision Cycle

Typically a consumer sales cycle occurs in one to four 30-minute intervals. The customer enters the establishment, begins looking at a variety of products or services and then starts to ask the most available person some questions. This Q&A period is almost always done standing and occurs in a relatively non-relaxing space (buying a stereo with four to ten different music sources going and a half dozen other 'decision-making conversations' going on at the same time can rarely be called relaxing). Typically in the sales process, the salesperson will be asked to step away (or will volunteer it), and a private huddle will occur. At this time the decision is made to buy, wait, or go somewhere else. After two to five of these occurrences the decision will be made, either offsite and then with a return visit, or onsite at the last visited establishment. A frequent reason for buying product A versus product B is simply being tired of looking.

A Corporate Sales Process Rarely Includes The Customer Visiting The Buying Location

Typically, in a consumer sale, the customer will visit the company that is selling the product or service. This is why the consumer sale is often confused with order-taking. Many people assume that since it is similar to going to the grocery store or the fast-food joint, the people there have similar qualifications. It is a real shame when the selling company makes a similar mistake and puts no more effort into their employees than the burger joint down the street. Do not make the mistake of thinking that just because the buyer enters the establishment, the people there don't have to be professional salespeople. Organizations that understand this distinction will win in the long run if they train their salespeople to be successful with techniques such as Trapping.

A great example of a consumer sale that requires skilled, knowledgeable salespeople that are in a storefront is real estate and insurance salespeople. It is common for these industries to pay little-to-no base salary and therefore the salesperson must sell in order to make an income. There are people in these professions that make six- or seven-figure incomes and have been doing this for many years. These are some of the best salespeople in the world.

Consumer Sales Is Difficult

The consumer sale is not a simple sales job, and I am not trying to be discourteous to these professions by saying this book may not be perfectly on target for consumer salespeople.

Think of how many times you have gone to several locations to buy a TV, a stereo, or carpet. These are not easy decisions for the buyer. They frequently get made after multiple trips to a variety of stores and many times end up with "no decision" at the end of a lot of hard work.

I am always impressed with a suit salesperson who has been in the business for years. I know this person is good because he has been able to feed his family and satisfy his goals in an incredibly challenging business environment. Similarly, I know insurance salespeople and real estate agents who have been in business for decades, and they are some of the best salespeople I have ever met. They consistently make their goals, and they prosper in good times and bad.

What Is A Trap?

Obviously, the first thing that comes to mind when we mention "trap" is the wilderness variety. This image may bring favorable impressions or distaste, depending on your feelings about game hunting and killing animals for food, skin or profit. It is, however, a fact of life that many people today and many more people in the history of mankind made their living by being trappers.

Some more favorable impressions may come from the tales of Daniel Boone and other early Americans. While it is not necessary for the reader to be an expert gamesman and to understand the different types of tools and techniques that these professions used, it is helpful to discuss them to some degree so that we can fully grasp the analogies used in this book.

Wilderness Analogy Of Traps

Undoubtedly, you have watched a movie or TV show that features a trapper or a fisherman (fishing is a type of trap). You do not have to be an expert in trapping wild game to be an expert at using Trapping techniques in sales. In fact, you don't even have to like meat or like the idea of killing wild animals. However, please bear with me as I compare the tactics of trapping wildlife to the techniques of the best salespeople.

Traps lure game to the trap, but the placement and care of the traps are essential. A poorly laid or created trap will not capture the correct animal or maybe will catch an animal that is not a suitable size. There are a variety of ways to accomplish this, so let's explore the idea a bit.

Some traps put food or fake food, known as bait, in them to lure the animal. This is what happens in most game fishing. A piece of meat (or an object that resembles meat) is used to attract the fish to the hook. In this example, the trapper/fisherman places the trap in a place that the preferred animal is likely to be located and presents the bait in an alluring manner for that kind of animal.

Some traps are placed on a game trail to catch an unsuspecting animal. This is most common in fur trapping, where the trap is placed along a game trail to catch the unsuspecting animal, but it is common in game fishing as well. In this case, the trapper/fisherman understands the habits of the desired animal and places the trap or hook in a spot that the animal is likely to pass through.

Some traps use a maze so that the animal cannot escape. This is common for catching certain water-dwelling creatures such as lobsters or crabs. In this case, the trap is usually presented with bait to act as a lure, but instead of being impaled, the animal is unable or unwilling to escape the trap after entering it.

Sales Analogy Of Traps

In sales, we are not trying to Trap our customers. Rather, we are trying to Trap our competitors to make them unsuccessful, or at least significantly inconvenienced.

The definition of a Trap for a wilderness situation is probably obvious, but it is less obvious in sales. Traps are perceived strengths and weaknesses that competitors precondition customers to believe.

In sales, we want to allow our prospects to believe that our competitors have a distinct disadvantage compared to our offering. This is a Trap. We want them to question our competitor's offering so that the competitor loses.

▼▼▼▼▼▼▼▼▼▼▼▼▼▼

Traps are perceived strengths and weaknesses that competitors precondition customers to believe.

▲▲▲▲▲▲▲▲▲▲▲▲▲▲

It is important to understand that Traps are not lies, nor are they evil. In fact, the best Traps are entirely correct, honest, and in the best interests of the prospect. You are doing a service to your prospect by placing the Trap.

Let's examine a quick example of how you are helping the prospect. Let's imagine that you sell printers. Your company has invested heavily in design and manufacturing and has created a printer that can print in color on both sides of the paper at twice the speed of any other printer on the market for the same price as any other printer on the market. Doesn't it seem like you are doing your prospect a favor to find out if she has to print a lot of double-sided documents? If she does, doesn't it then make sense for you to ask, "Ms. Prospect, have you checked the throughput of my competitor for double-sided printing? Do those specifications best fit your needs?"

In this printer example of a Trap, you are not evil; you are helpful. You are making sure that the prospect has appropriately looked at a feature that you feel will be of benefit to her. Remember, you sell printers every day, but she probably doesn't make a decision about the appropriate printers for her organization's goals every day. You are the expert and are only guiding her in the decision-making process.

Just like in the wilderness analogies above, not all of our Traps will work. In many cases, we will need to place multiple Traps to make our offerings look better than those of our competitors. We call using multiple Traps: Trapping the Process. You will learn how to Trap the Process in this book.

What Is A Trapper, Hunter, Gatherer, Or Farmer?

There are four types of salespeople in a corporate sale. Every salesperson exhibits traits of all four types, but invariably they gravitate to one or two. The goal of this book is to help salespeople develop Trapper-like tendencies.

The four types are:

A. Gatherer
B. Farmer
C. Hunter
D. Trapper

It is possible for a Gatherer, Farmer, Hunter, or Trapper to close an order. We have all heard the old adage: "Even the blind pig occasionally finds an acorn." Farmers, Gatherers and Hunters close orders and can have a successful career. Trappers, however, close more orders that are larger, and they do it more consistently. In fact, the most successful salespeople may self-identify with one of the other three traits, but invariably they end up looking very similar to a Trapper.

Gatherer

In some cases, a Gatherer is naturally another salesperson trait, but at the particular account in question, they act like a Gatherer. They act like they own the account and primarily try to be a trusted adviser to the company. They are the incumbent and therefore are susceptible to trying to protect the status quo. A Gatherer can also be a senior salesperson who has sold to the prospect earlier in her career while working for another company.

Because all traits are morphed to a Gatherer, their actual tendencies can be varied. In some cases, they can even be a Trapper who has gotten lazy. Typically, a Gatherer can only work for a great company and sell a great product deployed in many different use cases. They have generally established themselves with a lot of experience. Often the company that employs a Gatherer puts this person in roles that allow them to generate repeat business rather than new business because of their tenure and familiarity with the customer.

Gatherers are incredibly difficult to beat. Multiple studies have shown that selling more to an existing client takes a fraction of the costs of acquiring a new client. This reduced cost directly correlates to making it easier to win more business with the customer. A Gatherer has a significant advantage in any sales contest and even smaller or niche competitors can be difficult to beat once they have the benefit of an existing purchase relationship.

Farmer

Farmers can be quite successful in a territory. This is especially true if the salesperson is selling a well-known product and they are familiar with the majority of the companies and individual buyers in their territory. Farmers tend to grow relationships and use those relationships to introduce new technology.

The failure of a farmer is consistency, especially with new products and unfamiliar decision makers. A farmer will take quite a long time in growing a new patch simply because there is very little targeted prospecting or targeted selling. A farmer's revenue performance is typically shaped like a rollercoaster because they do not control the success of their prospecting and leave it up to the customer to decide the outcome of the sales campaign. Therefore they cannot regulate their successes and failures.

The Farmer is most susceptible to losing deals to "No Decision." If you squander 30% or more of your deals to "No Decision," then you must begin to think of yourself as a Farmer.

Hunter

Most hiring VPs instruct sales recruiters to find only Hunters. Hunters have developed the skill of 'stealing' to great advantage. A true Hunter doesn't have the patience to spend time on future customer projects, but rather focuses on prospects who have already identified a need for the product. Hunters will often have extremely short sales cycles because they like to find prospects who have been cultivated by other salespeople. The Hunter steals the forecasted deal from another unsuspecting salesperson.

The revenue stream for even the best Hunters can most easily be described as a rollercoaster because they work real hard to steal, leaving them little time to work on their pipeline of customers. If there are no existing salespeople who have created a new opportunity and convinced the prospect to solve a problem, the Hunter will starve. The Hunter needs prospects to come to the conclusion that a particular type of product is needed. Once the prospect has identified a goal to satisfy, the Hunter will aggressively pursue the opportunity.

The Hunter rarely loses to "No Decision." She rarely spends time worrying about opportunities that are not in an active buying cycle. Because of this late entry, No Decision is simply not a reasonable conclusion.

Trapper

The Trapper is a thinker, a planner, and a worrier. The Trapper is constantly worried about competitors that he knows and those that he doesn't know. Those competitors also include "No Decision," which is a perennial competitor in most early buying cycles. Because of this worrying, the Trapper plans for a battle with each and every competitor and lays Traps to be sprung on the most likely competitors.

The Trapper is constantly trying to understand the prospect's business. This is second nature to a Trapper because just like a "wilderness" trapper, the business Trapper understands his quarry and understands the environment. The Trapper studies the habits and peculiarities of his prospect as well as his competitor.

The Trapper isn't just versed in the obvious parts of the business, but also in how the prospect really makes money and, more importantly, how the prospect loses money. The Trapper knows that if he helps the prospect avoid financial losses, the funding for his project will be ensured. Also, by focusing on financial rewards and losses, the

Trapper is often in a completely different relationship with the prospect than the competition.

All of this worrying and thinking requires planning. The Trapper anticipates what is going to happen and makes plans to capitalize on it. He doesn't wait until the last minute to understand the prospect and cultivate relationships. Rather, the Trapper makes an effort to completely understand the politics and driving forces of the prospect so that he is extremely prepared when an opportunity comes up to sell more products.

Traits Of The Salespeople

As explained above, few salespeople are completely within one single trait. Just like there is no true introvert and no true Class A personality, every salesperson will have traits of all four types of salespeople. The self-challenge is to identify with which salesperson's trait you most closely align.

The following traits are people who are naturally self-taught to be these roles or are taught by their environment. If the person has been trained to be a particular type of salesperson, then it is possible that they can increase their score one level.

	Gatherer	Farmer	Hunter	Trapper
Aggressive	1	2	4	3
Willing to change	1	2	3	4
Prospecting skills	2	3 (tie)	1	3 (tie)
Ability to understand customer	4	2	1	3
Competitive knowledge	2	1	3	4
Understands own weaknesses	3	1	2	4
Understands Customer Business	4	2	1	3
Strategy	2	1	3	4

Figure 1-1: Traits of the types of salespeople – relative skill rated 1-4, where 4 is the highest. All figures are also available at http://www.thetrapper.com/book_figures

Overall Strategies To Beat The Other Types Of Salespeople: Gatherer

The most difficult competitor to beat in an account is the Gatherer. You must take a long-term approach to winning and perhaps you win by indirectly assisting other fringe competitors in winning and shake the Gatherer's control on the account. You also must analyze your strengths against the Gatherer's weaknesses and concentrate on areas of the prospect where this advantage is important.

Overall Strategies To Beat The Other Types Of Salespeople: Farmer

Plan and anticipate the next steps. The Farmer watches and responds to requests from the customer. The Trapper anticipates and controls the process.

Overall Strategies To Beat The Other Types Of Salespeople: Hunter

Make the opportunity move very fast in the last half of the evaluation process – this makes the Hunter panic and act out of desperation.

Do You Work For A Trapper Company?

A Trapper company anticipates and plans for what may happen in the future.

Companies often discuss the length of their sales cycle. They will quote a range of time for their average sales campaigns such as two to four weeks or three to six months or even nine to fifteen months. As we saw in the discussion about Trappers, Hunters, Gatherers, and Farmers, the sales cycle can be similar to the prospect's decision cycle or only a small portion of it. When discussing sales cycles with a company, it is important to dig a little to see if it is a Gatherer company, a Hunter company, a Farmer company, or a Trapper company.

A Hunter company will have sales cycles that are much shorter than the decision cycle because they are stealing prospects late in the decision cycle and not contributing much to prospects early in the cycle. Typically, the salespeople cannot handle more than 10 active opportunities in complex sales because they are spending huge amounts of time and resources trying to establish credibility and learn the roles of the decision makers. Their company pipeline is usually very heavy in the final stages of the decision process and very weak in the early stages. Hunter companies may have lots of inaccuracy in their forecasts. If you talk to their senior management, you will find quite a few orders happen the last few days of the selling period (month, quarter, or year) rather than being evenly distributed throughout the period.

A Farmer company has much longer sales cycles. The length tends to be very close to the decision cycle because they found the prospect very early in the decision process or perhaps initiated the decision process. Since the Farmer is doing massive amounts of work and cultivating the prospect all the way through the cycle, they can handle a similar amount of accounts to the Hunter. However, as we discussed earlier, the revenue produced by a Farmer is usually very similar to a Hunter after the Farmer has built up enough tenure for a few typical decision cycles to occur. At this point, the Farmer will have a pipeline that is fully developed.

A company that is composed of Gatherers will have sales cycles that are longer than the prospect. Since the Gatherer usually is calling on existing customers, it is common for her to anticipate the needs of the prospect. She can do this because she is working on very few accounts and often on only one account.

A company that has committed to the Trapper philosophy has a similar pipeline to the decision-making pipeline of their customers. Because they are following Trapper techniques, they do not have to spend as much time with the decision-making process of the prospect. They can touch the prospect often enough to maintain value, but since they are relying on their competitors to do some of the educating, they can keep more prospects going at one time. A Trapper company will have salespeople who are two to four times more efficient than the average in the industry.

Understanding This Book

This book is not simple, with one central theme that gets repeated differently in every chapter. Instead, it is an entire strategy and process that compels the customer to reject your competition, select your product, and buy your product at the maximum price.

The readers of this book will be a wide variety of salespeople in many different industries; it is important that I lay out a sample sales campaign that you can learn from and I can refer to in later chapters. To that end, Chapter 2 is a fictional account of a sales campaign. The story introduces a fictional company, GlueWorks. GlueWorks is one of the largest producers of adhesives in the world.

The story introduces four salespeople who are competing to sell a software package to GlueWorks. These salespeople use different styles to sell. They are:

A. Amy Gatherer
B. Ben Farmer
C. Carla Hunter
D. Dave Trapper

By following the sales campaign, you should readily see the problems with all of the styles except for Trapper. At the end of the chapter, Dave Trapper will win the order.

All of the examples in the remainder of the book relate back to this fictional sales campaign, which gives you the framework and understanding of the sales situation in case you are not familiar with the industry.

After we have set the stage with this case study, I will walk you through the thought process that occurs in an organization in identifying, selecting, and buying a product.

Understanding Complex Decisions

It is critical that you understand the product selection process. Most sales methodologies on the shelves of bookstores do not spend time trying to understand the buyer and the work that a company goes through to select a product. This leads to a one-sided view of the process and is inherently inaccurate. This contributes to the enormous number of unsuccessful salespeople.

I begin by explaining that no one ever buys the wrong product. Every purchase decision is a series of compromises and in the end, every prospect makes the best choice for them at that time. This leads to the discussion that there are no inferior products, there are no perfect products, and therefore, all salespeople can be successful.

Every purchase is essentially a decision-making process. Most prospects do not have a firm idea of what they should buy, how they should buy it, or their actual needs. This situation gives the salesperson the opportunity to structure the prospect's decision-making process and control the outcome. Typically, the best product does not win; instead, it is the salesperson who controls the decision-making process that wins.

The Buying And Selling Process

It is essential for a successful salesperson to understand the entire buying and selling process. Most salespeople can document their company's selling process and the various stages that their management tracks for forecasting purposes. However, truly successful salespeople understand what the prospect is doing and why they are doing it.

To aid you in your sales campaigns, Chapter 4 compares a selling process to the steps that the prospect is going through to show that paying attention to only the selling process and not the buying process is a mistake. Finally, each step of the buying process is analyzed, and the Trapper salesperson is given action items to accomplish to ensure a successful sales campaign.

Two of the many challenges in sales is finding the right people to call on and finding opportunities that fit your product. Chapter 5 gives many examples on prospecting and targeting appropriate organizations for sales campaigns. More importantly, it discusses how to completely understand the relationships within the organization after it is found.

Prospecting

Too many salespeople spend time on prospects who are not optimal for buying their product. This is a mistake, as it is critical to find the organizations most likely to buy the salesperson's product. These organizations have a strong fit with the salesperson's personal 'Sweet Spot.' The Sweet Spot organizations are composed of the best combination of geography, size, structure, and industry to allow the salesperson to excel.

Once the target organization is found, the salesperson must completely understand its politics and structure. To aid you, I will explain the concept of a Power Matrix. The Power Matrix is a convenient way to map out everyone in the organization, their relationships with each other, and their power in the company. It eliminates the false sense of security the salesperson can develop by understanding the prospect's organization chart, but not understanding who trusts each other within the organization.

Bait

To be an effective Trapper, you must learn to create and use Bait. Bait is information prepared to encourage the prospect to react in a certain way. Bait allows you to create a Trap that influences and controls a prospect.

Creating Bait may be very easy for you because your employer has adopted Trapper techniques. Others may struggle because your company has not realized how to perform many of the background steps of Bait development. Regardless of the tools provided by your company, the development and deployment of Bait is ultimately the salesperson's responsibility.

If you do not understand the true driving reasons behind the prospect's actions, you increase your chance of failure. Without this knowledge, you will only be delivering a pre-canned message to your prospect and will win only a small percentage of your sales campaigns.

Once you understand the exact reasons for the prospect's interest, you can decide which unique benefits to explain. To do this, you must evaluate the competition and deduce which benefits you offer that have an advantage over the competition and are of interest to the prospect.

▼▼▼▼▼▼▼▼▼▼▼▼▼▼

If you have no difference between you and your competition, you have nothing to sell. Identify those differences and focus your time on explaining the value of the differences.

▲▲▲▲▲▲▲▲▲▲▲▲▲▲

Upon understanding the prospect's reasons and identifying your unique benefits, you must deliver this information to the prospect in a way that is memorable, convincing, and persuasive. This will set up the prospect for a Trap that should help eliminate the competition.

Traps

There are three types of Traps:

1. Accidental Traps – this is honest information gathering by the prospect, not an actual Trap. It is an opportunity to lose the sale, and it is an opening to Trap the competition.
2. Unintentional Traps – In this case, the prospect doesn't know he is being used by the competition. This is the most frequent type of Trap.
3. Collaborative Traps – Competitors place these Traps with the full knowledge and assistance of the prospect. Collaborative Traps are relatively rare in most sales campaigns, but they are the most dangerous if misdiagnosed.

I not only explain the difference in the types of Traps, but I will also give you advice on how to set a Trap for your competitor and escape a Trap set for you. Remember, you are not trying to Trap your prospect; you are Trapping your competitors. Also, it is not a bad thing that you help your prospect find deficiencies in your competitor's offering; you are only helping them to make a sound decision.

The four steps in Trap setting are:

1. Develop the need with Bait.
2. Confirm that you meet the need.
3. Question whether the competition meets the need.
4. Request feedback on how the competition responds.

Escaping an intentional or unintentional Trap is much more critical and difficult to accomplish. The successful Trapper understands that he will lose the sales campaign if he cannot escape Traps.

The four primary steps in escaping a Trap are:

1. Clarify the meaning of the question.
2. Acknowledge the business importance of the request.
3. Respond to the request with a well-thought-out answer.
4. Using the tools above, set a Trap that is similar to the original request.

Closing The Deal

Negotiating the final terms of the sale and closing for the order becomes anti-climatic for a Trapper. By the time the opportunity gets to this stage it is almost a foregone conclusion that the Trapper will win the order.

The work of an effective Trapper is not done when the order is booked. First, you must celebrate that win and potentially do something constructive with the commission. Second, you must leverage that success to generate more momentum and excitement for your other sales campaigns and to sell more to this new customer.

Appendices

In the process of writing this book, there was some information that interrupted the flow of the topic. While the information is useful, including it in the various chapters simply made them hard to read and understand. This type of information has been moved to various appendices.

The Trapper Blog

Some concepts didn't warrant an entire chapter. In those cases, I have moved these conversations to a blog at http://www.theTrapper.com. Also, this channel gives me the opportunity to speak in much more detail about specific concepts from the book. Please check out the blog and

Chapter 2 – A Case Study

"We can try to avoid making choices by doing nothing, but even that is a decision."

- Gary Collins

This case study will help you to understand the Trapper selling methodology. This fictionalized case study will be used throughout the book to explain the more difficult concepts.

You are not required to read this chapter before proceeding with the rest of the book. You may want to go on to Chapter 3 and then come back to review this case study when you are confused. Also, if you have already read this book once, this case study may give clarity to the overall strategy that the first-time reader may miss.

The company in this case study is GlueWorks. GlueWorks doesn't know how to achieve one of its major goals and is looking for outside assistance.

In this case study, we follow four different salespeople who sell management consulting software that can help companies focus and align their products. This type of software replaces management consultants. In this case study, there are no major technical limitations in any of the four software products. Any of the four products will work, and therefore it is primarily sales skill that differentiates the products and influences the sale. While each product will work, there are individual features of each of these offerings that can be used to differentiate the products.

The four salespeople in this story are:

A. Amy Gatherer
B. Ben Farmer
C. Carla Hunter
D. Dave Trapper

Ivytown is a typical city, probably very similar to your city. It has its problems with keeping roads paved, keeping its parks clean, and providing adequate opportunities for its youth. Ivytown has had its share of very good mayors in the past, and it has also had a few mayors that probably should never have been elected. There are a few medium-sized universities in town that occasionally have a good year with one of their sports teams, and this incites quite a bit of pride in the community. Like your home city, the top weatherman can never seem to predict the weather but is still popular.

One of the largest companies in Ivytown is GlueWorks, Inc. GlueWorks is one of the largest manufacturers of adhesives in the world. The company started about 100 years ago and now has a very diverse line of glues and adhesives. Its products are sold to consumers and industrial companies. Their consumer products are a hit with young students, and the marketing of the consumer products is imaginative. The industrial customers range from book publishers to automotive companies. Their tagline on their website is "We Keep Everything Together."

Amy Gatherer works for Everything Consulting. GlueWorks is the largest of the five customers that she manages for Everything Consulting. GlueWorks is about 40% of her revenue.

Everything Consulting is a global consulting company with many different practices. Most of their revenue comes from the teams of consultants that advise companies on a wide variety of disciplines. A few years ago, Everything Consulting acquired a Scandinavian company that developed artificial intelligence software to help companies align the skills of individual people and job functions. This product is quite good, but it is competitive with the consulting operations of Everything Consulting. The software product, therefore, is typically only discussed with new prospects and not existing customers.

Ben Farmer works for DayDream Consulting. Ben has sold a few small consulting projects to GlueWorks. Ben always goes to GlueWorks on Mondays; he has a cup of coffee with Steve and Alice in manufacturing. Steve is an old college friend, and they enjoy talking about the status of their alma mater's sports teams. Steve was instrumental in helping Ben get the previous consulting engagements. Alice attends the same church as Ben.

DayDream Consulting is a regional consulting company with extremely talented consultants. They also re-sell, in an exclusive territory, a software product that uses artificial intelligence techniques to help companies align the skills of individual people and job functions. This product is quite good, and the publisher of the software is willing to help any of their resellers successfully sell the product. DayDream Consulting doesn't get many leads for the software, but it does receive a steady stream of RFPs (Requests For Proposal) to fill out. DayDream is very diligent about filling out these RFPs, but Ben regularly complains that they need better resources to complete those RFPs.

Carla Hunter works for Focused Software, where she won the top salesperson award for two of the last four years. Focused Software creates a software product that uses artificial intelligence techniques to help companies align the skills of individual people and job functions. Carla loves working for Focused Software because they give her a lot of latitude in going after opportunities, give her well-written collateral, and are extremely flexible on pricing and terms. Focused Software has never sold anything to GlueWorks.

Dave Trapper works for Premium Software. Premium Software creates a software product that uses artificial intelligence techniques to help companies align the skills of individual people and job functions. Dave doesn't think Premium Software has great marketing and always wishes for more leads, but knows that he needs to generate his deals. Dave is one of the top salespeople in the company and understands that the company's management is at his disposal to help him win business. Premium Software has never sold anything to GlueWorks.

We will watch these four salespeople as they discuss their territories with their management over the majority of a year.

36 Weeks Before The GlueWorks Purchase Order

Amy Gatherer meets with her manager every Monday morning, and the subject of GlueWorks comes up weekly. She details the consulting orders that she is billing, some personnel problems with the various onsite consultants, and a customer event that she recently hosted with some GlueWorks executives. The status of GlueWorks as a customer continues to be very profitable and the outlook is quite positive.

The subject of selling the new artificial intelligence (AI) tool to GlueWorks doesn't come up. Her manager is pleased with GlueWorks but is a bit distressed that Amy just had a 90% drop in billings at a different customer, ABC Plane Parts. ABC Plane Parts selected Premium Software. Amy explained her plan to her manager. "I think I can increase my billings at GlueWorks by taking some new business away from DayDream Consulting to offset the decrease in revenue from ABC Plane Parts."

Ben Farmer also talks to his manager every Monday, but his conversation occurs in the afternoon, as he has appointments on Monday morning. When the subject turns to GlueWorks, Ben tells his manager, "Steve and Alice are loving what we are doing. They are pretty adamant that they don't want to switch to Everything Consulting, even though there is some pressure from executive management. I think this initial consulting order will be successful, and we will grow that relationship, but we may have to drop our price to keep Everything Consulting out."

When asked about selling the artificial intelligence-based product, Ben replies, "GlueWorks is a solid, old-fashioned company that values human relationships. I don't think they are going to go for the new stuff."

Finally, Ben's manager asks if he had heard the rumor about ABC Plane Parts buying artificial intelligence-based software. Ben replies, "That doesn't surprise me. I am not close to anyone there. I know one guy in the human resources department, but we are not very close. I have tried to invite him to golf and various sports events around town, and he is never really interested. They seem to be much more cutting edge and hard charging. I will look into the rumor." Ben will look into the rumor, but he will never tell his manager what happened unless asked again. Ben subscribes to the theory that salespeople should only tell management about bad news when it is absolutely necessary.

Carla Hunter's meeting with her manager was filled with frustration. Carla had spent a lot of time over the last ten to twelve weeks at ABC Plane Parts but had come up short on a decision they recently made. She and her manager complained that the customer obviously made the wrong decision, even when given a massive last-minute discount. By the end of the conversation, they concluded that Focused Software was never given a fair shot at the business and it was wired for Premium Software from the beginning.

Carla and her manager never discussed GlueWorks, as she has never made a call there and isn't aware of any reason to discuss the account. She did mention several RFPs that she was responding to with the help of her inside sales team and her technical team.

Dave Trapper's meeting with his manager is more of a celebration than an account review. Dave, his extended team, and the management team just closed a very large sale at ABC Plane Parts. Much of the meeting was spent talking about that successful campaign, with appropriate congratulations to all of the team members who contributed to the success.

The meeting ended with Dave's manager starting to think ahead. "Great job on the deal! I hate to go straight to business but you are on a bit of a streak right now, and we need to keep building on that momentum. Let's skip the discussion on GlueWorks, Suncar Auto, Spinning Energy, Four Star Homes, and Hot Food Restaurants for this week. We can focus on those next week. My treat for lunch today at Tony's Steakhouse."

35 Weeks Before The GlueWorks Purchase Order

Amy Gatherer is still frustrated by her loss at ABC Plane Parts. She discusses her plans with her manager on increasing billing at GlueWorks. They both agree that introducing their new AI software product would be a detriment to the consulting revenue they currently enjoy. They develop a plan to visit every influencer at GlueWorks to discuss a new consulting product that Everything Consulting has developed.

Amy is aware of a small group within GlueWorks that has selected another consulting organization. She strategizes with her manager on how to discredit the group led by Steve Smith and Alice Andrews so that they are forced to use Everything Consulting.

Ben Farmer discusses GlueWorks with his manager. They are very concerned about the potential pressure from Everything Consulting. While Ben feels comfortable that his relationship with Steve and Alice will maintain the revenue stream, his manager is less confident. By the end of their meeting, it is agreed that Ben will take his manager to GlueWorks on the following Monday to meet Steve and Alice.

Carla Hunter continues to not worry about GlueWorks, and the subject doesn't come up in discussions with her manager.

Dave Trapper has finished celebrating his success at ABC Plane Parts. He treated his wife to a night at one of the boutique hotels in the neighboring city, where they ate a great meal, enjoyed a comedian at the local comedy club, and finished the weekend with a couples massage in the hotel spa. This activity is a ritual that Dave enjoys every time he closes an order for more than 20% of his annual quota.

When he sits down with his manager, they go over his plans for other accounts. When the conversation turns to GlueWorks, both he and his manager agree that the company has great potential, but they have not started to move forward in a meaningful way. Dave has identified eight people who are likely to be drivers in a decision to use artificial intelligence to drive employee skills issues and resource alignment. Dave's manager continues to encourage Dave to maintain his regular newsletter, mailings, and meetings to create a relationship with each of these potential Discoverers.

34 Weeks Before The GlueWorks Purchase Order

Amy Gatherer presents her GlueWorks "keep healthy" plan to her manager. The overall plan is to discredit the small rogue group led by Alice Andrews that is using DayDream Consulting. She thinks she can do this through pressure from the GlueWorks VP of Human Resources. She is going to invite that VP to a PGA golf tournament being held a short distance away. The VP is a huge golf fan, and Amy golfs with him at least once per month. Amy's manager continues to be amazed that she is so good at working executive relationships.

Ben Farmer didn't have a weekly meeting with his manager since he took him to GlueWorks to meet Alice Andrews and her lead manager, Steve Terry. Alice confided that their project is not influenced by HR as they work for the VP of Manufacturing, so it doesn't matter what HR wants to do for resource management, the Manufacturing Group of GlueWorks will continue to set its own direction for its needs.

During the meeting, Ben asked Alice about artificial intelligence. She admitted she didn't have much understanding of the technology and how it could help them. Ben promised to send some literature about a product that they sell.

Ben's manager feels good when they walk out of the meeting, but he has a sinking feeling that he may not know the whole story. When he relays that concern to Ben, Ben assures him that everything is fully under control because Alice would never steer him wrong. Also, he has known Steve Smith for a long time, so there is little risk of being blindsided.

Carla Hunter continues to not worry about GlueWorks, and the subject doesn't come up in discussions with her manager.

Dave Trapper excitedly tells his manager about his meeting with Terry Tram. Terry was one of the eight targets that Dave has been meeting with for the past several months. Terry called him last week and asked Dave to come by and chat over coffee.

During their coffee conversation, Terry said that he thinks GlueWorks needs to make a major change. Terry had been brought in by the VP of Human Resources to help the VP of Sales look for ways to improve the company. Officially, Terry is in charge of a new program to develop customers who are better references for other customers. Unofficially, Terry has been pushed to come up with suggestions to make the company more competitive and more responsive to its customers.

Terry has read all of the material that Dave has been forwarding, and he thinks there could be a significant opportunity to improve resource management of GlueWorks.

Dave and his manager agree that Terry has all of the signs of being a Discoverer. They discuss a variety of options to motivate Terry to continue his analysis and to create a Personal Vision Goal.

33 Weeks Before The GlueWorks Purchase Order

Amy Gatherer informs her manager that she received a phone call from Terry Tram. Terry works for the VP of Sales at GlueWorks and is in charge of customer references. She has never met with him but knows the VP of Sales quite well. She will meet with Terry, but she wants to set up another meeting with the VP of Sales to make sure that the 17 people that Everything Consulting has in the Sales department doing sales training are not at risk.

Ben Farmer reviews the previous week's meeting with Alice and Steve. Ben is very confident that their future revenue is secure and commits to his manager a continued pipeline of consultants. He also told his manager that he sent some marketing material to Alice regarding artificial intelligence.

Carla Hunter continues to not worry about GlueWorks, and the subject doesn't come up in discussions with her manager.

Dave Trapper's meeting with his manager was a little longer than usual. Since their previous meeting, Dave had spent a couple of hours with Terry Tram at GlueWorks. In that meeting, Dave guided Terry through the developments in the artificial intelligence industry. Dave specifically talked about how Terry's peers in other companies who had adopted this technology were recognized and rewarded by their company. During that conversation, Terry confided some of his personal career goals and personal goals.

Armed with the knowledge about Terry's relationship with the VP of Human Resources, Dave asked Terry for an introduction to him. Terry was impressed with Dave, so he offered to walk him by the VP's office on their way out of the GlueWorks building.

As luck would have it, the VP of HR was walking out of his office just as the two came down the hall. Dave had one goal aside from making the introduction: encourage Terry to move forward. Dave quickly summarized some of the industry successes using artificial intelligence and asked the VP if he thought Terry should pursue an investigation into the technology. The VP was impressed with the success stories and told Terry that he would be interested in anything that could be useful to GlueWorks.

Dave and his manager agreed on a consistent set of messages to keep in front of Terry that aligned with Terry's career goals.

32 Weeks Before The GlueWorks Purchase Order

Amy Gatherer informed her manager that she felt that their consulting revenue from GlueWorks sales department was quite safe.

She had met with Terry Tram, and she felt that his research into artificial intelligence was very early and not part of a funded project. She also met with the VP of Sales and was excited to learn that he may be increasing the number of Everything Consulting consultants in the next budget year.

Ben Farmer barely discussed GlueWorks with his manager. There was little change in the relationship, and everything was going fine.

Carla Hunter continues to not worry about GlueWorks, and the subject doesn't come up in discussions with her manager.

Dave Trapper met with Terry Tram again during the previous week. Dave continued to answer Terry's questions about the technology, but he also continued to talk about Terry's career goals. Dave gave Terry a book on early adopters of technology that he thought Terry would enjoy.

Dave also coached Terry that he might want to talk to others about his ideas. Dave knew that manufacturing was strongly aligned with DayDream Consulting and wanted to avoid his competitor's influence on the early direction of this potential project. To help Terry with a wider insight but without helping his competitor, Dave suggested three people that he had early conversations with but they didn't take up the role of Discoverer. He suggested Sally Sunderman from Accounts Payable, Keith Vandenburg in Marketing, and Jen Fremen in Product Development. Terry reached out to all three to discuss his developing ideas, and they were all interested in helping him.

Jen was particularly impressed with Terry's ideas and mentioned it to her manager, John Roundtree, the VP of Product Development. John had brought Jen into the company when he joined and was very impressed with Jen's creativity in solving problems.

31 Weeks Before The GlueWorks Purchase Order

Amy Gatherer told her manager that she received a phone call from Jen Fremen from Product Development on AI software. Amy thought it was probably a waste of time, but she answered Jen's questions. Jen suggested a meeting with John Roundtree, the VP of Product Development. Amy was going to take the meeting, but she was a bit skeptical because John wasn't a very powerful player in the previous deals that Everything Consulting had done with GlueWorks.

Ben Farmer told his manager that he received a phone call from Jen Fremen from Product Development on AI software. Ben was excited about the phone call, and he answered Jen's questions. Jen suggested a meeting with John Roundtree, the VP of Product Development. Ben immediately reached out to Alice Andrews for an understanding of how John relates to her department.

GlueWorks contacted Carla Hunter and her inside sales team sent out some marketing materials. She advised her inside sales team not to create an opportunity at this time, as it didn't seem to a funded project. She continues to not worry about GlueWorks, and the subject doesn't come up in discussions with her manager.

Dave Trapper tells his manager that he thinks that Jen from Product Development is potentially setting up to be a Coach in the sales process at GlueWorks. She called Dave and explained that she had talked to Terry Tram and then had a meeting with her manager. She passed on some specific questions from her manager that Dave and his technical team easily answered. She offered to introduce Dave to John Roundtree, the VP of Product Development.

30 Weeks Before The GlueWorks Purchase Order

Amy Gatherer's meeting with John Roundtree went well. He was quite interested in using AI to align his workforce with the company's needs. Amy explained that she was doing the exact same thing for Professional Plastic Products, Inc. using some of the most qualified consultants in the industry. She suggested that using consultants to achieve John's goals was a safer strategy. John said that he would reach out to the VP of Product Development of Professional Plastic Products Inc. to discuss their use of Everything Consulting.

Ben Farmer barely discussed GlueWorks with his manager. There was little change in the relationship, and everything was going fine. He had a meeting set up with John Roundtree that following week.

Carla Hunter continues to not worry about GlueWorks, and the subject doesn't come up in discussions with her manager. She did reach out to John Roundtree and agreed to stop by GlueWorks the next time she was in Ivytown.

Dave Trapper updated his manager on his meeting with John Roundtree. Before attending the meeting, Dave had researched John and understood that he played lacrosse at an East Coast university in college. Dave had a casual knowledge of the sport but spent a few minutes before the meeting reviewing the sport and the college that John attended, and came up with some sports-related questions to ask John. This preparation led to a 10-minute opening conversation on lacrosse and John's love of the sport and his alma mater.

Dave also had prepared a short slide deck that showed successes of using AI software in workforce management in the Product Development field but also how AI was starting to be used for other areas within Product Development. They ran out of time in the meeting due to the opening college sports conversations, and John asked if they could schedule a follow-up meeting on some of the topics.

After the meeting with Dave reached out to some of the vertical experts in Premium Software and they agreed to join via the phone in the next meeting with John. They helped Dave create a new slide deck using the acrostic device GAME to underscore the benefits of AI in Product Development. They selected GAME due to John's love of sports. They also sprinkled some lacrosse references throughout the deck.

29 Weeks Before The GlueWorks Purchase Order

Amy Gatherer was happy to inform her manager that she had spoken to the VP of Professional Plastic Products Inc. about John Roundtree. The VP assured her that he would speak to John. She felt comfortable that John would follow along with the previous direction of GlueWorks to hire more consulting from Everything Consulting. They began to discuss how big that order could be and how to fulfill it.

Ben Farmer told his manager that in addition to his weekly meetings with Alice, he also met with John Roundtree. Unfortunately, he wasn't able to answer most of his questions about AI uses in workforce alignment. Ben explained how successful Alice's efforts had been and suggested they talk about those types of consulting engagements. He also sent about a couple dozen electronic papers to John (basically everything that was in their literature stack). He would try to get on John's calendar again in a couple of weeks.

Carla Hunter continues to not worry about GlueWorks, and the subject doesn't come up in discussions with her manager.

Dave Trapper's meeting with John Roundtree, along with Dave's remote experts, went well. Jen called him after the meeting and told him that John was extremely impressed with his depth of knowledge and ability to apply his technology to other problems. Jen advised him to send her some more information on the subjects that were discussed, and she would make sure that she kept John up to date.

Dave's manager then started a conversation about competitors and a focused strategy for each. They identified how they were going to deal with the existing relationships of Everything Consulting and DayDream Consulting. They also identified weaknesses of each as they specifically related to GlueWorks and focused on those weaknesses where Premium Software had a corresponding strength. They also identified that GlueWorks' needs appeared to align well with Focused Software and were surprised that they had not seen activity with that strong competitor. They discussed a strategy to find out who the other competitors were at GlueWorks.

The biggest competitor identified was probably going to be Everything Consulting. They had heard of Amy Gatherer before and knew her to be a strong salesperson. Also, they knew that she managed a significant amount of business at GlueWorks. The basic plan for Everything Consulting was to focus on them as the primary competitor and let Everything Consulting take out the other competitors. It was quite likely that the final decision would be between Everything Consulting, Premium Software, and one other major competitor out of the several that were in the market. Dave planned to position himself against Everything Consulting and let the rest of the competitors eliminate each other.

One of the points that Dave's manager brought up was that Everything Consulting had a CEO who didn't come off well in quarterly analyst calls. They decided that if Everything Consulting made it to the final contenders they would bring in Premium Software's CEO to talk to GlueWorks' executive management.

To facilitate the conversations between various product experts and GlueWorks, Dave created a Relationship Map. This mapping tool would allow him to manage the conversations between various decision makers at GlueWorks with the best resources at Premium Software.

28 Weeks Before The GlueWorks Purchase Order

Amy Gatherer and her manager took several executives at GlueWorks out for dinner to celebrate a successful year and to thank them for their continued business. The CFO of GlueWorks was at the dinner and confided to them that she should probably spend some more time with John Roundtree, as artificial intelligence seemed to be gaining some interest in the company.

Ben Farmer updated his manager that he had found some additional reading material for Jen and John at GlueWorks and he was forwarding it to them.

Carla Hunter told her manager that she had met with John Roundtree of GlueWorks. It was an interesting conversation, but the project didn't appear to be funded for purchase anytime soon. She complains to her manager that her inside sales team needs to do a better job of prioritizing appointments.

Dave Trapper confirmed with his manager that Jen had confided to him that they were having conversations with Everything Consulting, DayDream Consulting, Focused Software and Premium Software. She also mentioned that there was some interest in three or four other vendors but, to the best of her knowledge, there had not been any formal meetings.

With the help of Dave's manager, Dave put together a specific attack plan regarding each competitor, including the less frequently seen minor competitors that Jen mentioned.

To assist Dave and his extended team to stay on message and focus on the important topics, they created an Issues Alignment chart. The first version had a lot of blanks, and they were confident that they didn't have all of the issues identified for each influencer. They knew that they were going to add to and refine this information throughout the sales process.

27 Weeks Before The GlueWorks Purchase Order

Amy Gatherer takes the CFO of GlueWorks' advice seriously, and she reaches out to John Roundtree at GlueWorks to set up a meeting. He tells her that he is going to be burning up some personal time, so his calendar is tied up but suggests that she talk to Jen Fremen. Amy downplays this advice because she doesn't want to go down a level in the organization chart. Instead, she reaches out to Greg Saterree in IT for a meeting. Greg says that he has heard of Roundtree's ideas and agrees to a meeting. In that meeting, Greg explains that they are primarily focused on human resources but will be exploring manufacturing and product development in the future.

Ben Farmer also took Alice and Steve out to dinner to celebrate the end of the year. They had a great conversation. They told Ben that they heard that there was a growing interest in AI within GlueWorks and quizzed him on his knowledge of the use cases. Ben made a mental note to spend some time reading all of the material that he had sent to John Roundtree earlier.

Carla Hunter continues to not worry about GlueWorks, and the subject doesn't come up in discussions with her manager. It is the week before Christmas, and she is desperate to get a few more deals done before everyone disappears for the holidays. She is stressed out, but she jokes with her team that closing business at the end of the year is what gets her blood pumping.

Dave Trapper received a phone call from Jen Fremen and asked him to come in. Also in that meeting was Terry Tram. They explained that it appeared that Information Technology might be getting involved in this entire project. They quizzed Dave on how his product would be received by IT. Dave assured him that this was fine and Premium Software had some great experts to alleviate any concerns from IT.

Jen also told Dave that she was quite upset with Everything Consulting. It seemed that their salesperson, Amy Gatherer, had been told by John Roundtree to call Jen and Amy never called. Then she heard that Amy was going to be meeting with Greg Saterree in IT. Greg was Jen's good friend and over lunch the day before, Greg said that he was surprised that Amy blew her off.

Dave's manager suggested that it was time to start documenting the GlueWorks opportunity with a Power Matrix. They had already created an Alignment Map, and this map would be customized to each member of the Power Matrix. Dave was well ahead of his manager and pulled out the Power Matrix that he had already started. Dave was comfortable that GlueWorks was going to be a significant order, so he had started with the template for a Large Power Matrix.

Dave also started to work on his Decision Timeline to present to GlueWorks. He knew that this timeline document would be revised, but he wanted to have a solid foundation. As with all good timelines, he needed to anticipate when the GlueWorks buying process would naturally finish. He estimated that they were still six to eight months out from placing an order. Dave wanted to drive a decision that didn't fall at the end of a fiscal quarter, as he didn't want to add to his stress trying to wrap up an order at the end of a fiscal quarter. To facilitate this goal, he developed a timeline that would conclude in seven months.

26 Weeks Before The GlueWorks Purchase Order

Amy Gatherer isn't meeting with her manager this week. It is Christmas, and none of her customers want to have consultants on-site. She is using her vacation time to enjoy her family.

Amy achieved 95% of her annual goal this fiscal year. Her revenue was down primarily because of a general eroding of her ability to raise billable rates on the assigned consultants. She also lost a few key accounts such as ABC Plane Parts, as they went to competitive technologies. This year is the lowest quota attainment that she has had in years. She resolves that she needs to work harder to increase the number of consulting assignments and protect her installed base.

Ben Farmer is also off this week, so he didn't meet with his manager. He also didn't meet with his buddies at GlueWorks or any of his other regular customers. It wasn't an especially good year for Ben, but it wasn't a bad year. Ben doesn't ever anticipate being the top salesperson at his company, but he is never the worst. He is perfectly content with spending time with his customers who appreciate him and value his ability to give them good deals.

Carla Hunter is supposed to be off for the holidays but, as usual, she isn't. She hasn't taken the holiday week off in her entire career. She still has a couple of deals to shepherd into the end of the fiscal year. Her manager is off, but they have a phone conversation on the status of the deals she is trying to close.

If Carla closes these last couple of deals, she will be at 110% of her annual quota. She is proud of how hard she works, and she knows that hard work brings success. She doesn't always exceed quota on an annual basis but this year was the third time in the last six years at Focused Software that she exceeded quota, with two of those years giving her the top salesperson award. She is proud that she didn't do another bad year of 70% of quota, but she is frustrated that someone else will be on stage at the awards event for the year.

It is the last week of the fiscal year for Premium Software and Dave Trapper. It is also the week between Christmas and New Year's. Dave is off this week on vacation with his family at his in-laws', enjoying the Christmas holidays because all of his deals are closed, and the paperwork has been completed. Dave doesn't like to take deals to the last minute of a fiscal quarter, so he always manages his deals to close early in the month and usually early in the quarter.

Dave was well over quota for the year, was the top salesperson for his manager, and thinks he is close to being the top salesperson for the year for North America. It will be a good Christmas for his family, and he is excited about them seeing their Christmas presents.

Dave is also excited about his charity project. Dave is a firm believer in sharing his good fortune with others, so his entire family is going to a local children's cancer center to hand out stuffed animals that he has purchased for sick kids. Dave knows it will be good for his family and himself to help others who are suffering, and he enjoys the big smiles of the kids with cancer when they open a gift of a massive stuffed animal. Dave cannot cure cancer, but he can ease the suffering of someone else, even if only for a few minutes.

Dave was a bit surprised when his manager called him while he was on vacation. The kids were with their grandmother watching a new video they received for Christmas while Dave was packing the car with stuffed animals for charity, so Dave took the call.

Dave answered, "Merry Christmas and Happy New Year! Is everything okay?"

Dave's manager replied sheepishly, "Sorry to call you on your time off. I hope your holiday has been good. Everything is fine, but I just want to give you a heads-up that North American Management wants you to present your win at ABC Plane Parts at the sales kickoff meeting. Do you mind if I tell them that you will do it?"

Dave laughed and accepted the honor of doing the presentation. He knew that he had a couple of weeks to prep and he knew the account details so well that he could extemporaneously do the talk if he ran short of time.

When Dave's manager hung up with a season's greetings, Dave's wife had come to the car and had heard the last part of the conversation so asked if everything was fine. Dave replied with a shrug, "North American Management wants me to talk about the ABC Plane Parts win at kickoff in a couple of weeks. I accepted."

"Really!" Dave's wife replied with a growing smile of pride. "That seems like a big honor. Do they frequently ask salespeople to do that kind of speech?"

"I have seen it once or twice before, and it was always with the best salesperson the company has ever had. She was the person that made me rethink how I do this job. It will be a hat-tip to her since her ideas have accelerated my success. Hmm, I wonder if I beat her in revenue this year."

25 Weeks Before The GlueWorks Purchase Order

Amy Gatherer doesn't have much of an update for her manager after the holidays. She will have several meetings this week and hopefully will know more.

Ben Farmer doesn't have much of an update for his manager after the holidays. He will have several meetings this week and hopefully will know more.

Carla Hunter continues to not worry about GlueWorks, and the subject doesn't come up in discussions with her manager.

Dave Trapper doesn't have much news for his manager after the holidays but does tell him Terry Tram asked him to come in for a meeting the following day. Dave promises to give his manager an update after the meeting.

Terry Tram wasn't the only person from GlueWorks in the meeting. Greg Saterree, Director of Information Technology, was also in the meeting. Greg quizzed Dave on the technical aspects of Premium Software's products. During that conversation, Dave was able to understand that Greg had been following the artificial intelligence industry for a while and was quite versed in many aspects.

Dave also guided Greg in some of the risks that GlueWorks might encounter with deploying artificial intelligence. He purposely didn't build a negative feeling around the technology, but he did warn of some potential pitfalls that GlueWorks would have to overcome. Terry and Greg both replied how impressed they were that Dave was giving a fair and honest discussion of the challenges GlueWorks might face.

At the end of the meeting, Greg explained that he was forming a small multi-department group to look at artificial intelligence uses within GlueWorks. Greg said that Terry Tram was going to be in that group. Terry spoke up and said that he was impressed with Premium Software. Greg impressed upon Dave that there were no current funds identified for anything; however, the CIO had asked him to spend time on this. Greg said that he was optimistic that the new fiscal year would have a funded project in the very near future.

During the meeting, Dave explained to Greg that he had been proactively thinking about GlueWorks and the various goals that had been discussed with him. Dave reviewed the Decision Timeline document with Greg and Terry. He asked them if the milestones seemed appropriate and were logical. Greg was impressed with the document but cautioned Dave that there was no current funding for the effort, so he would be unable to promise Dave an order in six or seven months.

Dave responded to this concern, "Greg, I completely understand that you currently do not have funding to achieve these goals. Isn't it likely that if you find that you can accomplish your personal goals and the company's goals, then you would find the funding?"

Greg replied, "You are probably correct. We aren't doing all of this investigation for nothing. If we can achieve our goals, then we will probably want to move ahead."

Dave continued, "Then let's not worry about the order part. Let's agree that we should work together to find a way to achieve your goals. If you think that this timeline makes sense, then I am willing to invest in the effort and the resources on my side, as long as you are willing to invest the resources on your side."

Greg had another question after reviewing the document in more detail. "What are the 'Decide to Proceed' entries?"

Dave explained that throughout the evaluation of the technology both companies are going to learn a great deal about goals and needs as well as the functionality of Premium Software. The idea is simply that on a periodic basis, Dave and Greg should sit down and agree that everything is going well and both companies want to continue to invest the time and resources required to proceed to the next step. If for some reason either company felt that it didn't make sense to continue, they would shake hands and wish each other well. Greg was quite surprised that Dave was planning this mid-process health checks and thought it was a great idea.

Everyone was happy with the arrangement and Dave agreed to send Terry and Greg an electronic version of the Decision Timeline.

Dave called his manager from the parking lot of GlueWorks. They both agreed that this was very positive news. They were both very familiar with decision-making processes as described in the book *Eliminate Your Competition* and it appeared to them that GlueWorks was about to move into the Unification Stage of decision making and Greg appeared to be taking a leadership role in the process.

Dave composed a letter to Greg Saterree that confirmed many of the points that he brought up in their conversation. Dave shared his confirmation email with his manager, and his manager agreed it was a great follow-up to the meeting. Dave's manager specifically liked the feedback that Dave requested to make sure that the subtle trap on multi-department uses worked.

Dear Greg -

Thank you for your time discussing your optimization project. I have put my notes into this email in the hopes of confirming what I heard and our next action items. Please let me know if I have missed anything. I would like to get your feedback.

You have made it clear that the new solution must:

- Assess the skills of each employee.
- Identify the skills that need to be developed for each employee.
- Allow a manager to create specific requirements for each headcount in his/her department.
- Allow a manager to create a specific skills analysis for each project and recurring activity in his/her department.
- Compare departmental needs to skills within departments and the entire organization.
- Create detailed reports on human skills available and skills needed on personal, departmental, and organizational levels.
- Analyze learning paths to identify best candidates for enhanced training for any skills detriment.
- You mentioned that it was important that the software be flexible enough that it can be applied to other use cases within GlueWorks.
- You mentioned that other people on the committee might have other specific needs, but these were the most important needs to you.

Do I have these needs itemized correctly?

I am confident that we will be able to show you how we accomplish all of these points. Please let me know if you have any concerns as we work together over the next few months.

We are very proud of our Intelligent Assessment Advisor (IAA), which can rate every employee in an automated peer-review 360-degree view. We think that we are the only company to offer this technology to the marketplace. I would be curious to hear your feedback if you see anything like this in your research.

I am specifically curious about the last bullet item of applying artificial intelligence across multiple divisional problems. To the best of my knowledge, no other product that can match us in Human Resources issues can also be applied in areas such as Product Development, Manufacturing, and Logistics. If you find that I am wrong, can you help expand my knowledge of the industry by letting me know of your research?

Can we put the review of IAA on the agenda for our meeting next Wednesday? I would enjoy hearing your comments on how we approach this problem compared to other potential solutions.

I am also attaching an electronic version of the Decision Timeline that we discussed.

I look forward to seeing you at 10A next Wednesday to review the Decision Timeline and the IAA.

Sincerely,

Dave

P.S. Don't forget to sign up for our webinar on improving efficiency on Friday. You can register at http://www.thetrapper.com.

24 Weeks Before The GlueWorks Purchase Order

The CEO of GlueWorks has recently created a new initiative for the company. The CEO stated this goal in a company-wide speech on the previous Friday: "We want to organize the company to be more market focused. We will accomplish this realignment by the end of the fiscal year."

The local business press picked up the story, as did the Wall Street Journal and several other international business newspapers. Also, one of the cable business news shows interviewed the CEO on the morning talk show, where he explained that this would be a project led by Product Development and Human Resources, with significant help from the CIO. The stock market had a favorable reaction to the announcement, and the company's stock saw a nice uptick.

Prior to the announcement, the CEO and his direct staff had some idea of how they were going to handle the reorganization. His VP of Human Resources was going to be the face of the reorganization, but all of them had decided that new organization was going to be driven by the VP of Marketing, working closely with the VP of Product Development. The CEO had worked with the VP of Product Development at a previous company and this was the reason he was asked to take a leadership role at GlueWorks.

Amy Gatherer and her manager received a phone call from her VP of Sales alerting her to the news about GlueWorks. She has been tasked to understand how this news will affect her existing projects and to make sure that this change doesn't affect her revenue stream.

Ben Farmer discussed the news about GlueWorks with his manager. He has been tasked to understand how this news will affect his existing projects and to make sure that this change doesn't affect his revenue stream.

Carla Hunter and her manager discussed the GlueWorks announcement. They agree that it may be time to focus more energy on GlueWorks. Carla commits to having some more information next week.

Dave Trapper and his manager both had a news feed at Google Alerts following GlueWorks, so they immediately saw the announcement by the CEO. In their Monday morning meeting, they confirmed that the various executives mentioned in the CEO interview were receiving Dave's monthly newsletter that covered the challenges of alignment and successful employees.

Dave had developed enough of a reputation with this group that he had a LinkedIn connection to all of them. He also reconfirmed that the CIO of GlueWorks used to work for Midwest Products. Midwest Products is a similarly sized business to GlueWorks. Midwest Products had spoken at the national user group meeting of Premium Software last year regarding their successes.

Dave also noticed that the VP of Marketing went to Brown University, which is where Premium Software's VP of Marketing attended. Also, Dave noticed that the VP of Product Development was active in the Make-A-Wish charity, a charity that the CEO of Premium Software also supported.

Dave and his manager quickly stepped up their efforts on GlueWorks:

- Dave shared the Midwest Products success story and video on his LinkedIn account and his Twitter account.
- He sent an email to the GlueWorks employees on his list, congratulated them on the new direction, and referenced his LinkedIn page. Two of them asked him to link.
- He ghostwrote a note from his CEO, Mary Standard, to the VP of Product Development, John Roundtree, referencing the Make-A-Wish connection and forwarded the note to his CEO. The CEO slightly edited it and sent it late Tuesday night.
- He sent separate emails to Greg Saterree, Terry Tram, Sally Sunderman from Accounts Payable, Keith Vandenburg in Marketing, and Jen Fremen in Product Development. In the emails, he referenced the CEO's announcement and

reminded them that Premium Software helps solve this exact situation. Dave asked each of them for a meeting that week.

Later that day, Greg Saterree invites Dave to a meeting. Dave assumes that the meeting is to review his points from the email that he sent previously. He is surprised that the CIO of GlueWorks is in the meeting. The CIO explains how Greg has been pitching the idea of artificial intelligence and there is a small group tasked with looking at the technology for some time and CIO thinks it is impressive. He also thinks GlueWorks will receive a lot of positive press attention if they solve this problem with software rather than pure consulting services.

Dave doesn't bother to correct the CIO that he has been meeting with this small task force for quite some time. He is simply thankful that his early work may result in a funded project. He realizes that either the CIO or perhaps Greg, in the CIO's absence, could potentially be the leader of this effort from this point forward.

Dave spends a few minutes discussing the difficulties of company realignment. In the past, companies tried to do this type of project using dozens or hundreds of consultants, with varied results. He suggested a few activities that would allow GlueWorks to better understand the technology and how it would affect GlueWorks. He offers to share a Decision Timeline for those activities in a letter to the CIO and Greg.

The CIO appreciated his insight and assured him that GlueWorks could not afford to make a mistake at this critical point. Greg interjected that this was the reason that GlueWorks was having conversations about artificial intelligence and that it seemed to be a way to avoid an expensive but fruitless effort at company realignment.

Dave calls his manager from the GlueWorks parking lot. He has just updated his Relationship Map for GlueWorks and aligned the CIO of GlueWorks to the CTO of Premium Software. His manager agrees that this is an excellent idea and upon hanging up with Dave, calls the CTO and enlists his help.

That afternoon, the CTO of Premium Software called the CIO of GlueWorks and left a message with his administrative assistant. He was surprised when he quickly received a phone call back. After pleasantries, the CIO complimented Dave Trapper on his understanding of GlueWorks and his understanding of the artificial intelligence industry. The CIO accepted an invitation to breakfast before an upcoming analyst event they were both attending in several weeks.

Dave's manager also reminds Dave to make sure his Power Matrix, Relationship Map, and Issues Alignment chart are up to date so that he can share them with the CTO of Premium Software.

23 Weeks Before The GlueWorks Purchase Order

Amy Gatherer informs her manager that she has spoken to multiple people about the GlueWorks initiative. She feels confident that her existing consulting revenue is safe. She did say that her sources suggested that she spend more time with Greg Saterree. She has reached out to Greg for a meeting.

Ben Farmer told his manager that he spoke to Alice and Steve at GlueWorks. They feel that his revenue will be safe based on the GlueWorks initiative. They suggested that he reach out to Greg Saterree, as he appeared to be leading an evaluation of ways to improve efficiency in GlueWorks.

Carla Hunter finally mentions GlueWorks to her manager. Several employees of GlueWorks have downloaded information from the Focused Software website. She tells her manager that she is going to start calling some of the executives that she sees listed on the GlueWorks website. She also requests that her inside sales team reach out to those individuals who have downloaded materials. She is also going to reach out to John Roundtree, whom she had met with several weeks earlier.

This is Premium Software's week for sales kickoff for the new fiscal year. Dave Trapper is in attendance, along with all the salespeople from across North America. It is a big week for Dave as he is a bit of a hero for closing ABC Plane Parts. As he was warned, he is asked to do a special session on the win, where he outlines the week-by-week sales cycle.

Dave started his comments with an acknowledgment of how he was able to change his sales strategies dramatically. "Before I get into the meat of this deal, I need to give a quick acknowledgement to Sally Superstar. We all know that Sally is the company's most successful salesperson. Last year, I was at this very same sales meeting, and Sally was kind enough to sit down with me and give me advice on how to guide a prospect through the decision-making process and eliminate the competition. I honestly would not have closed this deal had I not sat with Sally. Much of what I am going to share with you regarding ABC Plane Parts, I learned from Sally and a book that she suggested that I read titled *Eliminate Your Competition*."

Later in the day, after Dave's successful and enlightening presentation, a young salesperson came up to him. "Dave, I am Jerry. Do you have a few minutes to talk about your great presentation this morning?"

"Sure. I am happy to help. What can I do for you?"

"My biggest question to you is about the book that you recommended during your talk. Can you eliminate your competition like the book suggests?"

"Yes, but the competitors probably do not know they are eliminated until the very end of the sales cycle. In fact, in a lot of organizations, some of the people in the decision-making process may not even know that a potential vendor is eliminated until a final vendor is announced officially. Look, we all know that at the end, all of the competitors are eliminated and one vendor is chosen. The key here is to make sure that you are the vendor that is chosen and your competitors are the ones that are eliminated."

Jerry continued to ask Dave questions about how he manages a sales campaign as well as specific questions about his prospect, Black Gold. After about 45 minutes, both salespeople wanted to attend the next scheduled session on new features in a future release of their product, but Dave had a final piece of advice for his new friend. "Call me anytime to ask about how I handle a specific situation. You should also reach out to Sally Superstar and get her help. I need to ask you one simple question, though: are you going to buy the book *Eliminate Your Competition* soon?"

Jerry laughed as he pulled out his tablet. "I bought it online this morning while you were presenting, and it is already on my tablet! I hope to start reading it on my flight home tomorrow."

That evening, Premium Software held their awards banquet to finish up the week of sales kickoff. Premium Software offers a club trip to its top performers who are over quota. This year's club trip was announced as the Caribbean island of Nevis. Dave was excited to take his wife on a well-deserved vacation and started texting his parents to see if they could watch Dave's three school-aged children. Dave's mother enthusiastically replied back in a confirmation text before the awards speeches even began.

The last two awards of the evening were for North American Salesperson of the Year, preceded by Region of the Year for North America. Dave received the top salesperson award, and his manager received Region of the Year for North America. Dave walked off the stage, still seeing spots from all of the pictures taken with the company executives, when he saw Sally waiting for him.

"Congratulations on a great year! I hated coming in second this year, but at least it was to you! I just wanted to thank you for the kind words this morning about my tutelage. More importantly, I want to warn you that next year you will be no better than second, as I have no intention to be the first-loser again."

Dave hugged Sally and said, "May the best salesperson next year be number one."

When they broke the hug, Dave turned to walk to his seat. Standing to the side, he noticed Jerry. Jerry lifted his drink as a long-distance toast in acknowledgment to the current leader. Dave suddenly realized that his competition to repeat as the number one salesperson may be a bit more crowded than he and Sally originally thought.

22 Weeks Before The GlueWorks Purchase Order

This week is the sales kickoff week for Everything Consulting and Amy Gatherer. As is typical, she has a detailed plan for four of her five accounts, and she will discuss these plans with her management. She had to drop ABC Plane Parts from her list, as they didn't continue their consulting contract, but she will now add Suncar Auto. Suncar Auto is not as large a consulting contract as ABC Plane Parts was, but her quota for the new fiscal year was adjusted accordingly.

One of the sessions that Amy attended covered positioning the company's artificial intelligence offering into accounts. The general strategy was to position the offering to companies where Everything Consulting did not have a consulting practice or to position it to accounts where the existing consulting contracts were at risk.

Amy privately discussed this with some of her fellow salespeople, and they all agreed that introducing the AI product to existing accounts was a mistake, as the consulting revenue would drop precipitously. The best philosophy was to get closer to the top executives at an existing customer and use fear, uncertainty, and doubt to prevent artificial intelligence from gaining a foothold.

Daydream Consulting also was having their annual fiscal year kickoff meeting, and Ben Farmer was present. Daydream was not a large company, so the meeting was held in the adjoining state at DayDream's headquarters. They invited the publisher of their artificial intelligence product to hold some informational sessions and Ben attended all of them. He noticed a strong push for the technical aspects of the product but not a lot of positioning. This frustrated Ben, as his forte was to have great relationships with his best customers and to offer them highly-trained consultants that his customers could trust. He was a relationship salesperson and people bought from him because they knew and trusted him rather than his expertise on technology.

By the end of the kickoff meeting, Ben concluded that he probably should wait another year to push the new AI products, as it seemed too technical for his good customers. Ben's customers were really happy with Ben's service and offering a new tool might undermine that relationship.

Carla Hunter was also at her company's kickoff meeting. She dreaded the entire event. She always seemed to have a million things in the air, and she couldn't take the time for all of this product positioning and sales training. She spent most of the presentations in the hallway with her cellphone, trying to track down projects and understand what her prospects were planning.

Carla also didn't enjoy the awards banquet. She knew what it was like to be the best salesperson for the company and this year she wasn't going to get that award. She was happy she won a President's Club trip to Mexico but disappointed that she was only in eighth place for revenue for the company. When she voiced her frustration to her manager over dinner the final evening, he replied, "Carla, that is why I like having you on my team. You are my best salesperson, and I need the rest of my team to be more like you. I am confident that you will figure out how to be number one in the company and while you are doing that, I need to figure out how to get the rest of my team to follow your lead."

Dave and his manager do a complete review of the Decision Timeline, Power Matrix, Relationship Map, and Issues Alignment chart for GlueWorks. This effort only takes a few minutes since Dave already understands the benefit of these documents and has put them into one larger document. They agree on a couple of tweaks and a refinement of Dave's overall plan.

Dave also updates his manager on his follow-up with Greg Saterree. Not only did Greg attend the webinar that Dave invited him to, but he also had some feedback as Greg escorted him out of the building after their Wednesday meeting. Greg confided in Dave that he has yet to see anyone talk about using the same AI platform for multiple departments. Dave queried Greg if that was still going to be a top priority in his analysis, and Greg assured him that nothing had changed.

They concluded the conversation with a commitment from Greg to make sure that other influential people would see the content from the webinar. Greg suggested a few tweaks to the content that would help others understand the use of artificial intelligence to solve problems.

21 Weeks Before The GlueWorks Purchase Order

Amy Gatherer told her manager that she had a very successful meeting with the CFO of GlueWorks. She was able to mention that Premium Software had very few consultants so if artificial intelligence didn't work out, there was little safety net for the project. She was also able to mention that DayDream Consulting was a very small local supplier and they didn't have a lot of experience in big projects. The CFO asked if she brought up this information to Greg Saterree, and she reached out to Greg for a meeting. She also asked the CFO if he would send a note to Greg about their long relationship. The CFO agreed that this would be appropriate and Amy was happy that she has the account under control.

Ben Farmer met with Greg Saterree at the suggestion of his sponsors, Alice and Steve. Ben explained that DayDream Consulting has been in business for much longer than everyone else in the industry and that they have more local consultants than everyone else. Greg asked him about his artificial intelligence practice, and Ben said they were growing that business. He told Greg that he had sent a bunch of material to John Roundtree in the past and offered to send that same packet to Greg.

Carla Hunter informs her manager that there may be something interesting going on at GlueWorks. She has had a couple of phone conversations with several people who have requested information.

She asks her inside sales person to prioritize reaching out to the VP of Human Resources and the CIO at GlueWorks.

Carla also had a great conversation with John Roundtree at GlueWorks. They had met several weeks earlier. He told her that he thought that GlueWorks was serious about moving forward. He suggested that she reach out to Greg Saterree.

Dave and his manager had a meeting with Greg Saterree and the CIO of GlueWorks. This was originally intended to be a simple follow-up meeting from the informal conversations that Premium Software's CTO had been having with the CIO.

Dave's manager is pretty certain that Everything Consulting is going to have an opportunity to be involved in this GlueWorks project. Amy Gatherer and Everything Consulting have a long history with GlueWorks. Dave's manager decides to directly challenge Everything Consulting's inclusion with the CIO. Dave knows that his manager will be bringing this up due to their pre-call planning, so he takes the lead after the first question.

Dave's manager says, "I understand that Everything Consulting is going to be considered for this project. Is that correct?"

The CIO pauses for a second at this direct question but smiles and says, "Yes."

Dave steps into the conversation. "I will be blunt. Does Premium Software truly have a chance to be honestly considered for this project? Everything Consulting has been a trusted and good vendor to GlueWorks for decades. Why would you consider our products when you have such a long and successful history with Everything Consulting?"

The CIO leans back in his chair and looks at Dave and his manager, along with a glance over at Greg, "That is a fair concern. Yes, we have a long history with Everything Consulting, but I am not sure it has always been successful. We think that we can solve this problem with technology and, for the most part, Everything Consulting is a consulting company. They also have a technology solution, but we don't know much about it yet. We are a bit concerned that if it was that good then perhaps Everything Consulting should have suggested it in the past. You can be confident that if your product is better than the Everything Consulting product, you will be chosen. Maybe if it is a tie then Everything Consulting will have an advantage, but few things in life are truly ties."

Dave and his manager don't dwell on the discussion past this statement from the CIO. They don't want to say anything negative about Everything Consulting, and the CIO has just given them the opening that they need against their competitor. They know that they need to ask everyone they know at GlueWorks why Everything Consulting has not introduced artificial intelligence products to GlueWorks in the past.

20 Weeks Before The GlueWorks Purchase Order

Amy Gatherer meets with Greg Saterree. She thinks the meeting went well, but Greg seems to be rather aloof. He informs her that his job has nothing to do with bringing in consultants and if that is the decision of GlueWorks, then she will continue to use her normal contacts for that relationship. Greg agrees to listen to some of Everything Consulting's artificial intelligence offerings.

Ben Farmer followed up with Greg Saterree regarding the information that he sent on artificial intelligence. Greg agrees that it looked interesting. Greg agrees to have a presentation with some of the experts from DayDream Consulting.

Carla Hunter tells her manager that she is excited that her inside salesperson reached the VP of Human Resources, who has referred her to Greg Saterree. This is the second referral to Greg, as John Roundtree had also suggested she approach Greg. Evidently, Greg has been tasked with looking at methods to most effectively organize the company's resources. She has sent an introductory email to Greg asking for a meeting, copying both John Roundtree and the VP of Human Resources.

Dave Trapper tells his manager about his lunch with Jen Fremen, as well as a casual conversation with Greg Saterree. In both conversations, Dave was able to bring up the question of Everything Consulting's lack of use of artificial intelligence in previous projects. He also brought up some concerns about Everything Consulting's support capability.

Greg also asked Dave for some ideas on things to put into a Request for Proposal. Greg doesn't like RFPs but knows that GlueWorks' purchasing will probably require one. Dave offers to send over some sample RFPs to help Greg with some of the questions. Dave reminds Greg of the importance of thinking of artificial intelligence as not just a human resource management technology, but a platform to solve a wide range of issues, so the RFPs that Dave will send will have some focus on multi-departmental needs.

Dave didn't include an RFP in the Decision Timeline that he had shared with Greg a few weeks earlier, so they agreed on a few modifications to the timeline to accommodate the RFP. At Greg's request, the timeline was not extended, and he was able to now commit to Dave that at the end of the timeline GlueWorks intended to have a solution to achieve their goals, even if that meant acquiring new technology.

Once Dave heard that Greg felt that a purchase was likely, he knew he needed some more information. Dave quizzed Greg on how GlueWorks typically justified acquisitions. This information included the internal rate of return required as well as several factors that would need to be included in that analysis. Greg didn't immediately have that information for Dave but sent it to him the day after the meeting.

Finally, Dave and his manager reviewed the two onsite sessions that Dave's technical team did as a follow-up to the webinar from a couple of weeks back. Between the two sessions, there were 27 people in attendance. They agreed on which of those 27 people belonged in the Power Matrix and updated the Relationship Map so that everyone on Dave's team knew whom to focus on in subsequent conversations.

19 Weeks Before The GlueWorks Purchase Order

Amy Gatherer informs her manager that they presented the artificial intelligence offering from Everything Consulting. The meeting went well, and Greg Saterree was the host. There were about a dozen people in the room, but most of the questions came from Greg, Terry Tram (whom Amy didn't know well) and Jen Fremen.

Ben Farmer informs his manager that they presented the artificial intelligence offering from DayDream Consulting. The meeting went well, and Greg Saterree was the host. There were about a dozen people in the room, but most of the questions came from Greg, Terry Tram, and Jen Fremen.

Carla Hunter tells her manager that she had a phone conversation with Greg Saterree at GlueWorks and they were going to do a presentation on artificial intelligence in two weeks. Greg had suggested next week, but Carla was really busy, and she asked for the following week.

Terry Tram had met Dave for coffee outside of the GlueWorks facilities. Terry said that he heard Dave was concerned about Everything Consulting. Terry assured Dave that Everything Consulting was not in the lead simply because the more people learned about artificial intelligence, the more they realized that Everything Consulting was not helping them by only providing consulting rather than artificial intelligence capability. Terry finished the point with, "Look, there are some people at GlueWorks that think that Everything Consulting must have really bad software simply because they never brought it up to us in the past."

Terry told him that Greg Saterree was frustrated with Everything Consulting. It seemed that the salesperson for Everything Consulting had influenced the CFO to intercede with Greg and remind him of their long relationship. Greg then spoke to his manager, the CIO, and the CIO agreed to have a conversation with the CFO to allow the buying decision process to proceed unhindered.

Dave finished his conversation by bringing up a recurring conversation that he had with Terry regarding the market share and developer location of Everything Consulting.

Dave and his manager agree that this is great feedback and Terry Tram is a Coach that they can depend on for advice.

18 Weeks Before The GlueWorks Purchase Order

Amy Gatherer had spent most of the week dealing with some emergencies due to the GlueWorks consultants. She successfully handled all of the problems, but it was a huge time drain for her. She also responded to some questions that had come up in the GlueWorks presentation from the previous week. Luckily, Amy was well-connected within Everything Consulting, so she was able to delegate a lot of the research to others, and all she had to do was to forward their research.

Ben Farmer had a hard time responding to some of the tougher questions that came up during the GlueWorks presentation. He had never sold artificial intelligence, so he was dependent on others for most of his answers. He wasn't sure that some of these answers truly addressed the questions, but he sent them to Greg Saterree anyway.

Carla Hunter didn't have much of an update on GlueWorks. She was extremely busy with two RFPs that had just come out from companies that she didn't know very well. She reminded her manager that they had a presentation scheduled for the following week at GlueWorks.

Dave Trapper and his manager were interrupted during their normal account-planning meeting. Their CTO called during the meeting and updated them on a breakfast meeting with the CIO of GlueWorks. He appreciated all of the information that had been shared about GlueWorks and wished more Premium Software sales teams used a Relationship Map similar to the one that Dave managed.

Dave was surprised that more Premium Software salespeople didn't use Relationship Maps in their sales campaigns. Dave originally learned of Relationship Maps from the book *Eliminate Your Competition*, which Sally Superstar told him about. The amazing thing was that Sally had also given a copy of the book to the Premium Software VP of Sales and he was a big fan. It surprised him that more salespeople didn't take the lead of the VP of Sales and the number one salesperson at the company.

The CIO meeting went very well. The two of them spent 90 minutes over lunch discussing many technologies, including artificial intelligence. The CIO complained about the high cost of just using consultants and how he was hopeful that artificial intelligence would cut those costs and increase the accuracy of projects.

The CIO of GlueWorks mentioned to the CTO of Premium Software that while he was not in favor of a consulting-only project, he was concerned whether Premium Software had enough consultants to get GlueWorks up to speed. The CTO realized that this was the true metric for success, as opposed to the number of consultants, so he spent time explaining the Premium Software deployment methodology and gave some examples of successful deployments. He assured the CIO that Premium Software had the right number of consultants to successfully get GlueWorks going without so many that Premium Software felt the need to shove consultants at a project.

The CTO then asked the CIO of GlueWorks if he ever had a situation where a project seemed to be overrun with consultants and the budget grew out of control. The CIO nervously laughed that he had often seen it happen. The CTO boldly proclaimed, "That won't occur with Premium Software, and you should make sure that it doesn't happen with our competitors."

The CIO of GlueWorks agreed to correspond regularly in the future.

After the call with the CIO, the CTO called Dave and told him that a consulting company was a top competitor. It was fairly obvious that a salesperson from a consulting company had tried to create a trap for Premium Software regarding the number of consultants. Dave thanked him for the insight and agreed that the trap probably came from Everything Consulting or DayDream Consulting due to their history with GlueWorks.

17 Weeks Before The GlueWorks Purchase Order

Amy Gatherer and her manager met with the CFO of GlueWorks. They reviewed some of the challenges from the consultants that had come up over the last week or so. The CFO was pleased with how Everything Consulting had worked through the problems and he felt they were a great partner for GlueWorks.

Amy's manager took this sign of trust as a closing opportunity. He said he was aware that GlueWorks was looking at artificial intelligence. He asked the CFO to agree to a pilot of Everything Consulting's artificial intelligence offering. The CFO thought that this was interesting and asked if they had proposed the pilot to the CIO and Greg Saterree. Amy's manager said that they had not but wanted the CFO's endorsement first. The CFO of GlueWorks said that he was letting the CIO and his team make the decision and would support whatever the CIO decided.

As they left GlueWorks, Amy's manager voiced his disappointment that his trial close had failed. They discussed that this might mean that the CFO was not as strong as they had previously thought. After consideration, though, they realized that the CFO was probably just being polite to the CIO and would come through again in the end, as he had in the past.

Ben Farmer was frustrated with his support structure, and he complained to his manager. It seemed that some of the answers that he had provided to GlueWorks were not perfectly aligned with the questions. He wasn't knowledgeable enough about the software to truly understand all of the questions and the answers, and he was disappointed that his team let him down. He was hopeful that the newly submitted answers were sufficient.

Carla Hunter informed her manager that they presented the artificial intelligence offering from Focused Software. The meeting went well, and Greg Saterree was the host. There were about a dozen people in the room, but most of the questions came from Greg, Terry Tram, and Jen Fremen.

Dave Trapper met with his manager and described how he had further extended his influence on the GlueWorks evaluation. He met with Jen Fremen and John Roundtree in Product Development and discussed their challenges with developing new GlueWorks products. It was obvious to Dave that their personal goals of developing higher margin products were being hampered by the inability of manufacturing to respond to product changes quickly.

Dave discussed how the use of his software could not only make manufacturing more efficient but also make it easier for product development to spot needs in the GlueWorks customer base. John Roundtree questioned why manufacturing wasn't pursuing such options, and Jen pointed out that the group was tied to a relationship with DayDream Consulting. John encouraged Jen to become more active in the evaluation of AI and to discourage DayDream Consulting from becoming a finalist in the evaluation.

With the help of his manager, Dave customized four of Premium Software's product positioning papers and combined them with several customer success stories on manufacturing and product development. They put a plan together to send one of these documents to John Roundtree and Jen Fremen every week for the next four weeks.

They also rearranged the Power Matrix to accommodate the increased importance of John Roundtree. They agreed that they should align a product development specialist from Premium Software to John Roundtree and record that activity in the Relationship Map.

16 Weeks Before The GlueWorks Purchase Order

Amy Gatherer informed her manager that Greg Saterree was not open to the idea of just running a pilot of Everything Consulting's artificial intelligence software. He felt that this might be something that they would consider in the future, but it was too early at this time, as everyone at GlueWorks was still learning about artificial intelligence.

Ben Farmer told his manager that Greg confirmed that all of their questions from the presentation a week ago were satisfactorily answered. Greg told him to sit tight as they digested all of the information and made plans for the next step.

Carla Hunter informs her manager that GlueWorks is a real opportunity for Focused Software. She has met with Greg Saterree who appears to be the decision maker. Greg has informed her that GlueWorks wants to decide in the next three to four months. She has asked for Greg to introduce her to the VP of Human Resources and the CIO. She has also asked for meetings with several members of the virtual team. Greg has promised to do the best that he can.

Carla tells her manager that the presentation that they did for GlueWorks was very well received. She has just sent answers to some of the follow-up questions, and her team had researched for her.

Carla's manager is not very familiar with GlueWorks so he spends some time after their update call reading about the company.

Dave Trapper is away at President's Club in Nevis, and so is his manager. They made a pact not to talk about current business during the week.

15 Weeks Before The GlueWorks Purchase Order

Amy Gatherer didn't have an update for her manager on GlueWorks. The company seemed to go silent on her.

Ben Farmer told his manager that he had a meeting with Steve and Alice. They didn't have much news regarding the artificial intelligence project, as they were out of the loop. All of Ben's phone calls to Greg Saterree were not returned.

Carla Hunter is at her President's Club in Mexico but still working. It is typical of Carla that she cannot stop working on deals, even on her time off. She tries to reach Greg Saterree regarding meeting the CIO of GlueWorks. Greg tells her that it is a bit premature for that meeting and asks that she be patient. Carla is frustrated, as she is rarely patient. She convinces her manager to send an email to the CIO but not copy her so that she can deny knowledge if Greg becomes upset.

Dave Trapper and his technical team have some more meetings with various people at GlueWorks. Most of these people are not very high ranking but are new people that have recently been included in the evaluation process. Dave didn't ask permission from Greg for these meetings since Terry Tram suggested that he contact the individuals. Several of the people are Dave's old contacts from when Dave first met with Terry many weeks earlier. Dave is a bit relieved when Terry assures him that he will make sure that Greg doesn't mind the various side conversations.

Dave and his manager divide the conversations appropriately by using the Relationship Map so that no one is overwhelmed with the effort.

Dave also accompanies his product development specialist to a meeting with John Roundtree and Jen Fremen. They spend almost two hours talking through applications of the technology and drawing on whiteboards. At the end of the meeting, John asks Dave if it is okay if he has a bi-weekly conversation with the specialist to review his thoughts. They agree on a call schedule, and Dave sends out the recurring appointment.

14 Weeks Before The GlueWorks Purchase Order

Amy Gatherer tells her manager that she is starting to become concerned with GlueWorks. Evidently, there are some new people on the project, and she doesn't know all of them. GlueWorks asked her for a meeting, and there were a lot of new people in the meeting, and they were asking some of the same questions that were previously covered. At the end of the meeting, she was told that she would be receiving an RFP from GlueWorks. This greatly concerns Amy, as she was trying to avoid being lumped in with all of the other competitors.

Ben Farmer tells his manager that GlueWorks is frustrating and is a confused customer. He was invited to a meeting with Greg Saterree, and almost everyone was new. The only people that were the same were Terry Team and Jen Fremen. The new people asked many of the same questions that had previously been covered. Ben had a few questions that he couldn't adequately answer, so he asked for a further meeting to cover the information again. Greg suggested that they were probably okay at this time but would be getting back to him in the form of an RFP. Ben despises RFPs, as he doesn't think that DayDream Consulting does a great job of preparing the responses.

In Carla Hunter's weekly meeting with her manager, she expresses some frustration. Evidently, some of the people she met within the last few weeks have been moved off the project. There are some new people that have joined, but she doesn't know who these people are yet.

Carla does tell her manager that it appears that they will be receiving an RFP from GlueWorks. This is great news for her because she feels that Focused Software has a lot of great resources for creating impressive RFP responses.

Carla's manager tells her that he did receive a response from the CIO of GlueWorks The email response copied Greg Saterree. The CIO simply said that he was glad that Focused Software was interested in working with GlueWorks and that Greg was the point person within IT for the effort.

With the changes in the evaluation committee at GlueWorks, Dave Trapper and his manager do a complete review of the Power Matrix, Relationship Map, Decision Timeline, and Issues Alignment chart for GlueWorks. This only takes a few minutes since Dave already understands the benefit of these documents and has put them into one larger document. They agree on a couple of tweaks and a refinement of Dave's plan.

13 Weeks Before The GlueWorks Purchase Order

The CEO of GlueWorks was interviewed by one of the major stock investment TV programs. The reporter asked the CEO about his announcement at the beginning of the year. The CEO elaborated that GlueWorks was going to undergo a massive re-focusing on its most profitable and highest growth products.

The CEO told the reporter, "We want to organize the company to be more market focused. To do this, we will reorganize along four major verticals plus Consumer Products. We will accomplish this realignment by the end of the fiscal year and it will result in one hundred million dollars in additional profit in the form of cost savings."

When challenged by the reporter on how he was going to achieve this, he announced that he had just "green-lighted" a new project that was going to allow the company to more efficiently apply its resources.

Every consulting company and software company that thought they might be able to assist GlueWorks immediately started to call their contacts within GlueWorks.

Amy Gatherer and her manager called the CFO of GlueWorks as soon as they read the announcement. He assured them that they were already very plugged into this initiative via their existing relationship, as well as their work with Greg Saterree. They asked the CFO if GlueWorks should meet with them immediately to discuss the pilot that they suggested earlier. The CFO thanked them but suggested that they continue to work with Greg Saterree.

Ben Farmer told his manager that all of his hard work was going to be rewarded soon. They discussed the announcement, as well as the various meetings and presentations they had done earlier. Ben requested that he get the full support of DayDream when the RFP came out.

Carla Hunter's manager was ecstatic at the announcement that he read about regarding GlueWorks in the financial newspaper. He brought it up to Carla as soon as she walked into his office. For once, they seemed to be ahead of the competition and knew about a deal before the RFP was issued. Carla was also excited about the news that GlueWorks would surely be a funded project. She also informed her manager that she expected the GlueWorks RFP to come out within the next week or so.

Dave worked with his manager to compile all of their contacts at GlueWorks. Together, they had met with 51 people throughout the organization, and they wanted to make sure that their lists were combined and cleaned. Dave's manager then "ghost wrote" an email from the CEO of Premium Software to the CEO of GlueWorks congratulating him on the recent announcement. A similar congratulations email was "ghost written" for the CTO of Premium Software to the CIO of GlueWorks. In parallel to this activity by Dave's manager, Dave sent personalized congratulatory emails to the remaining 49 GlueWorks people that he knew.

The CEO of GlueWorks responded with a quick "Thank you" to the email from the CEO of Premium Software, but the CIO of GlueWorks actually called the CTO of Premium Software to thank him for paying attention to them.

Dave also put a press release of the GlueWorks announcement on LinkedIn and tweeted it to his followers. Dave's manager immediately shared and retweeted the social media posts, and by the end of the week the LinkedIn post had been "liked" or shared by 112 people, and the tweet had been shared by 407 people. Most significantly, both the LinkedIn post and the tweet were liked by both the CEO of GlueWorks and the CEO of Premium Software.

Dave Trapper hosts his first bi-weekly conversation with John Roundtree and the product development specialist from Premium

Software. The meeting goes extremely well, but Dave is concerned that the upcoming RFP will force him to cancel the recurring calls. John laughs, "No one is going to stop me from learning more about technology that I think is important. We can continue to have this call."

12 Weeks Before The GlueWorks Purchase Order

GlueWorks has now formally sent out a Request For Proposal to cover their needs. They sent the RFP to six companies, including the four that are followed in this case study.

Amy Gatherer, Ben Farmer, Carla Hunter, and Dave Trapper spend several hours reading the RFP and working with their internal teams to create a plan to answer the questions.

11 Weeks Before The GlueWorks Purchase Order

GlueWorks sets up a phone call for all vendors to ask questions about the RFP.

Amy Gatherer and her manager had a few questions that they addressed on the call. The questions were all about the requested support options of the artificial intelligence software covered in the RFP.

Ben Farmer and his manager asked more questions about the RFP than any other vendor. Since the format of the call was to introduce himself first, he wanted to make sure that GlueWorks knew that he was very interested in the RFP and giving it his full attention. His philosophy was to show his desire for the details to show his willingness to be flexible.

Carla Hunter does a lot of RFPs, and she rarely asks questions unless something is very confusing. In this case, all of the questions made sense and she stayed silent.

Dave Trapper and his manager were both surprised that there was so little in the GlueWorks RFP that concerned manufacturing and product development. Dave commits to his manager that he will try to find out why the questions didn't cover this area when they had spent so much effort with John Roundtree and Jen Fremen. Dave didn't address any of these questions publicly on the call and didn't ask any other questions.

Later that week, Dave sat with John and Jen before their scheduled phone call with Dave's specialist. They laughed when Dave asked about the lack of a focus on their areas of specialty. John stated that he didn't value formal RFPs in his department, so he told Jen not to respond to the request for formal questions to be added. Instead, John prefers to meet with vendors and read about their technology.

John explained that there were six vendors that received the RFP and in his opinion, two of those vendors didn't have the technology to address his needs, and he would veto any decision to purchase their solution. The Manufacturing team championed one of them, a product resold by DayDream Consulting, and they were significantly slowing down his operation, so he couldn't work with them.

John continued to explain that Everything Consulting had a decent product, but John was upset that they had never introduced artificial intelligence to him during the many years GlueWorks worked with them. Focused Software seemed to have a good product as well, except they had never called on him until recently and when he asked about ideas and examples in his area of expertise, the salesperson overloaded him with dozens of barely relevant documents.

"So," Dave asked, "how do you feel about our offering?"

John responded with a smile, "Dave, in my opinion, Premium Software is the best solution for my group and probably the best solution for GlueWorks. I am going to let the RFP proceed, but I will make sure that the results favor your product and possibly Focused Software."

Dave was feeling a bit confident after that statement, so he decided to find out how strong a champion John might be down the road. "If that is the case, why don't you eliminate everyone but Premium Software and Focused Software?"

John laughed at the directness of the request. "They are eliminated. They just don't know it yet. We will keep Everything Consulting in play due to our long relationship, but I will make sure that the decision is between you and Focused."

After relaying the conversation to his manager, Dave started to put a stronger strategy together to go after Focused Software. John Roundtree didn't know it, but Dave had already laid a major trap within IT to further discredit Everything Consulting.

10 Weeks Before The GlueWorks Purchase Order

Amy Gatherer and her team worked on their RFP answers. It was a fairly challenging RFP. In particular, Amy was concerned about the emphasis on the location of the development organization and the support organization. Amy thought she had effectively answered those concerns over the last several weeks, but now it was coming up again.

Ben Farmer continued to be frustrated with DayDream Consulting and their ability to answer RFP questions. He spent many hours collating the answers. His team was also frustrated the Ben was not able to give them much insight into why GlueWorks was asking many of the questions, so they were unable to customize many of the canned answers.

Carla Hunter and her team were experts on RFPs. For nearly every question, they had two or three canned answers that they were able to plug into the response. They didn't bother with personalizing any of the answers since they had "wordsmithed" the answers over dozens of similar RFPs.

Dave Trapper and his team worked on their RFP answers. It was quite easy to answer the questions since Dave had discussed nearly every question in the past with someone at GlueWorks. Everyone on Dave's team marveled that the RFP appeared to be written just for them, and Dave was able to personalize many of the answers to specific needs within GlueWorks due to his knowledge of the company and its culture.

9 Weeks Before The GlueWorks Purchase Order

Amy Gatherer told her manager that they had successfully submitted the RFP response to GlueWorks. She was surprised that she was given an immediate reply that GlueWorks would select a short list of vendors within the week. Both she and her manager assumed that this meant that the vendor selection was almost pre-determined and therefore her long history would serve her well.

Ben Farmer told his manager that he successfully submitted the GlueWorks response. He again complained that DayDream Consulting needed better resources for RFPs. Ben's manager replied that he had heard that complaint before but also passed on that Ben's team felt that he didn't have intimate knowledge of the inner workings of GlueWorks and that lack of knowledge hindered the team's effectiveness.

Ben was also optimistic that a quick response to the RFP would be helpful to his efforts. He had a long history with the company and was confident that this history would be rewarded.

Carla Hunter told her manager that she was surprised that GlueWorks was going to announce the finalists within a week. She saw this as a positive sign, as she knew that she could apply a lot of resources to the final contract negotiation.

Dave Trapper also submitted his RFP response to GlueWorks. He typically didn't do a lot of RFPs so he wasn't sure if he should be worried about a quick answer or not.

At the end of the bi-weekly call that Dave and his product specialist had with John Roundtree and Jen Fremen, he asked John if he could call him back privately immediately after the call. John suggested that they just continue the conversation since he had no secrets from Jen. Dave tentatively asked about the rationale for a quick answer after the RFP. John laughed and said, "Dave, surely you remember that I said RFPs are a waste of time. I have convinced everyone else to follow my guidance on this. We already know who should be on the short list and as long as those companies didn't screw up on a few key answers, then we need to get on with our business. I am confident that you will be happy with this next step, and we should plan on keeping our conversation that is scheduled for two weeks from now."

8 Weeks Before The GlueWorks Purchase Order

Amy Gatherer reported to her manager that Everything Consulting was selected as one of the finalists in the GlueWorks RFP. They were scheduled to present their suggestions to the committee in two weeks.

Ben Farmer reported to his manager that DayDream Consulting was not selected to continue in the GlueWorks evaluation process. He was confident, though, that their existing stream of business with manufacturing would continue, and Alice had asked him to come in later in the week.

Carla Hunter reported to her manager that Focused Software was selected as one of the finalists in the GlueWorks RFP. They were scheduled to present their suggestions to the committee in two weeks.

Dave Trapper reported to his manager that Premium Software was selected as one of the finalists in the GlueWorks RFP. They were scheduled to present their suggestions to the committee in two weeks.

7 Weeks Before The GlueWorks Purchase Order

Amy Gatherer spent the majority of the week fine-tuning the presentation for GlueWorks. She was very confident that her long history with the company was going to pay off again, just like it had done many times before.

Ben Farmer's meeting with his manager wasn't very happy. His meeting with Alice that morning didn't go very well. It seemed that the manufacturing department at GlueWorks had been told that they would likely have to drop their contract with DayDream Consulting, depending on the chosen vendor at GlueWorks.

Carla Hunter spent the majority of the week preparing for GlueWorks. She had a lot of other deals that she was chasing in other parts of her multi-state territory, but this was the biggest and hottest deal. She was very demanding of her presentation team to make sure they knew every possible detail about their product that could come up.

Dave Trapper didn't have his normal meeting with his manager on Monday. Instead, the VP of Sales came into town later in the week and wanted to review the region's biggest opportunities.

After reviewing GlueWorks, the VP challenged Dave as to why he thought that he had successfully disqualified Everything Consulting, since they had such a strong relationship with GlueWorks. Dave explained that he and his manager had analyzed Everything Consulting and realized that their product was a weak fit for GlueWorks and was likely the reason that Everything Consulting had not competed with itself and introduced artificial intelligence to GlueWorks after they acquired the AI product.

Dave then relayed a series of meetings that laid a very effective trap that he had individually with Greg Saterree and Terry Tram. The meetings were never together, but they both followed the same plan.

> Dave: I understand that Everything Consulting's revenue for artificial intelligence is much larger in Europe than here in the US. Any idea why that is true?

> Greg / Terry: Is it really? That doesn't make sense given the size of the market in the US.

Dave: Perhaps you should understand that reason. For us, our Americas operations account for 62% of our revenue. We also have development operations combined with support operations in California and North Carolina.

At the next meeting, the subject came up again.

Greg / Terry: I found out that the reason that Everything Consulting is so popular in Europe is that their largest customers are in the Scandinavian countries of Finland and Sweden.

Dave: That is surprising. Those are relatively small markets. I would never have thought that there was that many companies in that market that would use the product. You know the core product that Everything Consulting acquired was originally based in Finland. Do they still develop the product in Finland?

Greg / Terry: I am not sure. Everything Consulting is based in Texas, and all of their typical support for their work is based in Texas. I would think they do development in Texas also.

Dave: It is a modern world, so companies can do development all over the world. I am sure they do that as well. You may want to make sure you are comfortable with the development operations. Our product managers are located in California, and I would be happy to have you converse with them. Also, our lead support architects are located in North Carolina and California. You may want to see if Everything Consulting provides all levels of support out of Texas.

Next meeting the subject came up again.

Greg / Terry: It does appear that Everything Consulting has support operations in Texas, as I expected. Their developers and product managers are in Finland. Evidently, they did acquire the company that created their artificial intelligence product. The reason that there are so many companies in Scandinavia that use the software is that was the extent of the original company's marketing and sales capability.

Dave: That is interesting. So I am a bit confused. You have said that our support offering intrigued you. This offering includes two-hour response time with a lead support architect. How is Everything Consulting going to offer a similar capability? Our lead architects are co-located with our developers. Do they offer a similar capability and how are you going to compare our capability with their offering?

Finally, in a further meeting:

Greg / Terry: I am a bit concerned with Everything Consulting's support offering. It seems that their lead architect access is a bit limited due to geographical reasons. They have two people in Texas at that level, but the majority of product planning and lead architecture personnel are in Finland. Also, seven of their ten largest customers are in Scandinavia, and nine of the ten are in Europe. It seems like this Texas-based company is not ready to be Texas-based for this offering. Where did you say your support and operations were based?

After hearing the series of conversations, the VP of Sales laughed, saying, "It seems you were paying attention on how to lay traps when you read the book *Eliminating Your Competition*. Great job! I am going to relay this story to all of the other managers - especially if you close this deal!"

Dave was proud that his strategy was well received, but he knew he needed more help. "Our CEO is active in Make-A-Wish, as is John Roundtree. Can you have her call John and reinforce our relationship?"

During the bi-weekly call with John Roundtree and Jen Fremen, Dave asked if his CEO, who was also active in Make-A-Wish, could give John a call. John was ecstatic to take the call, and it was scheduled for the next week.

6 Weeks Before The GlueWorks Purchase Order

Amy Gatherer and her technical teams presented their RFP answers to the GlueWorks team. There was a high degree of comfort in their conversation due to the long relationship between GlueWorks and Everything Consulting. The purchasing manager for GlueWorks asked Everything Consulting to deliver a "best and final" proposal to him within the next two weeks.

Amy walked out of the RFP meeting with a nagging worry, though, as she felt like her long relationship wasn't making this an obvious win for her. She was so concerned that after the meeting she immediately called the secretary of the CIO to request an appointment.

Ben Farmer had nothing to report on GlueWorks since DayDream Consulting was not actively involved in the current sales process and there was nothing that Ben could do to save his consulting revenue.

Carla Hunter and her team did a phenomenal job at presenting their RFP response. It was obvious to everyone at GlueWorks that they were very good at discussing their software and their technology. Unfortunately, during the conversation, a few subtle items were missed regarding the culture of GlueWorks. Carla was able to smooth these over, but it was obvious that Focused Software did not have a long and deep relationship with GlueWorks and they had made quite a few assumptions in their presentation and RFP response. The purchasing manager for GlueWorks asked Focused Software to deliver a "best and final" proposal to him within the next two weeks.

Dave Trapper told his manager that he had been invited to a conference call with their CEO, Mary Standard, and John Roundtree. The call went remarkably well. They first talked about the work they do for their favorite charity, Make-A-Wish, but then proceeded to business. John questioned Mary on the focus of Premium Software in developing solutions in product development and manufacturing. Mary explained the amount of R&D that they were devoting to that critical area and John was very impressed. Mary took that as an opening and asked why he was considering Focus Software, since she didn't believe that they were putting as much attention on these use cases. She said that she might be wrong, but it wasn't obvious to her that this was an area where Focus Software was concentrating. John committed to her that he would investigate that commitment. Since Mary had read *Eliminate Your Competition* at the suggestion of her VP of Sales, she knew how to lay an effective trap and therefore confirmed that John would send her an email as to his findings.

Dave and his manager were both present for the RFP presentation to GlueWorks. They had spent time with the Premium Software technical specialists to not only answer the specific questions that were covered in the RFP response but to also include additional information on topics that GlueWorks did not specifically ask about, such as Product Development. Their presentation was well received, but just like all RFP conversations, it was meant not to be committal. The purchasing manager for GlueWorks asked Premium Software to deliver a "best and final" proposal to him within the next two weeks.

5 Weeks Before The GlueWorks Purchase Order

Amy Gatherer told her manager that she was quite concerned after the RFP presentation, as it felt different than any meeting that she had ever been to with GlueWorks. She had requested a meeting with the CIO of GlueWorks, which was later that week. She asked her manager to attend the meeting with her.

Later that week, when Amy and her manager met with the CIO, the conversation started with the status of the various consulting projects that Everything Consulting was leading. The CIO mentioned that Everything Consulting as doing a fine job of executing on those projects. However, he was surprised that in all of their years of working together, Everything Consulting didn't spend much time introducing GlueWorks to artificial intelligence.

After discussing the history of artificial intelligence at Everything Consulting, the GlueWorks CIO specifically asked about the presence of experts within North America. He said he had heard that most of the large implementations of Everything Consulting were in Scandinavia. Amy's manager then spent several minutes trying to explain how they were ramping up their Texas-based support offering.

Finally, the CIO asked Amy about Everything Consulting's expertise and use cases with product development and manufacturing. Amy explained that they were focusing their development on human resources use cases. She further mentioned that the RFP that they just finished didn't include product development. The CIO of GlueWorks confirmed this but said that there was a growing interest in expanding beyond human resources needs.

Amy's manager immediately sensed trouble and started to introduce fear, uncertainty, and doubt into using artificial intelligence for too many departments too quickly. He suggested that GlueWorks should probably focus on making human resources successful first and then tackle other departments later.

When the meeting wrapped up, Amy's manager looked at her and confirmed what they were both thinking, "We are in trouble. We need to find out what we are doing with product development use cases and also find out who at GlueWorks is pushing that agenda."

The same afternoon Jen Fremen called Amy with a request for more information on the product development capability of Everything Consulting. Amy advised her that she was going to compile a summary of the data.

Ben Farmer had nothing to report on GlueWorks since DayDream Consulting was not actively involved in the current sales process and there was nothing that Ben could do to save his consulting revenue.

Carla Hunter was in a bit of panic when she called her manager. Jen Fremen had called her for more information on the R&D focus of the company. Carla had provided some standard information, and Jen seemed less than enthusiastic with the response. Her manager offered to call Jen to see if he got a different response, but Jen never returned his call.

Dave Trapper told his manager that he had been involved in three important conversations regarding GlueWorks. The first conversation was with Terry Tram. Terry told him that he had just left a meeting with Greg Saterree, and Greg had said that he thought that the entire evaluation was over and the best solution was Premium Software. Terry advised Dave to keep the news quiet, but it was his order to lose.

The second conversation was with Jen Fremen in their bi-weekly phone meeting. John Roundtree typically attended these meetings but couldn't make this particular one. Jen asked why Premium Software was the only one in the industry that was proactive about the applicability of artificial intelligence in manufacturing and product development. Dave's specialist, who was on the phone, explained that Premium Software had realized early in the life of the product that it needed to develop expertise in many vertical markets. "Well," Jen replied, "it is obvious to us that not only is Premium Software the best choice but you, Dave, and your team are so valuable to us that we would be fools to buy from someone else. In fact, we would probably recommend you and your team even if you sold one of the other finalist products. Dave, you and your team personally have John's vote, and that means a lot!"

The third conversation was a phone call from Mary Standard, the CEO of Premium Software. She called to tell Dave that John Roundtree had called her back. She had challenged John to understand Focused Software's efforts on use cases in product development and manufacturing. John said that he was disappointed in the response that he had received so far. John also wanted to tell Mary that he felt that Dave Trapper was an incredibly valuable asset and perhaps even more valuable than the software. Mary finished the conversation with a challenge. "Dave, you have closed some great deals in the past but it looks like you have outdone yourself on this one. I expect this order to come in very soon! Let me know if you need my help in any way, but you are obviously doing a great job on GlueWorks."

4 Weeks Before The GlueWorks Purchase Order

Amy Gatherer met with the Director of Purchasing to explain her quote. The Director was quite pleased that Everything Consulting delivered a very large discount on their consulting. Amy further explained that Everything Consulting was offering a Premier Partnership program to GlueWorks so that GlueWorks could join with Everything Consulting to help drive the development of artificial intelligence use in manufacturing and product development.

The Director asked Amy how much of a commitment that would mean from GlueWorks and what the cost would be for those future use cases, and Amy said that all of that was still being discussed, as it was a new program. The Director was impressed but privately worried about telling John Roundtree that he would have to invest valuable expertise into that effort.

Ben Farmer had nothing to report on GlueWorks since DayDream Consulting was not actively involved in the current sales process and there was nothing that Ben could do to save his consulting revenue.

Carla Hunter met with the Director of Purchasing to explain her quote. The Director was very impressed with the professional presentation of the quotation. He asked her about a line item titled "New vendor discount" that was a significant percentage. Carla explained that Focused Software understood the costs of creating a new vendor in GlueWorks systems. This one-time discount was designed to overcome this cost so that it wasn't a factor in the decision.

Dave Trapper met with the Director of Purchasing to explain his quote. The Director explained that this was the highest price offer that he had seen on this project and questioned Dave if there might have been a mistake. Dave assured him that there was no mistake and that the offer was in line with what other Premium Software customers were paying.

Dave also produced a full ROI analysis of his software, covering human resources, manufacturing, and product development at GlueWorks. He showed how the implementation was a positive for the GlueWorks-preferred internal rate of return. When the Director of Purchasing asked how he knew of GlueWorks' required return rate, Dave explained that Greg Saterree had provided him with that information several weeks ago.

3 Weeks Before The GlueWorks Purchase Order

Amy Gatherer had another meeting with the Director of Purchasing. He explained to her that her offer was not the preferred choice and asked her if she could help him out by waiving some of the costs in the Premier Partnership program as well as committing to the costs of future use cases.

Amy called her manager from the GlueWorks parking lot. He immediately reached out to his superiors and by the time Amy was back in her office they had a plan. They would commit to a firm price for all future purchases in the next three years, and they would hold all planning meetings for manufacturing and product development in Ivytown so that the travel cost to GlueWorks was minimized.

Amy immediately wrote up this expanded commitment and sent it back to the Director of Purchasing. She asked for a meeting the next day, but the Director pushed back, saying that he had to review the offer with his team.

Ben Farmer had nothing to report on GlueWorks since DayDream Consulting was not actively involved in the current sales process and there was nothing that Ben could do to save his consulting revenue.

Carla Hunter had the unfortunate task of telling her manager some bad news during their regular account review meeting. The Director of Purchasing had just called her to inform her that Focused Software did not make the final cut. GlueWorks would be making final negotiations with two other vendors, but if those negotiations didn't work out, he might be calling her back.

Dave Trapper and his manager called their CTO to reach out to the CIO of GlueWorks. He laughed because the CIO had just called him that morning. The CIO had reached out, saying that Premium Software's price was the highest-priced software solution, and asking if he could help get the price down.

The CTO asked if it was an acceptable ROI timeframe based on the needs of GlueWorks. The CIO assured him that it was but then offered that Everything Consulting's offering was quite a bit lower, but the team preferred Premium Software. The CTO explained several of the main features of Premium Software and the trust that the GlueWorks team had in the offering and the Premium Software team. He also explained the reduced risk that GlueWorks would enjoy due to the depth of relationship formed between the two companies.

Finally, Premium Software's CTO asked if the GlueWorks CIO was able to speak at the annual global customer meeting for Premium Software and, if so, perhaps Premium Software could provide transportation and lodging. When the GlueWorks CIO thought that might be possible, the CTO said Dave would be confirming if that was possible.

The CTO assured Dave and Dave's manager that he felt the deal was going to happen, even at the higher price, due to the value that Dave had built within GlueWorks. He encouraged Dave not to discount the deal any further.

This feedback was useful, as Dave received a phone call from the Director of Purchasing at GlueWorks a short time later. The Director said that he was asking all of the final contenders for a better price on their offers. Dave explained that they considered their offer to be the best and final offer. Dave went on to suggest that if GlueWorks agreed to speak at their annual user group meeting, Premium Software would provide three free passes to the event and cover the travel and lodging cost of the GlueWorks CIO. The Director of Purchasing was appreciative of the goodwill offer.

2 Weeks Before The GlueWorks Purchase Order

Amy Gatherer had the unfortunate task of telling her manager that the Director of Purchasing had just informed her that they were going to go with another company's offer. Amy's manager immediately called his VP of Sales. The VP was very upset at this news and immediately asked for the phone number of the CIO for GlueWorks.

During the subsequent phone call from the VP of Sales, which included the CIO and the Director of Purchasing, he was able to get the Director of Purchasing to delay his final decision until he could visit him in person. Everything Consulting had a long relationship with GlueWorks and he should allow them one last conversation before a final decision. The Director agreed to the delay.

Ben Farmer had nothing to report on GlueWorks since DayDream Consulting was not actively involved in the current sales process and there was nothing that Ben could do to save his consulting revenue.

Carla Hunter had nothing to report on GlueWorks since they were eliminated. She spent her time discussing other deals that she had in the works.

Dave Trapper told his manager that he sat with Greg Saterree from GlueWorks. Greg assured him that GlueWorks was going to buy the software from Premium Software. There were people in finance and purchasing that were complaining about the higher price, but Greg had quelled their fears and explained that the Premium Software was well worth the higher price.

Dave also had reached out to Jen Fremen, and she assured Dave that her manager, John Roundtree, was not going to accept any solution except the one that came from Dave and Premium Software. John had educated himself on the use of artificial intelligence in product development as well as manufacturing, and he was convinced that Premium Software was a leader in the space and specifically, Dave Trapper had John's best interests at the forefront.

Terry Tram had also called Dave and said the decision was locked in. Terry had bumped into the Director of Purchasing, and Terry told him that Premium Software was awesome and not to mess with the decision. Terry told Dave that his final statement to the Director of Purchasing was "Premium Software is a great deal at three times the quote they gave us!"

The most difficult part of the conversation that Dave had with his manager on that Monday morning was convincing him that they could not sell the software at three times the list price!

1 Week Before The GlueWorks Purchase Order

Amy Gatherer, her manager, and the VP of Sales for Everything Consulting started the week in Ivytown sitting in the lobby of a local hotel. The VP of Sales had used his long relationship with GlueWorks to have a meeting with the CEO of GlueWorks, the CIO of GlueWorks and the Director of Purchasing of GlueWorks. They were going to offer an additional 20% discount on the current offer, as well as a 40% discount on future purchases for the next five years.

During the meeting in the GlueWorks CEO's office, they were surprised that Greg Saterree, Terry Tram, John Roundtree, and Jen Fremen were also invited along with the original three they expected. The GlueWorks employees all listened intently as the VP of Sales for Everything Consulting recapped their long relationship and their revised offer. The CEO of GlueWorks then asked Greg Saterree to explain the GlueWorks evaluation process. After that explanation, Greg asked John Roundtree to discuss his needs. John explained that his needs for artificial intelligence simply could not wait for the future development of new use cases if there was a product from Premium Software that was closer to maturity.

Amy realized that things were not going well, so she made a final request. She suggested that GlueWorks use the software from Everything Consulting for human resources and use Premium Software for manufacturing and product development. The GlueWorks CEO said that his team would consider that option and adjourned the meeting.

Ben Farmer had nothing to report on GlueWorks since DayDream Consulting was not actively involved in the current sales process and there was nothing that Ben could do to save his consulting revenue.

Carla Hunter had nothing to report on GlueWorks since they were eliminated. She spent her time discussing other deals that she had in the works.

Dave Trapper and his manager met with the Director of Purchasing to review the previously delivered proposal. The Director of Purchasing explained that GlueWorks had many options for this project and that Premium Software was the highest offer. Dave's manager assured the Director that this was a very competitive price to what other companies were paying. He also reiterated the many key points that the GlueWorks team had discovered. Finally, he shared a cost-benefit analysis that Dave had created with the help of the GlueWorks team that showed a financial payback that was extremely quick. Finally, he reminded the Director of the strong relationships that had been developed by GlueWorks with Premium Software.

The final statement from Director reassured them. "Well, I had to try to lower the price. I think you are correct that this is probably a fair offer. We will be communicating our decision next week, but I am sure you will be happy."

The Week Of The GlueWorks Purchase Order

Amy Gatherer called her manager to tell him that she just heard from the Director of Purchasing at GlueWorks. Not only did they not receive the order for their software, but also the Director explained that he would like her to come in to discuss phasing out their existing consulting relationship.

Ben Farmer didn't have a meeting with his manager. The Director of Purchasing called him into GlueWorks, and he brought his manager along with him. Ben knew the Director moderately well, since he negotiated their existing consulting contract with him once per year. Ben was quite enthused by the request, but his hopes were soon crushed. Ben was told that the services with DayDream Consulting would no longer be needed after this week and GlueWorks was exercising its right to cancel the current engagement immediately. All outstanding invoices would be paid and existing DayDream Consulting personnel should wrap up their open items by the end of the week.

Carla Hunter didn't call her manager on that fateful Monday. She simply sent him an email informing him that GlueWorks went with Premium Software. She also told him that she was taking the rest of the day off as a "mental health" day.

Dave Trapper called his manager to tell him that GlueWorks just gave him the purchase order for their artificial intelligence software. The deal came in at exactly the price that they all agreed to in the previous meetings.

Dave then called his wife with the good news. They agreed to once again make reservations for a weekend of fun and relaxation, just like they did for every major deal that Dave closed. She said that he was starting to spoil her with all of this attention, to which Dave affirmed, "That is my sole goal in life." To which his wife laughingly replied, "Such a salesman - don't worry, the deal with me is already closed too!"

Dave's manager knew of Dave's ritual after big orders and he rewarded his star salesperson. He called the hotel that Dave preferred and ordered two bottles of expensive champagne to be delivered to the couple's room.

1 Week After The GlueWorks Purchase Order

Amy Gatherer informed her manager that she had met with the Director of Purchasing and the decision was final. She lost the GlueWorks project to Premium Software, and all of their onsite consultants would be phased out by the end of the week.

Ben Farmer told his manager that GlueWorks had given the order to Premium Software. It was obvious to Ben that his manager was upset with him.

Carla Hunter took more than the previous Monday off. She took the entire week off, and she was going to take this week off as well. Her manager was more than a little worried, so he called his best salesperson to find out what was going on. She replied that she was burned out from losing and was re-assessing her methods, but she was not planning on leaving Focused Software.

Dave Trapper and his manager had dinner with Greg Saterree and Terry Tram. They discussed the project and how it was going to be implemented. They also received commitments that GlueWorks would attend their annual user's group meeting, and their CIO agreed to speak as the keynote customer address. Dave's manager asked if GlueWorks would be a reference for a few other companies in the area that were considering Premium Software and Greg committed to being helpful.

2 Weeks After The GlueWorks Purchase Order

Amy Gatherer was a bit apprehensive to walk into her manager's office for their weekly review meeting. In the last year, she had lost two major installed customers, and there was no way that she was going to make her quota for the year. She was a bit surprised when her manager didn't show any anger on his face when she sat down, but his opening words made her heart sink. "Amy, I had a long talk with the VP of North America earlier this week. We think we need to make a change in how we operate."

Her nervous reply came to try to head off what she thought was a plan to fire her. "Before you get too far, please remember that I have been a loyal employee of this company for a very long time and I have typically been among the top performers. I know that I am in a bit of rut right now, but I am sure that I can turn this around."

Her manager smiled with his response. "I'm sorry, Amy; we don't think it is you that we need to change. We support you. We think we need to change how we do business. We have been selling to customers the same way for the past 20 years. At the suggestion of my VP, I just finished a great book that we think we should use as the model going forward. The book is called *Eliminate Your Competition*, and I found it to be full of great ideas and processes that we need to start to use. Here is a copy of the book. Do me a favor and read it, and let's discuss it next week at our regular meeting."

Amy picked up the copy of the book and read the title: *Eliminate Your Competition - A Trapper's Guide to Increasing Your Commission*. She stood up and walked out of the office. She was determined to become a Trapper.

A similar conversation took place at DayDream Consulting. Ben sat down with his manager on that Monday, but Ben's manager was not quite as tactful as Amy's manager. "Ben, something isn't working. We like you, but you are consistently losing big orders and only closing small deals. This is resulting in you achieving only 80-90% of your quota, while we have salespeople over-achieving quota on a regular basis. Last year, we encouraged you to go to TheTrapper.com website and read their articles and read their book. My gut is that you haven't done that yet."

"No ma'am, I haven't."

"So here is the deal, Ben. We need you to step it up. Buy the book and expense it. Spend the next week reading the book and thinking about your business. Come in next week and let's put together a plan on how you are going to fix your business by the end of the year. If we haven't seen a major improvement in customer relationships and getting 'high and wide' in your accounts by the end of the year, then we may have to take some dramatic actions. I hope I am making myself crystal clear."

"Thank you. I will do exactly that," Ben replied as he sheepishly walked out of the office.

The situation was a bit different at Focused Software with Carla Hunter. Carla is a fighter. She hates to lose. She is also brilliant and knows when she needs to change tactics.

Carla walked into her manager's office and tossed a book on his desk, saying, "I am done losing! A friend of mine just read this book and said that it changed his career. I have read the first four chapters and it is amazing what I am missing. My friend said that is only the beginning, because the excellent stuff is in the last half!"

Her manager picked up the book and chuckled, "Another sales improvement book from another consultant. You know the old saying: 'those who can't - teach.' How in the world do you think this will make a difference? Besides, how do you eliminate your competition?"

Carla replied defiantly, "The author isn't a consultant or a teacher. He is a sales guy with decades of experience, and while he was writing the book, he was still selling for his employer every day. I have heard great things about it from everyone who follows his methods. This copy of the book is yours, as I have already scribbled notes all over my copy. I am going to take this week to finish this book and put a plan together. Next week, I want you to have read the book and help me find the holes in how I work. I have even reached out to the author on his site, and he has offered to help us. What do you say—will you help me?"

Carla's manager paused at that challenge. Carla was traditionally his best salesperson. If she was this enthused about making a change, he needed to help her. He was also tired of losing, and maybe this new methodology would be the secret to kick-starting his whole team. He calmly replied to Carla, "Let's make it happen," and opened the book to the first chapter.

Dave Trapper walked into his manager's office with a smile and a bit of spring to his step. He was surprised when his manager wasn't as happy.

"Dave, I have good news and bad news for you. I'm not going to ask which way you want it. The good news is that Black Gold down in Texas closed for four times what GlueWorks just closed for, and it looks like that southern region will be number one for the year."

Dave was elated. "That is great news for Jerry. He sat with me and talked strategy for Black Gold during kickoff. Glad that he closed it. What's the bad news?"

"Isn't that obvious? Right now, I am not the number one region this year, and you aren't the number one salesperson this year, even though you just closed the biggest deal of your career here at Premium Software. Also, Sally Superstar, your mentor here at Premium Software, is having a fantastic year and is currently ahead of you on revenue. You are likely to only be in third place this year! What have you done for me lately?"

There was a pause in the room, and then the manager gave a big goofy smile, and Dave laughed, saying, "We'll be fine. Let's talk about Four Star Homes as well as Hot Food Restaurants."

As every reader of this book probably understands, once you have closed the deal, you must continue to the next deal. Also, if you have lost, you need to figure out how to regroup, learn from your mistakes, and do better next time. That is the essence of the career that we have chosen.

Chapter 3 – Buying Is About Making Decisions And Choices

"If I had asked people what they wanted, they would have said faster horses."

-Henry Ford

Purchasing a product is ultimately just a decision and making a choice. The buyer chooses the product that best fits their needs, as they understand them. They then make the decision to buy the product. While this may sound simplistic, it is important to start with that simple concept and then complicate the discussion with greater detail.

It is critical that the salesperson understands how people make decisions. Most sales methodologies on bookstore shelves do not spend time trying to understand the buyer and the work that a company goes through to make a buying decision. This lack of understanding leads to a one-sided view of the process and is inherently inaccurate. Not understanding the buying decision contributes to the enormous number of unsuccessful salespeople.

Every purchase decision is a series of compromises and in the end; every prospect is making the best choice for them at that time. The reality is that there are no inferior products, there are no perfect products, and therefore, all salespeople can be successful.

Every purchase is essentially a decision-making process. When prospects first set out to buy a new product, many do not have a firm idea of what to buy, how to buy it, or their exact needs. This lack of understanding gives the salesperson the opportunity to structure the prospect's decision-making process and control the outcome. Typically, the best product does not win; rather, it is the salesperson who controls the decision-making process that wins the order.

▼▼▼▼▼▼▼▼▼▼▼▼▼
People work to attain a positive not to avoid a negative (pain).
▲▲▲▲▲▲▲▲▲▲▲▲▲

There is no such a thing as buying or selling. Instead, it is "decision-making" (buying) and "influencing the decision" (selling). This simple fact may change your whole approach to selling. We take the first step into Trapping by understanding that our role is to influence the decision-making process. Salespeople play an incredibly important role in the entire process. You will be a better salesperson by understanding that for the process to be as efficient as possible, you need to influence the outcome.

It is important to realize that the prospect has probably lived with the pain for a long time. It is very rare for a new pain to emerge that is immediately so painful that it reaches the top of the list of priorities. Rather, if the prospect is going to spend money on this effort, the pain had to evolve from merely a pain to a goal to eliminate or reduce that pain.

Organizations frequently are in pain. Individual people within the organizations are frequently in pain. Pain is simply that you wish that something worked better or perhaps the effort to perform a particular job function is difficult or tedious. That doesn't automatically mean that a prospect will spend money to eliminate the pain.

Many pains in business life and personal life are tolerated. Often this toleration is because we are used to the pain and do not notice it anymore. For instance, the Chief Financial Officer may wish that he didn't have to pay for maintenance people to clean and care for the building infrastructure of the organization. That is a pain. He cannot get rid of that pain entirely, solely because not cleaning the building could (among other things) endanger the health of the employees, could depreciate the assets of the company, and could create an environment his customers don't want to visit. So he has to tolerate this pain whenever he pays building maintenance bills.

To elaborate on our building maintenance example, the CFO will tolerate the pain of building maintenance costs until he thinks that he can get the same maintenance accomplished at a lower cost. That could be due to a peer study he read that shows other CFOs spending less for maintenance. That could also be because an enterprising salesperson showed him a way to reduce building maintenance costs. Regardless of how he comes to understand this, the pain only becomes intolerable when he has the belief that he is experiencing too much pain.

At the point the pain becomes intolerable, he will create a goal of reducing or eliminating the pain. It typically takes some outside influence or learning to make a prospect change a pain to a goal. Until that pain converts to a goal, there is probably no way to convince the CFO (or any Economic Buyer) to spend money.

As a resourceful sales person (a Trapper), you could be the catalyst for converting that pain to a goal. To do this, you will need very firm and demonstrable data that shows the level of pain a prospect is feeling is too much. It is wonderful if you have such data since it makes your product much easier to sell. Almost by definition, if you have that capability then you probably have a significant advantage over all of your competition.

Most salespeople do not have extremely substantial and demonstrable benefits that will transition a prospect in pain to a prospect with a goal. Instead, they have a product that is approximately as good as most of their competition. In those instances, you are probably not going to convert the pain into a goal. If your product is essentially equivalent to other products on the market, then your competition has surely tried to turn that pain into a goal with their approximately equivalent benefits.

If the prospect is not convinced that your benefits show enough reason to convert a pain into a goal, you must take a longer path to success. Chapter 5 on finding prospects will give you some insight on how to slowly nurture a prospect. It will also give you insight into maintaining contact with a prospect who is not currently fully motivated but may become so by outside influences in the future.

The process that we call "sales" is nothing more than one individual helping another individual make a decision. This reality applies to a complicated sales process composed of several distinct decisions that are coordinated to attain a goal. The adage in sales that 'people buy from people' is 100% valid and can be expanded to 'individual salespeople help individual buyers make decisions.' For complicated sales processes, we can have a corollary: 'Salespeople and their sales team help multiple individual buyers make multiple decisions that lead to one ultimate decision.'

Complicated sales processes are nothing more than a combination of individual events with individual people. In many sales organizations, these are random events and result in a sales process that is uncoordinated. This leads to frustrating goals, events, reactions and more importantly – endemic failure in the sales force. Many companies experience annual turnover of 20% or more in their sales force. Most companies have 30-50% (or greater) of their organization that does not make quota. Employing Trapper techniques in your sales process will allow you to be one of the overachievers the rest of the company respects and honors.

In a Trapper-led sales campaign, there are few surprises and fewer losses. When you map out all of the unique events, sales become more predictable and revenue increases. This management results in a much more enjoyable working environment where a majority of the salespeople make and exceed their targets and a sales department that performs well for the stockholders of the company.

No One Ever Bought The Wrong Product

One of the major mistakes that many salespeople make is believing that their product is the perfect product for the prospect. Some salespeople take this to the next step by believing that any other product is the WRONG product for the prospect. In reality, this does not make sense: Why would someone intentionally buy the wrong product? They never do! They always make a decision based on the information and beliefs that they have at the time of the decision. After weighing all of these variables, in a way that is unique to them, they make the decision. Since few products can boast of attaining a market share that is over 75%, we must conclude that no individual product on the market is the perfect product. You must shed the belief that you have the only viable product on the market if you want to be a successful Trapper.

The buying process that everyone goes through begins with looking at all of the available products, evaluating all of the variables such as price, performance, availability, and every other condition that is important to them. They decide which product best suits their needs. Only then do they purchase that product. No one goes through all of that effort only to buy a different product that satisfies fewer of his or her needs. Instead, they always chose the best product based on a multitude of variables that are unique to them and that specific buying decision.

There are combinations of factors that are unique to the individual making the decision. The buyer combines these issues in a way that is 100% unique to him and to that situation. To make matters more complicated, the same organization or person may buy different things in very different ways. This is particularly the case in a complicated sales environment where there will be many different buying influences in each opportunity.

A prospect never says, 'I am buying a product that is not the best for my needs.' Instead, they evaluate a variety of factors that influence their decision. These factors include (but are not limited to) price, functional fit, availability, and awareness of the product by the decision makers. In addition, the roles and personalities of the decision makers significantly influence the outcome of the process.

Here is an everyday example of this. If a consumer listed all of the features of a television that he may want to purchase, the list might look something like this:

- Costs less than $50
- Free delivery and installation in my home
- 10 separate HDMI inputs
- 10 separate HDMI outputs
- 5 separate RGB inputs
- 5 separate component video inputs
- 4 separate USB inputs
- 2 "universal" memory card slots
- 7 speaker surround sound
- Ability to run Internet apps
- Wide screen
- Ultra High definition
- Flat screen
- 160" diagonal screen
- TV must be no deeper than 1" and weigh less than 10 pounds
- A Wi-Fi and infrared combined remote that never gets lost
- Voice-activated remote capability
- Embedded DVR with a 250T hard drive and lifetime lookup of TV schedules
- Embedded DVD player
- 1 gigabit Wi-Fi and CAT6 Internet connection
- 24-month free subscription to at least four movie and TV subscription sites
- Programmable from computer both locally and remotely while traveling
- Made in the United States

As of the writing of this book, this TV does not exist. However, if we look at the features of every TV (or TV-like device) on the market, we find each of these features exists. This list is just a compilation of features that exist in the marketplace but do not exist together. The consumer must make compromises on one or more of these features since his perfect TV does not exist. Only he can make the decision to compromise certain features. He will need experienced and knowledgeable salespeople to educate him on the trade-offs and help him prioritize his desires with reality.

To make matters worse, many times the individuals involved in making the decision have never purchased this type of product before. In the very best cases, they have not done so in quite a long time, or they have not done it for the organization they are with at the time. For this reason, they often make conclusions that are not correct because they have not foreseen all of the consequences of their actions. The old maxim "The prospect is always right" is rarely true since frequently the prospect has never made these types of decisions before. This means that the prospect may be right, but just as likely the prospect is wrong and it is your job to point this out to the prospect in a tactful way.

▼▼▼▼▼▼▼▼▼▼▼▼▼▼
The old maxim "The prospect is always right" is rarely true
▲▲▲▲▲▲▲▲▲▲▲▲▲▲

In those cases where the prospect is always correct, then the salesperson is relegated to an order-taker and rarely offers any value to the sale other than providing a convenient place to purchase the product or service. This is a commodity-driven sale or a retail counter sale similar to buying milk at the corner grocery.

You, on the other hand, have been involved in dozens or hundreds of sales campaigns regarding your product. This means that you have more experience in the decision-making process regarding this type of solution than your prospect. By all rights, you should be dictating to your prospect how to evaluate the solution and its fit. Since this aggressiveness would not be received in a positive manner, you must constructively assist the prospect through the decision process. You do not need to assist them in understanding your competitors' good features since you can count on your competitor to accomplish this task. You must concern yourself in pointing out your product's positive traits, particularly if they line up to your competitor's weak points. The section on Bait development in Chapter 6 will assist you in developing this skill.

Let's revisit the above television example. If the prospect insists that he is correct and he can find that perfect TV, then every salesperson that he meets will fail to sell him a new TV. He is incorrect in insisting that the product exists and the salesperson who can convince him of this reality and show him a TV system that has a majority of his most important wishes will probably win the sale. The prospect is usually wrong and does not know it. The salesperson who helps the prospect understand their real needs and changes the wish list is usually the salesperson who wins the order.

With this type of unstructured buying process, it is not surprising that buyer's remorse is high. Quite often, the prospect did not have all of the information that they needed when they made their decision. A multitude of problems drive this situation, including lack of understanding of actual problems, lack of knowledge of the solutions on the market, lack of understanding of the product that they purchased, weariness of looking for a better solution and many more reasons.

One can almost conclude that the prospect hardly ever buys the perfect product or solution to solve their problems. Too many variables need to align for the buyer to select the perfect product. Instead, they buy something that is good enough to resolve the majority of their largest needs and most of the minor needs. This resultant product is usually adequate even if it isn't excellent, and they are satisfied with the result.

Due to all of this inexperience and lack of accuracy, salespeople should not worry about selling the perfect product or service. They also should never worry about satisfying all of the prospect's wishes because the prospect does not even know all of the issues. Therefore, no one sells an inferior product. No one is at a disadvantage in the market to be successful. You just need to know how to position your product correctly to win and position your competitors' products for them to lose.

We cannot count on the prospect to ask the pertinent questions to allow them to make a perfect decision. The Trapper realizes this and takes a predominant role in the decision-making process. You should lead the prospect to information they need to buy the best-fit product (which of course, is your product) and make sure that they see all of the reasons that they should not buy your competitor's offering. Your job as a Trapper is to eliminate the competition so that the prospect purchases your solution.

People make decisions constantly throughout their day. Many of the decisions that they make are significant and important, but most are mundane and routine. Many times these simple, low-level decisions dramatically affect the outcome of major activities. For example, you make the decision to listen to a CD or a podcast on the way to work, rather than the radio. This may seem like a simple choice, but it could mean not learning about a major traffic tie-up on that could cause you to miss a critical morning meeting.

The sales process is much like this as well. Small, everyday decisions dramatically influence the need for a product and the perception of that product compared to another. For this reason, you need to put all of your interaction with a prospect through your 'Trapping Filter' to decide how your actions and inactions may affect the outcome of your campaign. Also, it is important to look for activities and innuendo from the prospect to determine if you are 'Trapped' into some type of behavior

When people make a decision to spend their own (or their company's) money, they do so because their goals do not align with their reality. They wish that they were in a different situation and their desire to be in that situation is acute enough that they are willing to invest their time and their money to get closer to that goal.

Many people discuss 'pain' as the reason that people buy. This belief is not entirely true. Pain is the result of not realizing goals. Therefore, 'pain' is a 'lagging indicator' of the situation. In a competitive situation where there are no Trappers, pain may be a good driving force. Trappers try to get ahead of the situation and drive the buyer into a situation that is conducive to them winning the order. If you wait for 'pain' to occur, you run the risk of involving many more competitors and being much later in the sales process. Instead, you want to control the process, which means that you want to discuss the goals of both the organization and the individual people.

▼▼▼▼▼▼▼▼▼▼▼▼▼
Pain is the result of unrealized goals.
▲▲▲▲▲▲▲▲▲▲▲▲▲▲

In addition to 'pain' being a secondary and lagging situation, it also has very negative connotations. It is much harder to discuss an individual's 'pains' than it is to discuss the individual's goals. Goals have a very positive feel and therefore make you a valued partner to the prospect.

A similarity from your everyday life: if you have a knee pain then you may see a doctor. While you and your insurance company will likely give the doctor money to cure that pain, it does not give you a positive feeling about the doctor - it is more of a necessary evil. However, you may have a goal of getting into shape and losing weight and therefore join the local gym. You are more likely to develop a long-term friendship with that gym and its employees even though you may give them much more money over the term of your membership. The people who are working in the gym are helping you get to your goal whereas the doctor is solving a problem or a 'pain.'

Pain means that something is broken. It is a negative. While it may be common in this age of social media to whine and complain about broken things, it does not create a feeling of excitement or enjoyment. The excitement only comes when you are trying to achieve a goal.

The athletes on your favorite sports team don't work hard in practice because they want to avoid the pain of losing. Instead, they work hard because they want to win. Winning is the goal. The desire to accomplish a goal allows everyone to be motivated to work hard. Talking about pain with an athlete is to talk about losses, hard practices, and injury. The athlete is much more motivated talking about the game wins and the plans to win the next games. The same is true with your prospect.

Pain is also not the reason to choose one product over another. Pain may justify the purchase, or it may start an evaluation process. If all the products solve the pain, then ultimately price and 'terms and conditions' will be the deciding factors. However, most evaluations are more concerned about goals and achieving those goals. From our earlier TV example, if your pain is that you have a broken TV then any TV should solve your pain. If your goal is to watch sporting events and feature films on the best-looking and best-sounding audiovisual system on the market, then your list may be more detailed and may be similar to the one earlier.

Similarly, if your pain is that you cannot get to work in the morning, then hundreds of automobiles, along with some public transportation options, will solve your problem. If you have a goal of getting to work in a sporty red convertible, you will eliminate many of the choices, and the car salespeople must help you meet your goals.

▼▼▼▼▼▼▼▼▼▼▼▼▼▼▼
The chosen product will match the goals of the prospect, not just the pains of the prospect.
▲▲▲▲▲▲▲▲▲▲▲▲▲▲▲

In sales, we can use this to our benefit. We will center our initial questioning and needs development with our prospect on goals and the ability (or inability) to reach those goals. By doing this with the Discoverer (a role that we will discuss later in the book), we have the advantage of being a long-term and trusted ally. As the sales process evolves, other vendors are brought in to ascertain their possible remedies, but the prospect sees them as solutions to a problem (pain) that you have helped them identify because their reality was not the same as their goal. You, on the other hand, are a trusted confidant who only has their best interest at heart and you are willing to guide them as they explore their goals.

Too Much Information Doesn't Help Them

The prospect's role in the decision-making process is to collect information pertinent to their problems and find a solution for these challenges. Your stated role in this process is to provide information to the prospect that will allow them to purchase your product. Your unstated, but understood, role in this process is to affect the buyer in such a way that your competition loses the order, and you win. You are a combination of an information provider and a decision influencer.

You must give the prospect information to assist them or else they may not see value in you and may not purchase your product. You also must help them eliminate choices that do not benefit you. Therefore you must choose the information that you give them very carefully so that it not only helps them understand the benefits of you, your company and your solution but also helps them understand that your competition's solution is not a perfect fit. It does not matter if your product is a perfect fit since it is rare for any product to be a perfect fit. You are probably familiar with the adage 'putting a round peg into a square hole.' Unfortunately, most prospects do not truly understand what size hole they have, or the shape. Your goal is to make them see that they have a hole that is the size and shape that perfectly accommodates your peg.

Many salespeople will assist in the decision-making process by overwhelming the prospect with too much information about their product or service in the hopes that the prospect will make the decision that they want. How many times have we shopped for hours or days for a particular product (home, stereo, TV, car, etc.) to make sure we understand the pricing schemes and the features and benefits and then end up buying from the last store that we enter? Surely it was not random fate that the first salesperson that we talked to in each case was very incompetent and could not match us up with the perfect product. Rather, what happens is we start the process by gathering information. When we understand the specifications and the issues regarding our planned purchase, we start eliminating choices, then we delve into those few remaining products that we know we like and we make a decision to purchase one. However, we rarely go back to the first person who started the education process - we buy from one of the last few. We are simply too tired to go back to the first person - we have suffered from information overload, and that first salesperson is going to lose the sale.

You probably have purchased a house/condominium or rented an apartment. Invariably, your search began by driving around neighborhoods that you thought suited your needs. You may have evaluated your financial situation and decided on a price that you could afford. You also probably started looking at properties that might fit your needs and goals.

In your search for a new living place, it is doubtful that you selected the first place that you visited. Instead, you began to evaluate your options and change your criteria based on the available amenities. You started to look at flooring options, wall coverings, the sizes of rooms, the arrangement of rooms and dozens or hundreds more choices. As you looked, it is likely that you modified your list of needs and goals as you became educated. Eventually, after days or weeks of looking and changing your list, you decided on a place. Most house hunters do not go back to the first few places to compare them to this new, modified list – those properties have lost the sale to you.

So, what does a Trapper salesperson do in this situation? It is almost impossible to get only educated buyers, and in fact, we probably do not want to be in that situation. If we only have completely educated customers, then they will only evaluate us against their pre-determined conclusions and ultimately make a decision on price, terms, and conditions. Instead, you need to position yourself to educate the prospect, but never fully let the prospect leave your control. This applies to all sales situations - the consumer salesperson knows the prospect is going to leave and needs to make sure that the prospect returns. The corporate salesperson knows the sales cycle is going to be long and it is impossible to be at every meeting. So he provides enough information early on to be seen as being valuable, doesn't want to spend so much time on the company that he can't close other business, and still wants to make the short list to be involved in the close at the end.

▼▼▼▼▼▼▼▼▼▼▼▼▼▼

If we only have completely educated customers, then they will only evaluate us against their pre-determined conclusions and ultimately make a decision on price, terms, and conditions.

▲▲▲▲▲▲▲▲▲▲▲▲▲▲

We know that there are going to be competitors on the deal, so we need to anticipate that they are going to give the prospect information. We need to structure our information as being incredibly valuable so that we are seen to add value to the prospect's search but at the same time not spend all of our time educating the prospect on all of the minutiae. This is a delicate line, but experienced Trappers learn how to find this balance.

No one makes money by giving out information. So why do we do it? Why are we doing something for free? Simple - because we think we get value out of it. The goal should be to maximize the value that we receive. We do this by breaking our information into Bait. Bait needs to be benefit-based and not feature-based so that it is immediately 'tasty' to the prospect. The Bait is big enough to get our point across but not so big as to be confusing. Most importantly, Bait needs to lead to a Trap that makes the prospect think more highly of you, your company and your product and allows the prospect to see your advantages over your competitors. In chapters six and seven we will discuss how to break up features and benefits into Bait, but in the next chapter, we are going to see examples of how Bait is used in each step of the buying process.

Making a decision in an organization is a very complicated process. It is not like the criminal TV dramas where the wise old judge weighs the evidence and renders a sound decision. It is more like jury trials - relationships between individuals and their personalities are far more powerful than the facts. The reader is encouraged to read "12 Angry Men" or watch the movie starring Peter Fonda and George C. Scott. It is an excellent example of emotions getting in the way of making an impartial decision. It also shows that a poor salesperson (the defendant's lawyer) can blow the sale. Peter Fonda's character is an excellent example of a Champion who can sway the emotions of the decision-making group.

Decisions follow several steps that are simplified as follows:

1. Identify Problem
2. Preliminary Decision
3. Test Preliminary Decision
4. Implement

A Decision Triangle makes a great visualization model for these steps. You can see that the Decision Triangle has Identify Problem at the center, Preliminary Decision at the lower right corner, Test Preliminary Decision at the left corner and then Implement is at the top of the triangle.

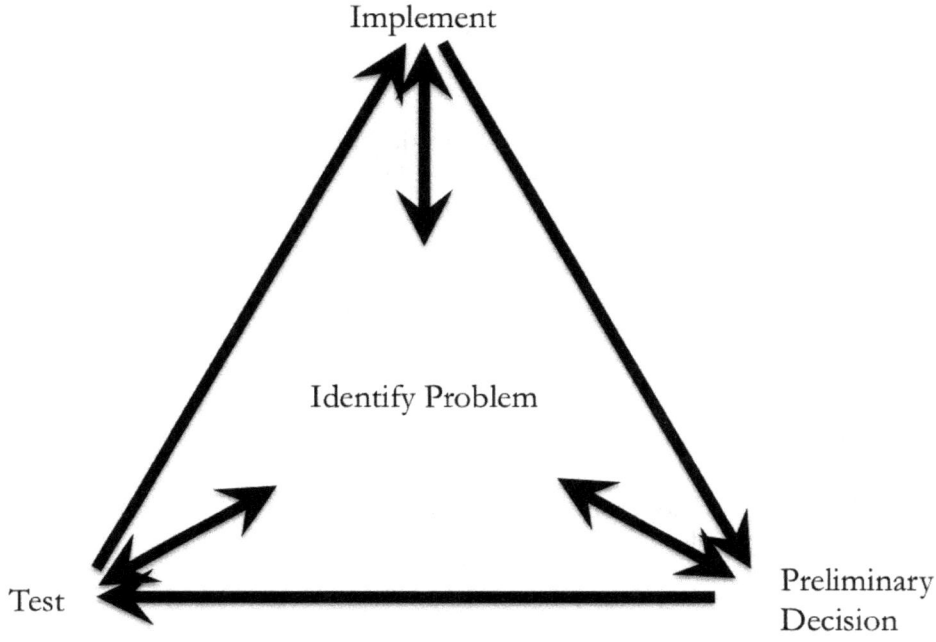

Figure 3-1: Decision Triangle. All figures are also available at
http://www.thetrapper.com/book_figures

The decision-making process begins with an identification of a decision the prospect will make. A preliminary decision appears to satisfy the requirements. Then we test the decision to check its validity. If it survives that test, it becomes an implemented decision.

This flow is similar to the 'Scientific Method' that you learned in your high school science classes.

- A problem is identified.
- A hypothesis is offered as to the answer.
- Tests are conducted to confirm or deny the hypothesis.

We can model decisions in organizations as large as Fortune 500 companies, or as small as a family, with a Decision Triangle. As with any diagram or process description such as this, remember that one individual can play multiple roles. Also, some roles can be individuals, or they can be a group. This is an important consideration. You should not assume that just because the explanation in this book refers to an individual that in your sales campaign it will be only one person. Often, multiple people will divide the role. Conversely, in some organizations, one person can fulfill the role of a group.

The Decision Triangle has the Decision Owner in the center. The problem at hand passes to one Decision Group for review and investigation. The group may be comprised of many individuals and may or may not include the Decision Owner. This group may recommend no solution, in which case No Decision wins the purchase. They also may recommend one or multiple solutions. The Decision Owner then will often get verification of these solutions from a Confirmation Decision Group (once again, the members of this second group may include the Decision Owner as well as some members of the first Decision Group). This group takes the work done by the first group and approves the solution, makes further recommendations or shelves the idea. Now there is a final set of recommendations returned to the Decision Owner. The Decision Owner then delegates the execution of the decision to an Administrative Group. The Administrative Group administers, announces, and follows through with the decision.

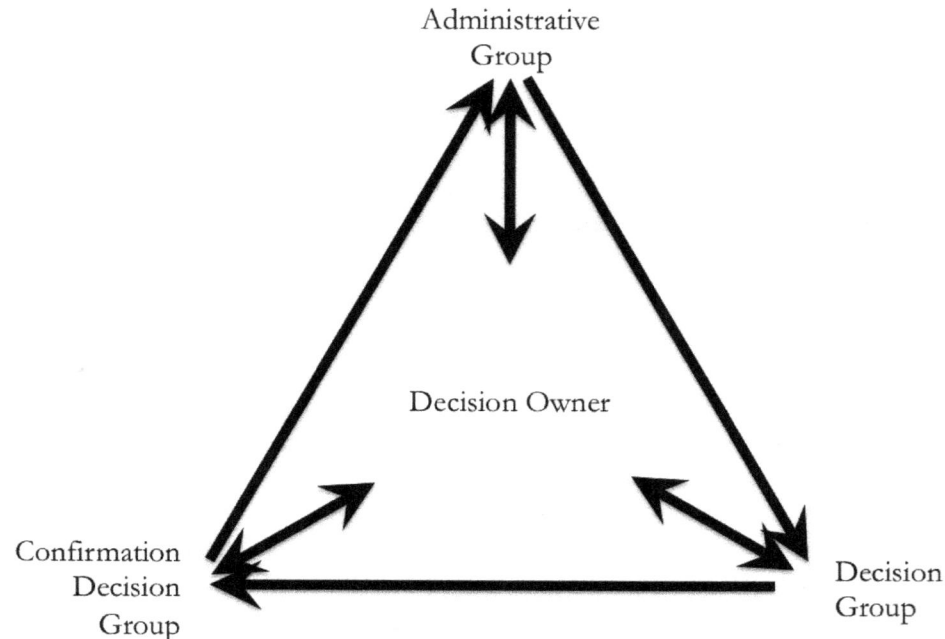

Figure 3-2: Decision GroupTriangle. All figures are also available at http://www.thetrapper.com/book_figures

Major decisions are composed of smaller decisions and elimination of options. For instance, when researching the available options for an audio system to listen to music in your home, you will most likely not consider the sound systems used in recording studios. This is not because these units are flawed; they simply do not fit the purpose that you need. By eliminating them, you have not made a final decision, nor have you significantly narrowed the field down to the select few that you will consider. We must understand this and realize that these smaller decisions can eliminate our competition or us.

You will note that in each of these steps, minor decisions accumulate to the major decision. For example:

- The Decision Owner decided to act upon the idea.
- The Decision Owner decided who was going to be in the first Decision Group.

- The two main Decision Groups decided which information was relevant, which choices to evaluate and how to make those choices.

These minor decisions also employed a Decision Triangle, but in many of these cases, one individual performed each function. This is very common, and it is important to understand. As Trappers, we need to influence these minor decisions to affect the major decision that will result in a sale. By breaking this process down into the smallest pieces possible, we can plan, control, and strategize a way to win the order.

There Are No Perfect Choices

The Decision Group is not trying to select the best solution but will settle for a product that satisfies the majority of their perceived needs. They will look at enough options to make themselves confident that they have a good sampling of the market.

If you have ever wondered why a company bought a competitor's offering and not yours, it is because perfection is not the goal in most decisions. In many cases, the goal is simply to make a choice that isn't terrible. It is your job as a salesperson to put your product into those decision criteria. This book will teach you how to be a Trapper, how to put your product in play more often, and how to win more of those customer decisions.

Chapter 4 – The Buying And Selling Process

"It's not enough that I should succeed -- others should fail."

- David Merrick

To be successful in life, you must have a plan and must follow that plan. A myriad of popular self-help authors, from Dale Carnegie to Brian Tracy to Zig Ziglar, have spent enormous amounts of energy explaining this to us. There is a very popular quote attributed to the late Thomas Watson, founder of International Business Machines, "If you fail to plan then you plan to fail."

It is essential for a successful salesperson to understand the entire buying and selling process so that you can achieve your sales goals. Most salespeople can document their company's selling process and the various stages that their management tracks for forecasting purposes. However, truly successful salespeople understand what the prospect is doing and why they are doing it.

This chapter starts with a typical description of the selling process that is familiar to most salespeople. It then compares this selling process to the steps that the prospect is going through to show that working only on the selling process and not the buying process is a mistake. Finally, each step of the buying process is analyzed, and the successful Trapper salesperson is given action items to accomplish to ensure a successful sales campaign.

This chapter further develops the Decision Triangle from the earlier chapter. It shows how a complicated sales process is multiple Decision Triangles that are part of a very large double Triangle. This double Decision Triangle is the entire decision-making buying process. It also shows that if the buying process does not follow this model, then it is unlikely that there will be a purchase at the end.

Planning is a top trait of a Trapper. A Trapper plans the sales campaign, the evaluation process that the prospect will follow, and ultimately, plans the competition's loss of the order. A Trapper understands that to win, none of his competition can win — they must lose.

A Trapper takes advantage of the environment of his sale. He will use the prospect organization's habits, characteristics, and behavior. The use of these clues guides his interaction and allows him to control the opportunity and eliminate the competition.

▼▼▼▼▼▼▼▼▼▼▼▼▼▼▼

A Trapper understands that in order to win, all of the competitors must lose and be eliminated from consideration.

▲▲▲▲▲▲▲▲▲▲▲▲▲▲▲

It is impossible to plan an activity without first understanding the mechanics of what is occurring. Since the Trapper must interact with and control the buying and selling process, it is critical to understand the prospect's process. This allows you to anticipate and take advantage of actions or inactions. This chapter explores this 'typical' process and lays out the first stages of your action plans for winning the order. Later in the book, we will refer to these stages as we lay out the strategies for Traps.

There is no perfect description of a process for all situations. In fact, one organization can purchase two different products with two different processes. It is also possible to accomplish a role in the process with one person or a group. This is why sales is both an art and a skill, not a programmatic, systematic recipe. It is the understanding of this variability in the entire process that gives you the competitive edge as a professional salesperson and — most importantly — a Trapper.

A Sales Cycle Is Part Of The Decision Cycle

It is imperative that you refer to Appendix A to understand the various roles and strengths involved in the decision cycle. We will explore how those roles evolve and interact throughout the stages of the buying process. Later, we will map out the various things that we need to anticipate in each of the buying stages so that we can create effective tactical Traps.

Often, there is a discrepancy between vendors and prospects on the length of a sales cycle. This is because the buying organization thinks they are in a buying decision cycle, not a sales cycle. The vendor thinks of it as a sales cycle, not a decision cycle.

Quite often a sales manager will brag about a rep who just won an order with a three-month sales cycle when the average cycle is six months. More often than not if you ask the prospect, he thinks that the decision cycle took nine months. Why is there such a large discrepancy between views? The sales team did not align the sales cycle with the prospect's decision cycle. A Hunter controlled the sales team, and this one opportunity was late in the process, and it was stolen from the competitor. Congratulations on the win, but how many of the competitors' wins happened that they did not know about and therefore did not steal?

Companies often discuss the length of their sales cycle. They will quote a range of time for their average sale such as two to four weeks or three to six months or even nine to fifteen months. When discussing sales cycles within a company it is important to dig in a little to see if it is a Gatherer company, a Hunter company, a Farmer company, or a Trapper company.

A Hunter company will have sales cycles that are much shorter than the decision cycle because they are stealing prospects late in the decision cycle and not contributing much to prospects early in the cycle. Typically, the salespeople in complex sales cycles cannot handle more than ten opportunities because they are spending huge amounts of time and resources trying to establish credibility and learn the roles of the decision makers. The company pipeline is usually very heavy in the final stages of the decision process and very weak in the beginning stages. They typically win fewer deals than they lose and tend to discount heavily. They also have a great deal of inaccuracy in their forecasts. You will frequently find quite a few orders happen the last few days of the selling period (month, quarter, or year) and are not evenly distributed throughout the period.

A Farmer company has much longer sales cycles. The length tends to be very close to the decision cycle because they found the prospect very early in the decision cycle or perhaps even started the decision process. Since the Farmer is doing massive amounts of work and cultivating the prospect, the Farmer typically cannot handle large numbers of active opportunities. Typically, they can handle a similar amount of accounts as the Hunter. However, as we discussed earlier, the revenue produced by a Farmer is usually very similar to a Hunter after the Farmer has built up enough tenure for a few typical decision cycles to occur. At this point, the Farmer will have a pipeline that is fully developed.

It is fairly rare for a company to be made up entirely of Gatherers. Typically, a salesperson will gravitate to Gatherer status from a different trait. In the few times that Gatherers are predominant, the company is usually quite mature, with very long-term customers. A company that is composed of Gatherers will have sales cycles that are longer than the prospect's decision cycle. Since the Gatherer usually is calling on existing customers, it is common for her to anticipate the needs of the prospect. She can do this because she is working on very few accounts.

A company that has committed to the Trapper philosophy also has a similar sales cycle to the decision cycle. Because the sales teams are following Trapper techniques, they do not have to spend as much time with the decision-making process. This will allow you to influence the decision-making process and eliminate your competition. They can touch the prospect often enough to maintain value but since they are relying on their competitors to do some of the educating, they can keep more prospects going at one time. A Trapper company will have salespeople who are two to four times more effective than the average in the industry.

Steps Of The Sales Process In A Typical Company

Trappers understand the entire decision-making cycle as well as the sales cycle. They map their action plan to both cycles. To accomplish this, you must understand the typical steps of the Sales Process mapped out by most companies. Later in the book, we will review the decision-making process that the prospect implements. Then we will correlate these two processes to each other and use this map to manage the sales campaign effectively.

This correlation of the two processes is critical for you to understand as you transition from a Gatherer, Hunter, or Farmer to a Trapper. As we will see, the standard models employed by most methodologies do not adequately describe the decision-making process that the prospect organization is going through, therefore leaving the salesperson open to error.

Most sales methodologies describe approximately eight steps to the sales process. Different experts and organizations may give a variety of names to each step, but the meanings are essentially the same. Most companies will have developed a term for each step; you are encouraged to write the term that your company uses in the margin.

1. Suspect - Prospect – Lead - Potential Lead - Cold Lead - Name
2. Developing Lead
3. Early stage technically qualified
4. Early stage ROI Qualified
5. Formal Evaluation
6. Solution refinement
7. Final proposal refinement
8. Closing

1. Prospect – Lead - Potential Lead - Cold Lead - Name - Suspect

In this stage, you have identified an organization that may have a fit for your type of solution but often the prospect organization does not know it yet. They simply fit the profile of organizations that would benefit from your solution due to one or many factors. You have little understanding of the specific needs of the organization and the influences of the various players.

2. Developing Lead

This stage is where you begin to develop an understanding of the organization as well as to determine the likely players. As we will see later, this is the longest portion of the decision process for your prospect in some methodologies, but in many sales organizations it is the shortest portion of the sales cycle. In fact, many sales methodologies and pipelines do not even measure this stage.

We can easily see if a salesperson is a Hunter because his accounts will go through this stage quite quickly because a competitor has already developed the needs of the organization. Gatherers, Farmers, and Trappers will have many prospects in this stage. Those prospects will stay there for quite some time, as you will see when we explore the decision-making cycle.

This stage is where we will begin to develop the goals of the organization as well as to determine who the players will likely be. We also begin to set Traps for our competition at this stage, as well as the No Decision competitor. Hunter competitors are probably ignoring the opportunity at this time and therefore not in place. This is the point where we must anticipate that they will arrive later, and we must find an advantage over them.

3. Early Stage Technically Qualified

At this stage, there appears to be some alignment between the prospect organization's goals and your product. You and the prospect organization may not have explored all of the issues yet, but you believe that there may be a good fit. Also, the prospect organization has enough knowledge of their goals, issues, and needs, as well as your product, to believe that there may be a fit. It is important to understand at this point that your intention is not to be eliminated and at the same time to understand as much about the prospect as possible. The prospect is only going to eliminate obvious non-solutions, so you should be judicious about the amount of product information and your company information that you give out at this stage. Review the sections on creating Bait to explore how to feed information to your potential prospect efficiently.

4. Early Stage ROI Qualified

You now have some confidence that your product can help the prospect and they can financially justify the purchase. You believe a reasonable Return on Investment (ROI) exists even if the prospect does not have to accept this ROI at this time. Just as important, you have the confidence to understand that the prospect is willing to spend the amount of money that you need to charge.

5. Formal Evaluation

Now the prospect is officially involving all of the competition and trying to find the best possible solutions. This is where every type of salesperson (Gatherer, Hunter, Farmer and Trapper) is firmly in play. At this stage, the prospect has some type of evaluation plan in place. There is a general belief within your company that the prospect will make a purchase.

6. Solution Refinement

The prospect organization now has some understanding of the types of solutions for their needs. They have narrowed down their selection to a chosen few types of solutions and are trying to understand the advantages of each. They are also genuinely trying to understand the potential benefits of each. They are also trying to understand the potential downsides of each solution. The vendors are fine-tuning the proposals and aligning their products with the prospect's requirements.

7. Final Proposal Refinement

At this stage, the prospect has narrowed the potential solutions down to the best-understood choices. They are in the process of determining the final configuration. They also are discussing the pricing of the solution. You are now actively involved in trying to extract an order from this organization and internally they are justifying the cost of the solution compared to the size of their budget. This stage is where terms and conditions are beginning to be reviewed.

8. Closing

At this stage, the prospect decides on a solution and to purchase this solution. The philosophies of the Gatherer, Farmer, or Hunter encourage an inordinate amount of work at this stage. This flurry of effort and lack of planning also causes extreme stress. However, as a Trapper, you are essentially done at this time. You have eliminated your competition. You receive the order at high margins with little or no negotiation.

The Steps Of The Buying Process

Unfortunately, the preceding sales cycle does not map to the decision-making process that the prospect undergoes. It is vendor-oriented and therefore does not help the sales organization control the decision-making process. To consistently eliminate the competition, you must understand the decision-making steps and map your activities to each of these steps.

The buying process encompasses two Decision Triangles that we discussed in Chapter 3. The first triangle is the Discovery Stage of the buying process and the second triangle is the Unification Stage of the buying process. During the first Decision Triangle, the prospect organization is trying to decide if they have a goal to achieve. If there is no need, then there is no solution. The second Decision Triangle is seeking to solve this need and to unify the organization on one product.

It is important to understand the reason there are two Decision Triangles. The first triangle is to justify to the original Discoverer and her close associates that the missed goal is worth pursuing. The second triangle is for the organization to acknowledge that there is a missed goal and collectively agree to address the issue.

By understanding that there are two separate decision processes that must occur, you can appropriately target your activity. Also, you can use the correct resources from your company at the correct time. There is little reason to spend a huge number of resources in the first triangle if you are only going to have to repeat that effort in the second triangle.

▼▼▼▼▼▼▼▼▼▼▼▼▼▼
If the prospect does not have a need, issue, or missed goal then there is no reason to find a solution, and therefore there will be no purchase.
▲▲▲▲▲▲▲▲▲▲▲▲▲▲

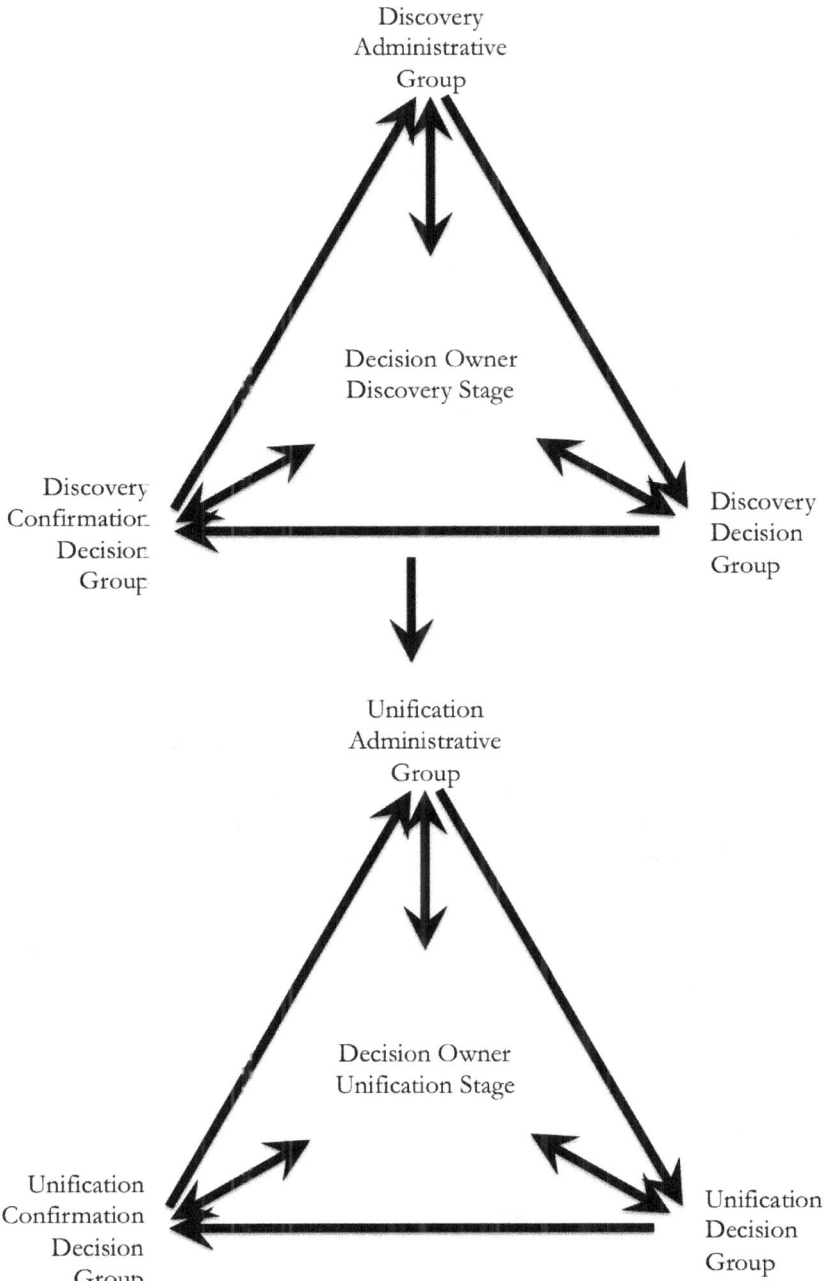

Figure 4-1: Buying Process Decision Triangles. All figures are also available at http://www.thetrapper.com/book_figures

These steps are:

Discovery Stage

1. Discover - Individual (the Discoverer) at the prospect level realizes that there is a potential need, issue, or missed goal.
2. Individual Clarification - Discoverer clarifies in his or her own mind the meaning of the need, issue, or missed goal.
3. Initial Communication - Discoverer communicates the need, issue, or missed goal to a small group of people (Decision Group) in the organization.
4. Initial Impact – Decision Group does an initial impact study of the need, issue, or missed goal.
5. Initial Prioritization - Decision Group prioritizes this need with other known organization issues.
6. Promotion of Problem - Decision Group promotes this need, issue, or missed goal to a wider audience and potentially a new Decision Owner is chosen. This new Decision Owner is the Administrative Decision Owner.

Unification Stage

7. Initial Assignment – Administrative Decision Owner assigns duties to find a solution to the need, issue, or missed goal.
8. Initial Evaluation – Decision Group finds possible solutions.
9. Initial Ramification – Decision Group evaluates solutions for possible ramifications.
10. Re-evaluation of Duties – Decision Owner adds more appropriate team members to Decision Group.
11. Formal Evaluation – Group narrows down search to the best few solutions.
12. Short List – Focus on the best few solutions.
13. Final Ramifications – Decision Group decides on the best solution.
14. Negotiation – Deciding what will be purchased
15. Decision – Administrator purchases product.

The Buying Process and the Sales Process may vary slightly in how they are correlated, but overall it looks like Figure 4-2. In particular, the Suspect and Developing Lead steps in the Sales Process occur whenever you find out about the prospect organization. For this discussion, though, we will assume that you are a Trapper; therefore, you are driving the decision rather than letting it proceed on its own accord.

The final steps of the traditional Sales Process map closely to the Buying Process. This correlation is due to the traditional strategy approach that this is a Sales Process and not a Buying Process. Unfortunately, most salespeople do not spend enough time in the early stages of the Buying Process and therefore always feel like they are behind the proverbial 'Eight Ball' during most of the sales campaign. A Trapper understands and leads the prospect through the process.

Buying Process	Selling Process
1. - Discover	1. - Suspect
2. - Individual Clarification	
3. - Initial Communication	2. - Developing Lead
4. - Initial Impact	
5. - Initial Prioritization	
6. - Promotion of Problem	
Unification Stage	
7. - Initial Assignment	
8. - Initial Evaluation	3. - Early stage technically qualified
9. - Initial Ramification	4. - Early stage ROI Qualified
10. - Re-evaluation of Duties	
11. - Formal Evaluation	5. - Formal Evaluation
12. - Short List	6. - Solution refinement
13. - Final Ramifications	
14. - Negotiation	7. - Final proposal refinement
15. - Decision	8. - Closing

Figure 4-2: Buying and Selling Processes alignment. All figures are also available at http://www.thetrapper.com/book_figures

At each stage of the Buying Process, a Trapper must take specific actions. Also, there are critical mistakes that Gatherers, Hunters, and

Farmers will make, and you need to capitalize on these errors. This understanding will enable you to take advantage of their blunders.

The following discussion assumes that you uncover the opportunity at the very first step of the buying process. This is quite often not the case if you have just started to adopt the Trapper methodology. Initially, you will probably have no opportunities at that step. While being late is not ideal, it is a Trap that you must understand, and you should prepare for this Trap. I cover escaping Traps in a later chapter, and that should assist you in dealing with this Trap.

Eventually, you will develop a pipeline of opportunities that you started early in the decision-making process. Even when you are a proficient Trapper, you will undoubtedly find opportunities later in the process. You will need to backtrack and cover most of the critical steps that you missed. One of the benefits of the Trapper Methodology is to have the time to dedicate to an opportunity that requires it.

Appendix B has a checklist of the actions that you will need to perform at each of the steps in the decision-making process. This list will help you stay on track as you are moving the prospect to an order. If you have joined the process late, it will also assist you in covering previous decisions and catching up to the prospect.

Discovery Stage - First Decision Triangle

1. Discover

Explanation: This is the first step in all buying processes. The organization must understand that they have a need or issue to make a decision to change. Companies are simply groups of individuals; therefore, one person, the Discoverer, is the first person to realize that a need, issue, or missed goal exists. This, of course, does not mean that this individual will develop the solution.

Gatherer: If the Gatherer is managing her business well, she will be ahead at this point. Since the Gatherer already has sold something to this customer, she should be able to understand the political relationships with the account. She should be able to easily map out which portion of the organization would be more likely to embrace a different product within the organization or the same product in a different area of the organization.

If the Gatherer is initiating this idea, it is likely that she has already lined up supporters for her campaign among her existing relationships. This is why the Gatherer's sales process is often longer than the prospect's buying process – the Gatherer is leading the decision-making process.

The good news for you is that it is easy to find Gatherers and in most industries, you will rarely find them. You should understand your top competitors by looking for those with multiple offerings and investigate if the prospect already owns something from the competition. You can turn this into an advantage because it is likely the Gatherer will not know that you are there, but you will be aware that they are talking to the prospect simply because of the long relationship.

Many Gatherers also are more motivated to maintain existing revenue streams than to expand into new areas of the company. This complacency is a weakness of familiarity. This mistake is what happened in our GlueWorks example in Chapter 2.

Farmer: Quite often the Farmer will initiate this step of the process because he is excellent at building and developing the need within the prospect organization. His competitive advantage is his keen understanding of the prospect and their problems. Often the farmer will make the critical mistake of only having a relationship with the Discoverer and not develop relationships with other influential people in the organization.

The Farmer may also suffer from being too random in his efforts of spreading the ideas. Much of his effort is wasted and often cultivates the wrong people. This mistake was evident in the GlueWorks example in Chapter 2

Hunter: Rarely does a hunter know anything about this step of the process and only finds the Discoverer by luck. The Hunter sales methodology places little or no emphasis on the Discoverer. Hunters want decision processes to be more refined and developed.

Trapper: It is important that you identify the Discoverer. This way you can appeal to him/her later in the sales process. It is critical that you set Traps immediately that tilts the Discoverer to be a friend. Friends recruit friends and, as we will see later in the decision process, the Discoverer plays a significant role in choosing the players on the team.

At this stage, the Trapper is very similar to a competent Farmer or a competent Gatherer. The significant difference between the three types is that you will intentionally build the need into a financially fundable course of action that leads to a purchase of your product. The Farmer and Gatherer will allow the need to develop on its own. Since many opportunities have the potential to die at this point, your experience in your industry will assist you in choosing problems and companies that will not let the process die but will end up going all the way through the decision process.

It is essential that you chose your Discoverer whenever possible. While it is possible to succeed by responding to the Discoverer, this will force you to join the Buying Cycle much later in the process, and then you spend a significant amount of time trying to understand the organization and what has already happened. When you look for Discoverers, you should look for people who are motivated to propel their career with their personal successes. These people will work hard to make sure that they can claim successes in projects and are self-starters. They will also look for opportunities to use your wisdom to increase their standing.

Your goal is to develop a friendship and a high level of trust that you can utilize later in the process. You are trying to show the Discoverer that you are helping his / her career.

In Chapter 2, Dave Trapper had a list of potential Discoverers that he was corresponding with in several prospective organizations. His goal was to befriend these potential Discoverers, educate them about how he could help them, and ultimately, have them create sales opportunities for him.

2. Individual Clarification

Explanation: This step occurs quickly, but it is crucial. If the Discoverer does not clearly understand the need and its possible implications, then the entire decision-making process will stop here. This is easily the biggest reason the buying process dies early - lack of follow-through by the Discoverer!

Gatherer: This step should be easy for the Gatherer because she is so far ahead of the Discoverer. In fact, the Gatherer often will choose the Discoverer because of her ability to influence and control him. The Discoverer's relationship with other people in the organization will allow him to quickly ensure that the Discoverer understands the ramifications of the problem. The consistent problem with the Gatherer, though, is that she is so focused on maintaining a stream of revenue she frequently doesn't spend the time developing new opportunities.

Farmer: Farmers tend to fail in this step on a regular basis since they sow the seeds haphazardly, without regard to making sure that the decision process continues to the end. As the Farmer develops into a Trapper, he will learn to only begin processes that he knows he can win and more importantly, he will have a strategy to move the Discoverer past this stage. A pure Farmer will likely miss this stage because he hasn't explicitly chosen the Discoverer.

Hunter: The Hunter will not be involved at this stage since the Hunter only works on opportunities developed by someone else. She places little value on the Discoverer and justifies this by looking at her Farmer brethren and the amount of work they do on opportunities that do not develop. As she becomes frustrated with low win ratios and constantly being behind in the sales process, she will experiment with some Farmer techniques and then eventually evolve into a Trapper.

Trapper: When you have fully adopted The Trapper Methodology, you will only start a sales campaign that will result in an order. This is so that you do not waste time. You must map out this problem for the prospect organization so that you can lead them through the logic of why they need to try to solve this issue. You must make this a personal win for the Discoverer. Obviously, individuals will occasionally do things altruistically, but more often than not, they need some real personal benefit to motivate the Discoverer to action. You will do best to have several things that will give them a personal win so that you can have many chances of success.

This personal win must be in keeping with a Vision Goal that you will define in Chapter 5. While it is true that pain avoidance is a prime influencer in behavior manipulation, a person will be far more motivated to work toward achieving a Vision Goal. A Vision Goal is one that motivates the individual or the organization.

3. Initial Communication

Explanation: At this point, the Discoverer needs to validate the problem. He will contact a small group of people (perhaps as few as one person) for verification that he has discovered a situation that needs rectifying. There are three reasons this group is extremely important to you:

- First, this group will likely be composed of people the Discoverer trusts. They will probably continue to operate as one entity throughout the decision process. Occasionally, they will informally huddle in small groups outside of the big committee to discuss their concerns and their conclusions. They will then return to the main group with a consensus.
- Second, you will learn in Chapter 5 that someone from this group will be your best chance for finding a Coach during the decision-making process. Since these people are the first to become intimate with the problem, they will draw certain conclusions as to the correct solution very early. If they

conclude that you have an appealing product, then they will help you succeed. One or more of these people will start to confide in you and coach you in how to win this opportunity.

- Third, the group will create a de facto leader for themselves. This person is not necessarily the Discoverer, but instead is often the first person the Discoverer consults after identifying the need. You should determine this leader as soon as possible and recruit him as your first Champion. Your Champions will help you drive the decision to purchase your product. This person will likely be the Decision Owner for the Discovery Decision Triangle.

Gatherer: This, potentially, is where the Gatherer will make her first critical mistake. She will often assume that every buying process in the organization is the same. She will conclude that this new group will be comprised of the same people or the same types of people as her previous campaigns. She may miss some of the individuals who join this first Decision Group or become Influencers. As a Trapper, you will want to identify that there is a Gatherer in the account and make strategic suggestions that place these new players who were not part of previous pro-Gatherer decisions into prominence.

Farmer: The Farmer rarely has a strategy for this step, and this is the underlying difference between him and you early in the decision-making process. He does an excellent job of planting seeds for opportunities but does an inadequate job of controlling the outcome. He may already start to lose control of the prospect if the new leader of the group is not the Discoverer.

Hunter: This step is still too early for the Hunter to be interested.

Trapper: The extremely successful Trapper will take the 'bull by the horns' and influence who is on this Decision Group. By developing a relationship with the Discoverer, you can steer him to people that you know will be receptive to the cause and will be advocates for you personally or for your company's reputation. This way you will control this very important step of the process.

You will need to identify the possible recruits for the Decision Group as early as Step 1. Choose people who will benefit from your version of a solution or those who will have an affinity for you, your company, or your solution. You may want to use your executive level contacts from the previous step to populate this group. Be careful to save some of these executives for later in the process and the formation of the next Decision Group; you do not want to use up all of your goodwill too early in the sales campaign.

In Chapter 2, Dave Trapper did this quite effectively by suggesting several people to his new Discoverer, Terry Tram. This suggestion assisted Dave in structuring the initial stages of the evaluation and effectively positioned him in a very competitive sales campaign. The other competitors did not control this early stage of the process and therefore were always trying to 'catch up' to the opportunity.

4. Initial Impact

Explanation: In order for the Decision Group to work together, they must first rationalize the problem and 'buy in' that there should be a solution. This rationalization will happen every time a new member joins the group. Some individuals will not join the group because they cannot rationalize its importance.

To educate themselves on the 'state-of-the-art' on the market, occasionally the Decision Group may contact vendors of solutions and investigate their websites and literature. If they are not already involved, this will trigger the Farmer and Gatherer into action. They may have been working on the account to generate interest in the problem. Sometimes, the Hunter will notice this activity as well and she may show up at the account, but will not put a lot of effort into the campaign at this early stage.

Gatherer: The Gatherer does not benefit from a long evaluation process. Rather, it is in his interest that the prospect accelerates the process and puts a large emphasis on the existing relationship. Therefore, the Gatherer may not be helpful to these new players. The Gatherer may also spend too much time with the Decision Owner named in Step 6 or the Administrator from Step 14, and this may offend the current Decision Group.

Farmer: The Farmer is very active in this step. He will use his relationship with the Discoverer to develop this need and make sure that the goals of the committee align with this solution. He will try to be a sounding board to the potential members of the group, to convince them that there is a problem. He may even try to 'close' the group for a purchase or a trial, not realizing that this project will probably grow. The Farmer fails to control the situation and the first contact competitors.

Hunter: The Hunter will take some interest in this step if the decision group approaches her. She will also check to see the likelihood of the order and will respond to the early questions. She may categorize this opportunity as a Lead or Opportunity within her company's tracking system, but will not aggressively work on driving the process. This apathy leads to her consistent problem of the rollercoaster revenue stream. This rollercoaster effect happens because she is so busy trying to close opportunities where she is behind that she can't put herself into a position where she can easily close business in the future.

It is possible she will not spend enough time on the opportunity to want to register it or list it in her pipeline. This is probably due to a fear that her management will want more information than she has or can afford to take the time to obtain. She also does not like to have opportunities die in her pipeline and so does not list young opportunities.

Trapper: This is where your skills as a Trapper start to shine. Remember, you understand that there will be competition and they must lose so you will win. As discussed in Chapter 3, the Decision Group is not going to search forever to select the best solution but will settle for a product that satisfies the majority of their perceived needs. Chapter 6 builds on this concept and helps you prioritize your resources.

There are three types of competitors for each sales opportunity:

1. Competitors who are as qualified to solve the Decision Group's concerns as you.
2. Competitors who have some of the advantages that you offer but are in an adjacent market.
3. All other initiatives that consume resources for the customer and distract the Decision Group or the organization.

You have three main goals at this stage. First, you want to identify the pool of potential competitors; second, you want to control the list of competitors that the prospect considers; and third, you need to start setting up the competition to fail.

You know that the prospect is going to look at more solutions than yours. You also know that human nature will limit this list of potential competitors. You can help yourself with these goals by suggesting competitors that you are relatively sure are applicable but are not the top competitors in the industry. You may also want to suggest some minor players in the market, also known as B players. You should be careful in this case since your information on a B player may not be perfect, and they may be more of a fringe player than you realize. You do not want to suggest a fringe player that will pull the evaluation process into their area of strength, and potentially, your weak area.

By suggesting B players for consideration, you will fulfill the prospect's desire to comparison shop but they will find out that the B players are not as good a fit as your product. This way you may not have to face your toughest competition in the opportunity, and you will look like the best product on the market. This is a very effective early strategy if you are a major player in the market with two or three other major players complemented with a large number of niche, regional or small players. This strategy can backfire if your B players are on the verge of being a major player, so you should pay very close attention to your competitive intelligence.

After gaining experience Trapping over enough time, you will deduce which vendors are most likely to be viable for your ongoing opportunities. In this case, divide your list of competitors into three groups:

A. This competitor will definitely make the cut.
B. This competitor has a reasonable chance to make the cut.
C. This competitor has virtually no chance of making the cut.

Picking the top competitors is a common practice that you see almost every day in the professional and college sports worlds. At the beginning of the season (and virtually the entire length of the season), sports writers will offer a list of teams that will be the top teams at the end of the season and the teams that are going to struggle all season long. Sports talk radio and cable TV shows spend hours prognosticating the season in the beginning and then proclaiming or defending their conclusions all season long.

You need to do the same thing as the best sports writers. Who are your toughest competitors that you know you will see in all of your most competitive deals? Who are the weak competitors that you absolutely should beat and if you lose to them it is practically an insult to your capability?

You can assume that all products are very good at something, so you should compare their list of abilities with your solution. A Venn diagram such as Figure 4-3 is very helpful to visualize this alignment. Your product's capability is the center circle, and it signifies your product's features, strengths, and weaknesses.

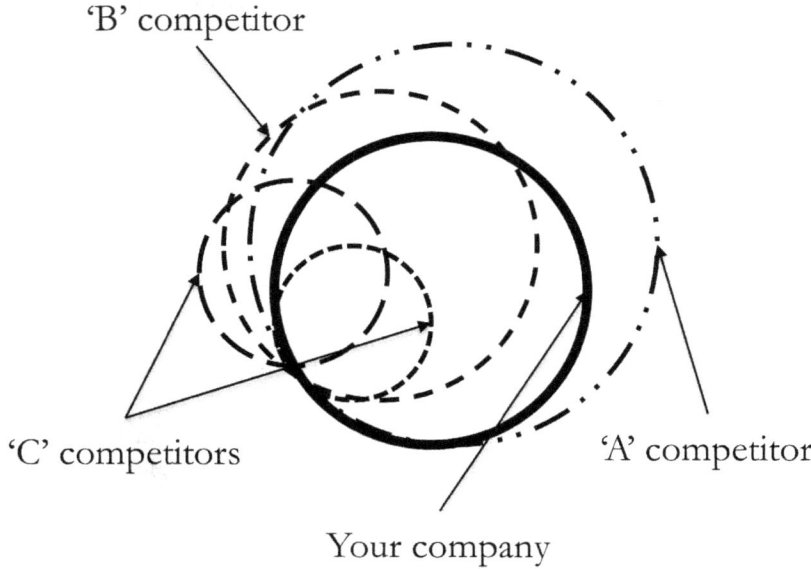

'B' competitor

'C' competitors

'A' competitor

Your company

Figure 4-3: Competitor Venn diagram. All figures are also available at http://www.thetrapper.com/book_figures

Your A-list competitors have nearly the same circle as your own even though it is likely that they will have some features that yours does not have and will not have some of your features.

Your B-list competitors will share a significant percentage of advantages with you but with less alignment than the A-list vendors. They may have other capabilities since they serve a slightly different market segment.

C-list vendors can include niche or new, underdeveloped competitors that are not interesting to most of your prospects. These competitors typically have a small benefits list, or their offering is very unproven.

Fringe vendors are C competitors as well. They may be strong vendors in a related market, but offer some capabilities that your market may appreciate. Their benefits list only partially aligns with your list, as they have just as many advantages but they address a related market. This complicates your Trapping process since you need to be careful not to divert your prospect's attention to other areas where your product does not offer an adequate solution.

▼▼▼▼▼▼▼▼▼▼▼▼▼▼
A fringe vendor can move the criteria to cover other needs that your product doesn't address. If a fringe competitor is involved, be very wary of scope creep.
▲▲▲▲▲▲▲▲▲▲▲▲▲▲

If a Gatherer has a relationship with the prospect, her company will always be an A-list competitor on this opportunity due to her history with the prospect. This categorization is true even if they typically are not one of your feared competitors.

The Gatherer will work very hard to eliminate competition and will typically be the favored vendor unless you bring out an inherent deficiency in her offering. A reasonable strategy when a Gatherer is involved is to survive as she eliminates your mutual competitors. To accomplish this, you will center most of your Traps on the Gatherer, to be sprung later in the sales process, and you will let her eliminate the rest of the competition. You will recall the Dave Trapper did this in his battle with Amy Gatherer's company in Chapter 2.

After the prospect has compiled a list of potential vendors, you must obtain this list. This is critical for you to be successful in your sales campaign. Using the techniques in Chapter 5, you will identify and develop a Coach within the Decision Group to assist you with this list. You will need to develop a strategy that will systematically eliminate the competition by pointing out their weaknesses compared to your strengths.

▼▼▼▼▼▼▼▼▼▼▼▼▼▼
If a Coach does not give you this list of competitors then you must find a new Coach.
▲▲▲▲▲▲▲▲▲▲▲▲▲▲

You should efficiently apply Traps. At this early stage of the Decision Cycle, it is fruitless to eliminate an A competitor because they will likely be able to recover later in the Decision Cycle. In addition, if you do not eliminate your B and C competitors early, then you will have to fight them later, as well as the A competitors. B and C competitors typically have enough of a difference in features that your prospect may change the criteria to match their products. This will confuse the Decision Group and cause them to be susceptible to making an error – buying your competitor's product.

Through conversations with the Decision Group players, it should be easy to deduce if a C vendor has a chance at making the cut. Focus your Traps on this C vendor to quickly eliminate them from the campaign. This will allow the Decision Group to feel that they are getting closer to a solution. You should spend the greatest amount of effort preventing this since you have the highest chance of success at doing this. In addition, if a C vendor makes make the cut, you are probably not in the strength of your product.

If the prospect has a strong affinity with a C-list vendor, then you may not be in an opportunity that you can win. It is extremely rare for a prospect to consider A-list and C-list competitors in the same evaluation. Usually, this means that one of the two vendors is significantly outside of their Sweet Spot that is discussed in Chapter 5. You should evaluate if you need to re-align the Decision Group's needs to fit your product or if you should withdraw from the sales situation. Withdrawing from the situation is not dishonorable and should not be a sign of weakness. Instead, you are conserving resources for those opportunities that you can win. In turn, you are doing the prospect a favor by eliminating choices that do not fit their needs.

5. Initial Prioritization

Explanation: By this step, the prospect has identified the need and ascertained they might have a solution. Also, they feel the solution will benefit the organization more than other known expenditures occurring in the organization.

Gatherer: The Gatherer, if she isn't ignoring the opportunity, will continue to try to accelerate through this step. It is to her advantage to control the process and lead it to a conclusion as quickly as possible. She likely knows more about the customer than any other vendor, so she will try to get the opportunity closed before real competition develops.

Farmer: The Farmer will allow the prospect to make this decision and wait for their results. If the prospect does not feel the solution will be up to the internal standards of the organization, the project will be called off, and he will have to start over.

Hunter: The Hunter may have knowledge of this stage in the process, but is usually watching to make sure that the project survives. Since this is a common area for the project to die, she is not concerned about the project's justification and, in fact, this is part of the reason that the Hunter does not get involved in early opportunities.

Trapper: You, however, will have anticipated that the Decision Group will have to prioritize this problem compared to other organizational initiatives. You, therefore, will have documented many more potential problems if this issue does not receive the highest attention. In fact, you will try and make this problem seem urgent so that the next steps go faster. This will make potential Hunter competitors seem more desperate when they join the battle late since they will have to play 'catch up' and will struggle building credibility.

The Decision Group will quickly move through this step if you can show executive sponsorship. Earlier in the buying cycle, you began to establish relationships with executives in areas of the organization that will benefit from your solution. You will have documented how the achievement of their goals maps to your solution. This documentation will be invaluable to you and the Decision Group. A short memo or phone call to executives in the organization at this point will probably be all that is required to move the Decision Group through this step. This documentation will be invaluable to you and the Decision Group. In addition, your credibility will increase since you have offered so much real value to this Decision Group and to the entire organization.

Dave Trapper did this quite effectively in Chapter 2 when he persuaded the Director to encourage the original Decision Group. This encouragement empowered the group to move forward. The Director also felt that Dave was adding a significant benefit to GlueWorks and that he was a valuable partner.

6. Promotion Of Problem

Explanation: At this point, the Decision Owner may find a new Decision Owner with enough political importance in the organization to carry this solution to a conclusion. The group will promote this problem, and its preliminary justification for expenditure, to the new Decision Owner. The new Decision Owner will form a new Decision Group.

It is possible that no one steps up to be the Decision Owner at this stage, resulting in no solution for the problem and therefore no purchase. This is one of the most likely times for No Decision to occur, simply because there is no one to drive the buying process. This is most often caused by lack of justification or conflicting resource commitments.

Gatherer: If a Gatherer is in the account and working the opportunity then it is rare that the opportunity will die. Typically, she has too many relationships to allow this to happen this early in the decision cycle. She will often have the Decision Owner picked and will be leading the group to that conclusion.

The one exception to this is if the Gatherer has a weak product in this area of interest. She may deliberately damage the project if she feels that the focus of the group will highlight weak areas of her products, services, or company. Her logic will be that she does not want to damage future credibility and good will with the organization by selling them something that is not best in class. Since all companies have limited resources, she may be better off in preventing the purchase from happening.

Farmer: The Farmer becomes very frustrated if nothing materializes. He will often try to re-grow the opportunity again in the organization, perhaps with a new Discoverer. The mistake that he makes is that he does not lay the groundwork for the project to survive this test. Farmers inherently allow the buying process to evolve on its own and then try to respond to those challenges.

If the project does survive this test, then the Farmer will probably lose all control at this point. He has spent much of his time working with the Discoverer, but it is very rare for the Discoverer to still be the Decision Owner at any successive stage. The Farmer will now be in a reactive mode and unable to affect or guide the buying process.

Hunter: The Hunter is still not actively involved in the buying process at this stage. She may be aware of the potential opportunity, but she is too busy trying to steal other opportunities to spend much time on this one. If the opportunity dies at this point to No Decision, then she will foolishly use this to justify her strategy.

Trapper: You have anticipated this step of the process and have already helped to recruit the appropriate Decision Owner in the organization to carry the process forward. Later in the process, it will be very helpful if this new Decision Owner is in the inner circle of friends with one of the executives that you have already contacted. The closer you are to the executives of the prospect organization, the more likely you will win.

Be wary of a Decision Owner who is friendly with a Gatherer. This is the Gatherer's strength. If this is the case, the Gatherer will gain inertia. You may need to start recruiting coaches and champions that can fight this turn of events.

At this point, you need to start getting the customer involved in developing the Decision Timeline for the remainder of the buying process. The new Administrative Decision Group will need your advice to advance their directive. Your market expertise will help your prospect through all of the coming intricacies. This Decision Timeline is a critical guide to the Traps that you will set and will be a Trap. The Decision Timeline will be a Trap since you will drive its creation instead of your competition. The Decision Timeline allows you to:

- Allocate your resources appropriately
- Align the prospect's decision-making process to your offering
- Create a guideline for the timing of your Traps

Chapter 6 discusses the details of this Trap in much more detail, with a sample Decision Timeline included in Appendix C.

The decision-making process now has a life of its own. From this point on, you are less concerned about the decision-making process project dying and more concerned about losing the sale. You need to be very honest with yourself at this stage: Do you have a solution for this need? If you do not, then you need to make some critical decisions:

1. Should you try to force-fit your product to fit the Decision Group's goals? Keep in mind that this may mean that you are a C competitor in this opportunity. Being a C competitor will make your chances of success more difficult. If you chose this alternative, then you must be ready to walk away from the opportunity when it is obvious that you are going to lose. It is better to save your time by leaving a lost order than to 'throw good money after bad' by pursuing a losing campaign.
2. Should you try to break up the order into smaller parts and only compete for one part? There are times that the goal, issue or need has grown so large that your solution was not applicable. If this is the case, you may want to try to isolate your solution from the larger project. This new focus will require starting the process over with a new Discoverer. This new Discoverer needs to understand that there are multiple problems and each deserves the attention of the organization. This means going back to Step One of the buying process, but that is better than losing the sale completely.
3. Should you withdraw from competing for the order? This drastic step may accomplish two goals:

- Not spending time on this opportunity could allow you more time to compete in other sales campaigns. This is a perfectly valid conclusion since your most precious resource is your own time. No matter where you are as a percent of quota achievement, working on an opportunity that is outside of your product's comfort zone is a difficult way to catch up. You should focus on opportunities that you can win.

- Withdrawing from the opportunity may convince the Decision Group prospect that they are straying from their originally intended direction and therefore make them re-think their direction. This result is possible when the Decision Group has mentally connected your products with their problem. If you withdraw, stating that you do not feel there is a fit; they may re-evaluate their situation. This is similar to the 'doomsday' gambit that we discuss later in this book, but it is less ominous since you are still very early in the buying process.

▼▼▼▼▼▼▼▼▼▼▼▼▼▼▼
A Trapper only focuses on opportunities that can be won.
▲▲▲▲▲▲▲▲▲▲▲▲▲▲▲

Unification Stage - Second Decision Triangle

Your opportunity has now progressed from the first Decision Triangle to the second. You have reached the Unification stage of the project. From this point forward, the people you are selling to are concerned with trying to solve a problem and find a solution. Before, they were investigating whether the problem existed and whether it was worth solving. Individuals in the organization that encounters this problem may still need to evaluate the problem and its importance, but by reaching this point, there is enough inertia within the decision-making process to withstand most of these discoveries.

7. Initial Assignment

Explanation: The second Decision Triangle begins with the assignment of the Administrative Decision Group to investigate possible solutions and learn about the consequences of solving the problem. Invariably, this Decision Group will include some or all of the Players from the earlier stage. Due to this association, the first Players not directly assigned to this new Administrative Decision Group will still maintain some involvement and insight. This means that these earlier group members become Influencers of the Administrative Group even though they may not formally be part of the group.

To effectively control the decision-making process, you need to control the members of this Decision Group. Your relationships with others in the prospect organization and understanding of the organization's problems will assist you in identifying likely Decision Group candidates. If you have helped reinvent the new Decision Owner, you will be able to influence the selection of the members of the Administrative Decision Group.

Gatherer: The Gatherer will try to load the group with her friends in the organization who have been successful with her product in the past. If she is not able to do this, she will recruit a large group of Influencers to shadow the group and keep her in the lead.

The Gatherer may make a very critical error at this stage. If she has a strong relationship with the current Decision Owner, then she may minimize the importance of the rest of the Decision Group and therefore ignore them. This can hurt her as the group begins to investigate the problem and look at potential solutions. She will likely recover from this as the Decision Owner advises her on the status of the investigation, but it will cause her to spend precious time catching up.

Farmer: The Farmer is now ecstatic since his vision is becoming a reality. Since the Farmer is great at building relationships with people, he is trying hard to develop a relationship with this new Decision Owner. He may think that the Discoverer is still in charge and may not realize that there has been a transfer of power in the guidance of the project. This is a tactical error that will be compounded in future steps as he fails to see the new roles that everyone is now playing in the decision-making process.

He will also have difficulty with any previously placed Traps. He is particularly sensitive to Traps that undermine his credibility with the new Decision Owner since he has spent most of his time developing relationships with the Discoverer and may not be prepared to start over as the decision process enters this stage.

Hunter: The Hunter is now starting to get interested in the opportunity since it is entering a more formal stage. She will begin to make significant inroads into the account, but if there is a Trapper involved, then she will face some significant obstacles. She will be most at risk with Traps that undermine her lack of knowledge of the organization or the work that has occurred to date. Since she will be on the defensive on these issues, she will waste her valuable time in developing more relationships.

Since she is late, she will be likely to make inroads at the top-level management of the organization. You can use this predictable step against her with the Decision Owner and the members of the original decision group to portray her as being brash and uncaring for their particular problems or wins. Once again, this forces her to respond to these issues rather than promote her agenda.

Trapper: Now is the time for you to go into high gear as a Trapper. By this step you must have several Traps in place for your most likely competition.

In Chapter 5, we discuss the Power Matrix of the organization that you will use to map out the Decision Group decision makers and its Influencers. At this step of the process, you should begin to use the Power Matrix to keep track of whom you know and how well you know them. You will need to put a plan together to meet and understand the people who are openings in your Power Matrix and understand their goals and issues.

8. Initial Evaluation

Explanation: It is at this stage that the Decision Group formally begins to evaluate solutions. They begin to call vendors, investigate websites, proactively host sales calls, and go to trade shows and conferences. Their mission is to find products, services, or technology that may solve their problem.

Gatherer: The Gatherer may begin to panic at this point. She does not want competition on this deal since it will diminish her importance in the account and it may affect her previous victories. Her goal is to have such a strong relationship with the customer that they will not look at competitors.

Her first recourse will be to approach her friends who are not in the Decision Group and encourage them to be Influencers. If their influence is not strong enough to stop the invitation of competition, she may look like she is trying to manipulate the sales process and may create enemies within the Decision Group. The Decision Owner is especially susceptible to hard feelings for this act.

Farmer: Farmers have been involved for quite some time now, but they have just incurred brand new competition. Up until now, they have been competing with No Decision and other Farmers, but now they have Hunters getting involved, and they tend to spend more time trying to cement their relationships. They may have been dealing with Trappers at this point but typically a Trapper is hard to detect until too late, and the poor Farmer simply thinks that you are another Farmer.

The Farmer may respond to this new level of competition by trying to accelerate the opportunity. He may also bring in other salespeople in his organization who have more of a Hunter philosophy. This is quite effective since the combination of Hunter and Farmer techniques is the first step in becoming a Trapper.

Hunter: This is where most Hunters begin to get involved and interested. They typically respond to the requests of the organization and begin to evaluate the various players in this group. Unfortunately, they spend so much time responding to requests for information and trying to meet the members of this committee that they often will miss the Influencers from the earlier groups. Hunters who get involved in this step feel like they are getting involved in the early

142

stage of the cycle, but in reality, they have missed major portions of the buying cycle and are not typically even aware of the Decision Owner unless someone points her out to them. They also may not be aware of the Discoverer if she has taken the role of an Influencer. A Discoverer who is an Influencer remains very powerful, as she may still be controlling much of the buying process behind the scenes.

Hunters will continue to join the sales process from this point until the final decision. They may even join in after the final decision but before the organization has put forth a lot of effort in implementing the decision. Hunters pride themselves on being thieves and try to steal orders late in the process. As a Trapper, you must recognize this behavior and be able to quickly respond to new competition as they join the battle. This is one of the reasons you should keep your competitive database up to date and understand that the A vendors on your list may join in at any time.

Trapper: Trappers, of course, are in a good position. Since you anticipated this step, you knew some of the people who were going to be in this Decision Group; in fact, you should have helped influence the choices. You will also have new competition from the Hunters, but you anticipated this and laid Traps so that the competition is spending a great deal of time responding to Traps and not being proactive.

Competitors are typically good for you; so do not worry about their involvement. Competitors will help you teach the prospect about the market, your industry, and your overall technology. This will save you valuable time and money since much of what they discuss will be relevant to your offering. For example, GlueWorks had to learn many of the industry-related issues. These issues were nearly identical for all competitors; therefore, it was effective for Dave Trapper to suggest his competitors as a source for that knowledge. This allowed Dave to spend time discussing the features that made his offering different. Dave did not need to discuss common features that all the vendors offer that will not win the order. This is a critical component to the Bait discussion that we will have in Chapter 6.

▼▼▼▼▼▼▼▼▼▼▼▼▼
A feature that is not unique is not a feature worth discussing.
▲▲▲▲▲▲▲▲▲▲▲▲▲▲

Competitors will also help you to evaluate the level of serious consideration that is involved in the organization. If there is no competition, then you must always be concerned that the prospect may not be serious. Typically, if you know that there are two or more competitors talking to a Decision Group, then someone will usually make a purchase. This means it will not be lost to No Decision and eventually, a transaction will occur. If there are no competitors, you may find that the prospect was going through a learning exercise rather than a buying exercise.

▼▼▼▼▼▼▼▼▼▼▼▼▼
Competitors help to confirm that the prospect is serious about making a decision to buy.
▲▲▲▲▲▲▲▲▲▲▲▲▲▲

The organization may choose to send out a request to possible vendors to discuss their products or services. This request may be called a Request For Information (RFI) or a Request For Proposal (RFP). This request can happen as early as this step or be delayed until later in the process, potentially as late as Step 11. It is imperative that you understand if this is going to occur and if it does occur, help the prospect write the document. This is one of the most effective ways to eliminate competition from consideration in the following steps of the process. Chapter 6 will assist you in creating the items that you should consider for your RFP Traps. Chapter 7 will help you with ways to put your Traps into this formal request.

9. Initial Ramifications

Explanation: The Decision Group has begun to be educated about your market. At this step, the prospect will eliminate some of the weaker potential solutions or solutions that are on the fringe of their need. This is where most of the C vendors will fall off the radar.

Their lack of features will cause their elimination, and the Trapping techniques that you learn in this book will assist in removing them.

The Decision Group will investigate how this decision may affect other areas of the organization. These issues will likely grow over time and will compound themselves when we get to the next step, where there may be changes to the Decision Group or changes to the Influencers.

Gatherer: The Gatherer will try to convince the Decision Group that the biggest ramification of not choosing her solution will be to put the existing investment with her company at risk or to trivialize its savings to the organization. She will use her existing knowledge of the prospect to point out other topics for consideration, further strengthening her position with the Decision Group.

The Gatherer's strength is also her weakness. Remember that no implementation of a product is perfect, no product is a perfect fit to a prospect's needs, and a prospect rarely understands all of the issues that are pertinent. Therefore, the Gatherer is at risk by pointing out these deficiencies in her existing implementation to the prospect. You can also point out the deficiencies of logic, timing, or circumstance that caused the organization to choose her product over yours. This Trap potentially opens the door to expand the scope of the search to include replacing the Gatherer's previous implementation.

If the Gatherer sells a C product, then you may have luck in eliminating her at this step. If the product is an A or B competitor, then she will survive this step. Your goal is to make her start to feel like she has tough competition because she is probably not used to it and did not plan for it.

Farmer: By now the Farmer knows that there are new players from the organization in the process and has started to develop a relationship with them. His weakness at this point is the acceleration of the decision. Since he has to develop new ties to the new players, you must make this challenging for them by convincing your friends that you put on the Decision Group to move quickly. You must also place Traps for all of your competitors that are unique to them and your market.

Hunter: Time is working against the Hunter at this point. She is new to the organization and is trying to quickly learn who the players are and develop a strategy to win. Her biggest fear is not knowing what she does not know. Aside from product and company Traps that are unique to your industry, she is very susceptible to Traps that cause her to waste time or go on wild goose chases. You should have several of these in place to cause her problems.

The Hunter is struggling to build personal credibility even though her product or her company may have credibility. This causes her to do extreme amounts of work to try to gain credibility. It also causes her to try to get special consideration, extended preparation time, and potentially to complain about unfair treatment. You must anticipate this and lay a Trap for the Hunter that commits the prospect to not allow for delays.

Trapper: By this step, you must have placed at least one, if not many, Trap for every one of your competitors. You are in a very tenuous position at this stage since you are now dealing with the majority of the competition. At this stage, you need to eliminate as many competitors as possible as soon as you can.

Aside from Traps that are unique to your market and industry, your top goal at this point is to accelerate the process. Most of your competition will not understand the organization, the players, or their problems well enough to win the order at this stage. If you have been following the Trapper process, you are ahead at this point, and you need to maintain that lead. By accelerating the organization's decision-making process, you have a better chance of maintaining this lead at the end of the process.

The easiest way to accelerate the decision-making process is to look ahead at the next steps, contact those potential players, and convince them of your product's superiority. In fact, in the next step, the

Decision Group will change some members, and you can use this opportunity to 'stack the deck' in your favor and include the final players from the next steps.

10. Re-Evaluation Of Duties

Explanation: Quite often, not all of the appropriate people will be on the Decision Group. New members join to add expertise. This reorganization is usually due to a better understanding of the possible solutions and the ramifications of those solutions. The Decision Owner will bring in subject matter experts to advise the group on these ramifications and occasionally, these subject matter experts will officially join the group.

It is also possible that team members will leave the formal group at this point. They may find that their attention to this issue is not justified. In this case, those members will relegate themselves to Influencer status and will only become involved if the final decision does not represent their best interests.

Gatherer: This step is very good for the Gatherer. She should know more people in the prospect's organization than any other type of competitor. She will use this opportunity to stack the Decision Group with more of her supporters. She will also firm up her relationship with Influencers who can control the Decision Group.

If the Gatherer feels that she is ahead at this step, she may try to accelerate through this step. She will do this by suggesting to the Decision Owner that the Decision Group has considered all of the facets of the organization and further delay will be costly. She will typically get her Champion to echo this argument and try to force the acceleration.

Farmer: This is a good step for the Farmer. He will take this opportunity to cement his relationship with the existing decision group, and he may have a relationship with the new players because of his earlier work with the account. This time delay will assist him in getting closer to the primary decision makers.

The downside for the Farmer is that this is part of your Trap. You may have noticed that your competitor is still active in the account, but due to your competitive knowledge, you know that you can place people in the group who will hurt the competitor. Your Trap in this case is to approach the subject matter expert who may have an issue with your competitor and convince them to force their way onto the committee.

Hunter: This is also a good step for the Hunter. Up until now, she has been trying to catch up and learn the organization. This break in the activity may allow her the time she needs to meet enough people to make up for being late. Also, these new players may want to proactively meet her, which will ease her ability to network in the organization.

Similar to the Farmer, though, the Hunter is susceptible to the new experts being your Traps to eliminate them. They may have spent so much time getting to know the current decision group that they could not prevent being blindsided by a new subject matter expert who causes them further work and consternation.

Trapper: If you are ahead then your primary goal is to skip this step. If you have done your job well in earlier steps, then you included all of the subject matter experts who typically affect your decisions. If you did not accomplish all of your goals or you are behind, then this is your opportunity to fix this error. By adding more friends to the Decision Group, you may eliminate a competitor who did not fall to an earlier Trap.

This step is a prime example of the prospect organization's inexperience in your market. After the dozens or hundreds of sales campaigns that you have been on, you know that there will be issues that impact different portions of the organization. The Decision Owner, however, did not foresee this and did not include these people. These people should have been on your list to include at step 7, and it should be obvious from your Decision Timeline to consult these people. You can gain a significant amount of credibility with the Decision Owner by politely reminding him that this was your suggestion all along.

If you did not accomplish all of your goals or you are behind, this is your opportunity to fix this error. If you contacted these new Influencers in advance, you will be significantly ahead of your competition and will have accelerated the decision-making process. By contacting these people, you can cement your relationship with them and give them the impression that you are the 'de facto' choice. Setting Traps for your competitors before joining the Decision Group gives you the opportunity to put your competition on the defensive immediately. If successful, the competition will react antagonistically to these new members and assume they are enemies.

The key point at this step is your opportunity to have your friends brought into the team, thereby keeping your enemies off the Decision Group. Just like a high-priced trial lawyer, you need to 'stack your jury' with people who will vote for you and keep out the ones that will vote for your competitors. Great sources of new entrants to the Decision Group are the members of previous Decision Groups who are now Influencers. You may want them brought into the group since they may have also told you their feelings about your solution.

Dave Trapper did a very effective job of this in Chapter 2. He added three new people to the refined group. He also convinced the Decision Owner (Greg) that the Vice President of Manufacturing did not need to be on the team. Dave's strongest enemies in the account were in manufacturing, and he needed to reduce their influence.

11. Formal Evaluation

Explanation: At this step, most of your competitors are vying for the sale although the Decision Group may have already eliminated some competitors in the earlier steps of the process. From here forward, the prospect will follow one of three major scenarios:

1. Many times the prospect will use an organization-wide developed formal evaluation process to be followed. This is designed to be fair, but it rarely is fair. It is also frequently inadequate, and often fraught with ways to bypass motivated employees.

2. The Decision Group may create an evaluation process unique to this search. Typically, they take the suggestions of the various competitors and then create an evaluation process.
3. The Decision Group may not follow any formal process at all but instead respond to events, sales calls, and demos.

Once the creation of the criteria for formal (or in step 3 above - the informal) evaluation is set, the Decision Group will use these tests to assess the potential vendors. If it is a formal assessment process with rules and scores, then your salesmanship will not help you win the purchase. Your product will have to compete on its own merits, strengths, and weaknesses. This lack of control is why it is so important that you influence these rules.

Gatherer: The Gatherer prefers the third type of evaluation, an informal process. The informality will allow her to use her strong relationship with her customer to monitor the Decision Group. A formal evaluation will force her product to compete on its own merits, and it may not adequately account for her existing relationship with the account. If a formal evaluation is chosen, she will frequently try to circumvent any rules that hurt her chances.

Farmer: Many Farmers have dropped out by this time. The Farmer needs to have an A product to get to this point and not succumb to one of your earlier Traps. He rarely controls the prospect, so he simply follows along in whatever process the prospect chooses. His strength from this step forward is being the nice and cooperative salesperson. In fact, he will often use the line "The prospect is always right" as a Trap against you. He will portray you as terribly aggressive. You must be very careful to not fall into his Traps! You must make sure that all of the help that you are giving the prospect is welcomed and desired and therefore the prospect will ignore the Farmer's criticism of you.

Most Farmers will prefer an unstructured evaluation process, as this allows relationships to be the driving factor of the decision. They are very accustomed to making frequent sales calls on the Decision Group to gauge their mood. They will also not have many prospects at this stage of the buying process, so they can afford to invest their time. They will not push the prospect into one type of evaluation.

Some new Farmers may join the fight at this late stage because the prospect may issue a request for information to everyone in the industry. For him to survive very long, he will act more like a Hunter from this point on, but he will continue to sell the same basic way - by being the nice and cooperative salesperson and letting his product or service stand on its own merits. He will still not understand that the key to success is to control the sales process and not just respond to it.

Hunter: The last of the Hunters will join the fight now. These newer Hunters will be very aggressive and may ask for delays in the process to catch up. Overall, the Hunter's strategy will be to try to get the top of the organization to modify the decision process to favor her product. Once the evaluation process is established, she will follow every step to the letter and will involve many portions of her company in the campaign.

Trapper: This is where your skill as a Trapper must emerge. In many respects, the sale will be won or lost at this point. The formal evaluation will essentially remove your selling skills from the equation and leave your product to compete on its own merits, strengths, and weaknesses. You must actively set up the evaluation process before this step to make sure that you win. You must use your influence with the prospect to design the evaluation to show your strengths and highlight the weaknesses of the competitor.

▼▼▼▼▼▼▼▼▼▼▼▼▼▼▼

The salesperson who writes the evaluation criteria will win the decision-making process and will frequently win the sales opportunity. You must use your influence with the prospect to make the assessment show your strengths and highlight the weaknesses of the competitor.

▲▲▲▲▲▲▲▲▲▲▲▲▲▲▲

You must determine the typical evaluation at this organization. If scenario number one above is in play, then you must understand the organization's standard methodology and ensure a fair evaluation of your product. If it does not give you an advantage, then you must influence the Decision Owner to modify the normal process.

In the case of the second scenario, your early relationship with the organization will start to pay off. Use your influence with the organization to make sure that your product's pre-developed standard evaluation plan is a major factor in the prospect's evaluation plan. This document, filled with Traps for the major competitors in the market, can easily make the difference in a successful sales campaign.

▼▼▼▼▼▼▼▼▼▼▼▼▼

If you do not have a standard evaluation process filled with Traps, create one. Your success depends on it.

▲▲▲▲▲▲▲▲▲▲▲▲▲

The third scenario can be the most frustrating to the Trapper. In this scenario, the prospect will often make a decision out of frustration and weariness. This can mean that the last vendor to make a presentation can win the decision-making process. You need to have Traps set up well in advance of this step to prevent this from occurring. Your first goal is to convince the prospect to use a more formal process, i.e., scenario one or two above. The fundamental argument, in this case, is that you are an expert at evaluating this type of solution and they should use your counsel in creating a fair and complete evaluation. If this argument fails, you have two choices:

1. You must make a dramatic effort to make sure that you are always in touch with the mood and current of each Decision Group member. The more people you know in the decision-making process, the more likely that this will result in a successful campaign. You will need to vigorously use the skills discussed in this book, which, if applied vigorously, will help you to win this campaign. By doing this, you must be prepared to react quickly if the prospect gives up and makes a decision based on emotion and frustration.
2. Your second choice is much more drastic and should only be deployed if you cannot keep close tabs on the prospect. In this case, you withdraw from consideration by the prospect.

This is a very dramatic gesture, and you should reserve it solely to draw attention to you and your plight. You must ensure that your champions, coaches, and friends in the organization will defend you. In Chapter 6 we will discuss this 'doomsday' Trap in much more detail.

12. Short List

Explanation: In all likelihood, the formal evaluation will show one or two products as winners, with the balance of the vendors as a distant third place. The Decision Group will now focus on these top vendors and will make a buying decision from that group. If the prospect fails to create this gap between the leaders and the rest of the field, the prospect will either start the process over or will compromise their selection criteria to consider options with the second tier of players.

The prospect will typically put the top vendors through a more in-depth series of tests and evaluations. They do not want to do this with the earlier larger group of vendors, due to the costs and effort that this testing entails. This more involved test will find holes and deficiencies in the products or companies. This testing will help the Decision Group decide which one is the 'best fit' for their organization.

Gatherer: The Gatherer will already know the Administrator, so she will try to skip this step and accelerate to step 14 if she thinks she is ahead. If not chosen as a finalist, she will try to change that decision by using her Influencers. She will likely have new Influencers you have never seen and have not covered. These Influencers will be the management and leading team members from her existing installation within the organization. As a Trapper, you must cry foul to this inclusion and appeal to the wisdom of the group that arrived at a decision.

Even complaining that the criteria has been modified unfairly will probably not work if you try to raise the issue after the fact. Instead, you should be challenging the Decision Group about administrative interference before this step. If you have convinced the Decision Group that a product is not a good fit, you need to challenge them so that top management or other influences do not come in to restructure the decision-making process. If you cannot get this assurance of safety from outside influence, then you can be assured that either your Champion is not very influential or your product, your company, and/or you are not well respected by the prospect.

Farmer: The Farmer will be ecstatic that he made it this far. Similar to the formal evaluation step above, he will react in much the same way as he did in step 11. If the previous step eliminated the Farmer, then he will appeal to the goodwill of his friends in the organization to have him included. As a Trapper, you must cry foul to this inclusion and appeal to the wisdom of the group that arrived at a decision. As above with the Gatherer, this Trap is best placed before this step with assurances that outside influences cannot sway the decision of the Decision Group.

Hunter: The Hunter is probably already starting to cash her commission check at this point. She may drop every other activity to close this sale. It is normal for her to have forecasted this win to her management. She will pull out all the stops to win this order now that she has made it to this stage. Since she does not spend a lot of time growing prospects, then she must win this order to preserve her income and maybe her job.

Her most likely strategy is to expand the scope of this stage. If the prospect asks for three similar references, then she will give them six references. If the prospect wants to speak to someone from the management of the vendor, she will arrange a meeting with the entire management team. At this stage, it is critical that she wins and she will not stop at anything to close the deal.

Trapper: Early in the sales process, you understood that there were many vendors vying for the order and you were careful with your Trap selection. You saved enough Traps to compete effectively after the final cut. Early in the process, you did not want to set all of your Traps against the A competitors that you knew were going to make the final list. You will want to set the foundation for Traps early in the process (steps 5-9 above) so that you can launch them against these final competitors.

You should have worked out these Traps in advance while you were working on the evaluation criteria for the previous steps. If this is true, then this step is simply a logical extension of the last. Since you surmised the final contestants for this sales campaign, you should have already laid the groundwork for this step. You must use every skill at your disposal to point out the weaknesses of your competitor.

This is where the final A list must be eliminated. If you have done your job correctly, you predicted this list many steps ago and placed Traps for these competitors. You can assume that each of the solutions will work to some degree to solve the prospect's problems. What you want to do at this stage is show the prospect that there are significant ramifications in buying another product.

You usually cannot eliminate an A player purely on technical merit; otherwise, they would not be an A player and still be at this stage of the process. You need to show a tighter fit between your products and the prospect's goals. You do this by emphasizing your close fit and every weakness of the competitor. This skill is developed in the next several chapters of this book.

▼▼▼▼▼▼▼▼▼▼▼▼▼▼

You cannot eliminate 'A' competitors on technical merit alone; otherwise, they would not be 'A' competitors. You must show a stronger fit to the prospect organization's goals, issues, and needs.

▲▲▲▲▲▲▲▲▲▲▲▲▲▲

13. Final Ramifications

Explanation: The Decision Group is evaluating the preferred solution and trying to find out if they made a mistake. This ramification avoidances step often means bringing in other people in the organization as Authorities that may give a VETO or ACCEPT the decision. These Authorities cannot decide to make a purchase; they can only reject or accept the recommendation of the Decision Group. These new Influencers will differ depending on whether we are dealing with a Corporate Sale or a Personal Sale. For a Corporate Sale, the other Influencers will include other department heads, vendors of the prospect, the management of the prospect (especially the CFO if the dollar value is significant), etc. The Personal Sale will typically be friends, neighbors, and extended family of the prospect.

To avoid wasting everyone else's time and energy, generally the Decision Group goes through this step with only one solution and keeps the other 'best fit' offerings on hold. In rare cases, it is possible that the top two or three choices will be so close that all of the top contenders are circulated to find some significant reason to select or eliminate a choice.

Gatherer: If the Gatherer is behind she will make sure that her friends in the organization become Authorities and VETO the decision. She is very vulnerable in doing this since it is likely that this new project will have its own supporters. You must prepare your Champion for this onslaught. Warning your Champion of this act is often enough for him/her to politically neutralize the attack. This is an instance when the strength of your Champion must overcome the strength of your competitor's Champion.

If the Gatherer is ahead, then she will continue to try to accelerate the process, and your strategy will be to influence the Gatekeepers to VETO the decision. Your relationship with members of your Power Matrix, described in Chapter 5, will be critical now. A loss at this stage of the decision process can be devastating since you have invested so much time in the decision. You must use every tool at your disposal to overcome the Gatherer.

Farmer: If the Farmer makes it to this stage then he will capitalize on his relationship with the organization. He may be surprised that there are more steps to go through, having made the final cut. He will also know that he is out of tools to use to win the order, save one: price. The Farmer's goal at this point is to accelerate the process to the point of trying to skip this step. Often the Farmer has made a relationship with the Administrator, and he will try to skip this final step and proceed straight to the next step. His most viable strategy at this point is to offer steep discounts or incentives, which only the Administrator can take full advantage of.

Due to the Farmer's early knowledge of the organization, it is possible that the Farmer will know some of these outside influences. If you anticipate that a Farmer's product will make the final list, then you need to make sure you have identified his friends and make the extra effort to equal his relationship with these people.

Hunter: The Hunter will often panic at this stage of the process. She most likely will not know all of these new players. This will cause her to put pressure on the core group of people she knows well. It will also cause her to put extreme offers in front of the prospect to try to accelerate the decision. Her number one fear at this stage is the lack of control because she did not anticipate the players who now have an effect on the order. As a Trapper, you will want to capitalize on this and warn your prospect that she may do things in a panic. By predicting the actions of the desperate Hunter, you can make them look foolish and second rate.

Trapper: As we have discussed earlier, each of these solutions will probably make the prospect happy in the end, and none of these solutions is 'perfect' for the prospect without some compromise in one area or another. Therefore, do not be intimidated by your competitor's strengths. Since you are at this stage, you have an acceptable solution, and you must capitalize on your strengths.

During the entire sales process, you developed the other players who will likely have an impact on the final decision at this stage. These Shadow Influencers are familiar with you, your company, and your products. These Shadow Influencers should be on your Power Matrix from Chapter 5, and you or other members of your team should be regularly having high-value conversations with them. This coverage ensures they will not be surprised when asked to comment on the potential impact to their area of responsibility. In fact, you have shown them that there are personal advantages and wins to selecting your products. This relationship could be your greatest Trap if your competitors are trying to appeal to this group for the first time.

Now is the time for you to 're-launch' any of your Traps that you have laid out in the past. Revisit these substantive issues with each affected decision maker. If you found a Trap that was slightly effective for some of the decision makers, you need reiterate that Trap to all decision makers in the process. As discussed in Chapter 6, Traps are most effective if there are multiple Traps laid out for the competitor to trip over. You also want to increase the nuisance factor to your competitors by making them constantly respond to your questions, thereby eliminating their own agendas.

▼▼▼▼▼▼▼▼▼▼▼▼▼▼
Traps are most effective when they work in tandem with other Traps.
▲▲▲▲▲▲▲▲▲▲▲▲▲▲

14. Negotiation

Explanation: This is the domain of the Administrator, with oversight by the Decision Owner. The Administrator may be one person or multiple people who are conferring with each other. There may be more than one vendor involved at this stage, but there is always one preferred product. The Decision Group has already addressed the biggest challenges. Traps should be in place that will effectively neutralize the competition and make this step easy. If you have not followed the Trapper methodology, the prospect will decide based on monetary issues, delivery, terms, and conditions. This will reduce the selling price of the product or force other considerations that make the sale less profitable or smaller in magnitude.

Sometimes, the Decision Group will select the best few solutions and leave it to the Administrator to negotiate the final order. In this case, the Administrator is the final negotiation authority. The Decision Group assumes that all of the vendors are technically feasible, but there are ramifications to each solution that need to be negotiated. Your coaches must tell you these ramifications, with both your product and your competitors, so that you can use this information to your advantage.

Gatherer: The Gatherer is forced to discount at this point if there is competition. There are cases where she will reconfigure the existing implementation to accommodate the needs of this new project so the net cost is minimized. She will emphasize the relationship that exists and the need to continue that relationship. She may also use the argument that her company is an 'evil' that they know rather than your 'evil' that they do not know.

Farmer: The Farmer usually concludes that the only thing for him to do is to cut the price at this point. He has run out of tools to use and will resort to discounting. He is now at the hope and prayer stage of the sales process. He is unable to forecast and predict the outcome of this sale, so he is beginning to get quite frustrated, and his management is compounding this fear by their lack of comfort in the success of this campaign.

If the Farmer has just been eliminated or is being stalled while negotiations continue with a competitor, then the Farmer will likely give up and move on to another prospect. He simply does not have the tools to win an engagement where he is not on top.

Hunter: The Hunter is also in a state of panic. She does not have enough opportunities in her pipeline to afford to let this one slip. She will offer very steep discounts to close the deal quickly. She will be more aggressive if she is not involved in the process. She will offer aggressive discounts on the theory that if you win, you will not make any profit on the transaction because she will drive the profit out of the deal. She also will appeal to the highest levels possible for reconsideration, even to the point of accusing you and the Decision Owner of unethical behavior. Her tactics are self-justified by the conclusion that she has already lost the order; therefore, she has little downside to a 'mudslinging' contest.

Trapper: Move fast! You are on top, and everyone else is now gunning for you! You must anticipate desperate behavior by your competitors. Many times, simply warning the Administrator to anticipate the unreasonable behavior by your competitor will be enough to make the competitor look foolish. However, the competitor's tactics may be effective against you, so you must conclude this step as quickly as possible.

Often the most formidable competitor enters the campaign again at this point. The name for this competitor is No Decision. This competitor competes with every category of product, across all industries and markets. You must lay Traps for this competitor throughout the entire sales process, but typically, No Decision will not get in the way until this step if the process has already made it past step 7.

15. Decision

Explanation: At this step, it is time to make the decision, and there is little for you to do. In fact, there is a fallacious belief in many sales organizations that the end of the sale should be the most stressful and require the most work. This is not the case for Trappers. The end of the sale is almost anti-climatic since you have successfully convinced the prospect to purchase the product all through the decision-making process and you have eliminated all of the competition for the order. This combination results in an extremely high-margin order delivered with very favorable terms.

Gatherer, Farmer, and Hunter: They are immaterial at this point! They lost, and they are trying to figure out what they are going to tell their management. If they are intelligent, they are wondering why they keep losing to you, and they may start to emulate your tactics and modes of operating. In short, they are trying to figure out how to be a Trapper. Your biggest fear is that they will find a copy of this book and will evolve into a Trapper!

Trapper: You are done. Congratulations! You won! You must make sure that all of the paperwork is processed and that the prospect lives up to the terms of the deal. It is now time to focus more time on other campaigns. You know that your manager will be calling you soon to ask, "So what have you sold lately?"

Chapter 5 – The Game Trails - Finding Prospects

"You were born to win, but to be a winner, you must plan to win, prepare to win, and expect to win."

- Zig Ziglar

One of the many challenges in sales is finding the right people to call on and opportunities that fit your product. This chapter gives many examples on prospecting and targeting appropriate organizations for sales campaigns. More importantly, it discusses how to understand the relationships within the prospect organization.

The first part of the chapter discusses how to find the best organizations to buy the salesperson's product. These organizations have a strong fit with the salesperson's personal 'sweet spot.' The Sweet Spot organizations are composed of the best combination of geography, size, structure, and industry to allow the salesperson to excel.

After finding the target organization, the salesperson must completely understand its politics and structure. To aid the salesperson, we will discuss the concept of a Power Matrix later in the chapter. The Power Matrix is a convenient way to map out everyone in the organization, their relationships with each other, and their power in the company. It eliminates the false sense of security the salesperson can develop by helping him or her understand the prospect's organization chart but not how the organization makes decisions.

It is the job of salespeople to sell a product or products. As we have discussed, this is a difficult job, and many people fail at it. This is because we have many things working against us:

- Customers struggle to make a decision.
- Competitors are trying to make us lose our deal.
- Products that may not be the absolute best in the market.
- Difficulty in finding prospects for our products.

Of all of these issues, the one that salespeople most frequently complain about is the last item. Depending on the product that you sell, finding prospects for our products can range from "challenging" to "almost impossible."

This chapter is about finding the places to sell your product. In the wilderness Trapping example that I spoke of earlier, the wilderness Trapper will understand the species and habits of the animal he is trying to capture. He will lay the perfect Bait and the perfect type of Trap at the perfect spot to lure the animal into the Trap.

You need to perform the same analysis. You need to identify the target prospect, and then you need to put a plan in place to win the order. This chapter will help you detect and close the opportunity to allow you to get your commission.

As we have seen elsewhere in this book, the art of Trapping is to anticipate that events and decisions are going to happen in your absence and control those events and decisions without your presence. Nowhere is this more evident than when you are prospecting for new clients.

You will not be present for the entire decision to include your product in the company's search for a solution to their goals. At times, you may not even know the decision is being made for you or against you until much later. A group of individuals could create a list of potential vendors and your inclusion on that list is not certain.

Many salespeople will insist that being included on the list is the job of their marketing department. In many ways, this is true since the ultimate goal of marketing is to create awareness among prospects. However, a successful Trapper doesn't depend on other people to enable their success. Instead, a Trapper will create circumstances to enable success.

▼▼▼▼▼▼▼▼▼▼▼▼▼▼▼
A Trapper will create conditions to enable success.

▲▲▲▲▲▲▲▲▲▲▲▲▲▲▲

Marketing Is Probably Going To Fail You

A complaint that I hear from salespeople far too often is that their marketing department doesn't help them enough. Specifically, the marketing department:

- Doesn't provide enough leads.
- Doesn't have appropriate collateral.
- Cannot provide reference customers.
- Doesn't sponsor suitable activities to publicize the company and products in the salesperson's territory.

In short, the marketing department doesn't do everything required to deliver a customer with money in hand to the salesperson.

The easiest rebuttal to the above is to declare the salesperson to be correct. Of course, the marketing department doesn't do enough for any given salesperson to close orders quickly. If they did, the salesperson wouldn't be necessary.

Many products do not require a salesperson. These are widely used products, and the features and benefits are universally understood. These products are typically called commodities. Commodities in the general consumer market are things like most groceries, but could also include gasoline, electricity, and water.

Think about this issue and relate it to your personal experience. No salesperson convinces you to buy the above products. You choose the brand or place of purchase exclusively due to marketing messages that you receive. In these cases, marketing does everything required to deliver a customer who is ready to buy to the salesperson. In these cases, the salesperson is a clerk at a retail store or virtual counter who makes little commission for the sale. Also, the salesperson doesn't provide any actual value to the consumer aside from taking care of the transaction process.

If a salesperson wants the marketing department to do all the work, the salesperson should apply for a job as a teller in the local grocery store. If the salesperson wants to add value to the sales process, then s/he should choose products that need a more personal touch.

Enhancing The Marketing Message

In a complex B2B sale, the salesperson's job is to enhance and personalize the marketing message for the buyer. The salesperson is supposed to deliver the information from the company to the decision maker in a way that effectively shows the product and company in the best light for that particular prospect.

The easiest way to show this is via a vector diagram. While I understand that vector mathematics may be scary for some readers, they are not that difficult to comprehend.

As we can see in Figures 5-1 and 5-2, the goal is to convince the prospect that the company's product is the best product for this purchase. Marketing has to deliver content to all prospects, so it cannot perfectly align the message to the specific goals of the individual prospect. Also, since Marketing has no knowledge of which competitors are in play in that particular situation, they cannot efficiently deliver Traps in most cases. Therefore, we see that the messaging from Marketing is not the shortest distance from your company to the finish line of winning the decision by the prospect.

In Figure 5-1, the product sold is a commodity type product. In this case, the marketing message is entirely adequate to convince the prospect to buy the product. Even though the message is not perfectly aligned to the prospect's specific needs, the product's benefits are sufficiently understood to get across the line.

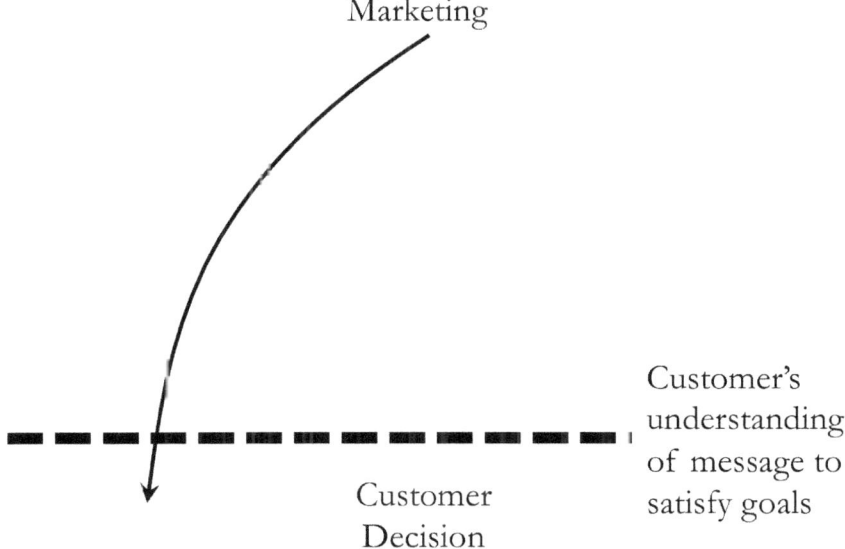

Figure 5-1: Marketing message for commodity products. All figures are also available at http://www.thetrapper.com/book_figures

In Figure 5-2 this is not the case. In Figure 5-2, the message is still not perfectly aligned to the prospect's needs, and it is not adequate to make a decision. It may not be enough information, and it also may not be the correct type of information. Therefore, a salesperson needs to fill in information to cover the gap.

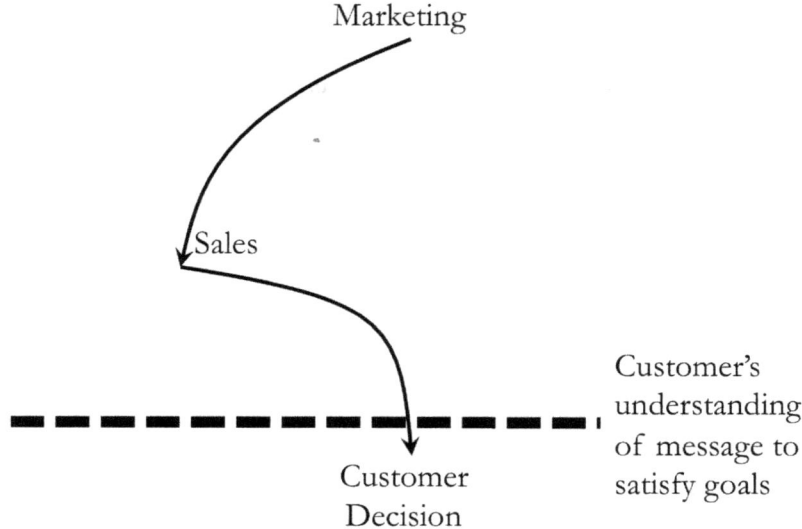

Figure 5-2: Marketing and sales message for non-commodity products. All figures are also available at http://www.thetrapper.com/book_figures

This information gap is why it is so important for salespeople to be Trappers. They need to take the information that is created by the marketing department and efficiently deliver it to the prospect. Trappers need to package information so that the prospect can make the desired decision.

It is impossible for the marketing department to create a targeted value pitch to every prospect. The more efficient the Trapper is in packaging this information to control the buying process, the more products that salesperson will sell and the higher his or her commission.

The above analysis is not to give the marketing department a break in delivering fantastic content. It should be the goal of all marketing departments to provide content that can be easily repackaged and tuned to the needs of the Trap-setting salesperson. The marketing department needs to acknowledge that they are unable to convince the majority of the prospects to make a favorable decision and understand that if they work with Trapper salespeople, sales will come more frequently.

Let me try to explain this with some sports metaphors. In American football, the quarterback and team don't go straight down the field. They do a series of plays going left and right but always trying for a net forward position. Some plays will be a run to the left, a pass to the right, or a run up the middle.

Football is very analogous to a sales campaign. The amount sideways that the player travels doesn't matter. It is only the forward progress that matters. The goal of the football team is to advance the ball to cross the end line, and it doesn't matter if that is through the middle of the field or in either corner.

Your goal is the same as the football team. You are responsible for getting the ball into the end zone or, more accurately, for closing the order. In football, the offensive team has the goal of moving the ball down the field to the touchdown. They have this goal if they receive the ball on the 50-yard line. They also have this goal if they receive the ball on their 2-yard line. The goal doesn't change based on the position of the ball on the field. It also doesn't change for you based on the quality or source of the lead.

By accepting that you cannot use the excuse of a bad marketing department in your success or lack thereof, you will become more successful. Your job is to take the leads that you receive and make them orders. Your job is to take the content that you receive from the marketing department and make it understandable and persuasive to your prospect. The ultimate failure is yours, not your marketing department. It is your job on the line. It is your commission on the line. You must take what marketing has prepared and use it to be successful.

It is not the fault of your marketing department if your literature and website are not perfect matches for your prospects. You need to bridge the gap between the standard marketing message and the fine-tuned and tailored message that will resonate with your prospect.

You and your competitors are likely finding that you are being lumped together into the same basket while your prospects perceive little difference between each supplier. Often researching online, customers trawl through website after website comparing the latest offerings, making up their minds about who and what they want with little or no help from the supplier companies. This perceived similarity leads to one variable becoming the main point of difference and negotiation: price. This sameness also leads to the erosion of margins and loss of business for suppliers.

The problem is that you and your competitors likely have distinct points of difference that can deliver real value beyond the product. It takes the salesperson customizing the marketing message to highlight the genuine value beyond product and price in a compelling value proposition.

Unless you have a clear and inspiring value proposition that captures the imagination of a prospect, chances are you are going to get the standard response and be told something like: "We're happy with our current supplier." Or worse, the salesperson will be 'used' by the customer as leverage for or against the current supplier to get what they want or need at a lower price. Having a clear and effective value proposition is crucial to sales success.

Your personalized value proposition should address issues that are relevant to the prospect. This may mean that you don't cover every point created by marketing and it may mean emphasizing a benefit that would be less important to other prospects or the market at large.

When we put ourselves in the shoes of our customers and think about what they want to achieve, all of a sudden, we can see how we can help them be more effective and efficient, or how to help them reduce risk and thus help them be more successful. We do this not just with our products and services, but also with our personal experience and knowledge.

Once we are engaged with a prospect and have understood their business goals, we can tailor a value proposition that is unique to that customer's situation using their language. Start by finding out how your prospect measures success. What are they expecting to achieve in the next 12 to 18 months? Maybe they have to lower supply-chain costs, or perhaps they're projected to boost customer retention or to reduce time to market on new products. Whatever it is, these are the business drivers for a value proposition.

Every sale involves changing something. The offer to a prospect must do something faster, better, more efficiently, etc., than the status quo of not making a change. The lack of correlation to business issues is why No Decision is such a big competitor: the reward for the change is not significant enough to offset the increased benefit. The key to making the value proposition is to use a verb that supports the targeted business driver.

Your customized value proposition should focus on the monetary value creation Where monetary figures aren't appropriate or possible, use percentages, but in all instances, there needs to be a timeframe to show the expected number of weeks, months or years the prospect can expect it to take to achieve the kind of results being promised.

The customized value proposition should be tailored in a language and value that your customer needs to hear for their situation. You need to make the value proposition sound like it came from a top executive of the prospect's organization.

When you have learned to develop a customized value proposition, you will find that your prospects treat you like a trusted adviser. The prospect will become involved in the sales process, see the benefit of talking to you and take the sales process to the next stage.

Prospecting For The Sake Of Prospecting Is Probably A Waste Of Time

Too often, a sales manager will tell the sales team that they have to make some number of prospecting calls per day (or week). I hate to be insulting to your manager, but this is typically a sign of a manager that doesn't understand the value of salespeople.

Instead, salespeople should find prospects who can buy the product and are open to evaluating new offerings. Lazy salespeople are financially poor salespeople, but activity for the sake of activity is not the goal.

I would much rather the salesperson identify great prospects and then spend a lot of activity trying to put a targeted and customized value proposition in front of that prospect. You may still make 25 or 50 calls per day, but the metric should be lots of activity in front of great prospects rather than just a lot of activity.

Who Is A Good Prospect?

In the wilderness, a Trapper understands where to find the best prey. He does this by understanding the habits of the quarry and the terrain. He plans and puts Traps in the most optimum place to be successful. The Trapper doesn't place his Trap directly in front of the animal but instead anticipates where the animal is going to be in the future and places the Trap in that location. You will need to follow this same pattern to be successful.

You need to define the sweet spot for you to prospect. Trying to prospect to people who will never use your product is simply a waste of your precious resources. You need to maximize your investment so that you can maximize your commission.

Your personal sweet spot will be different from that of any others reading this book. It may be similar to your co-worker, but it is likely that there will be differences even among co-workers. Your personal sweet spot combines the benefits of your products, your employer, and your personal skills.

It is impossible for me to tell you your personal sweet spot in a mass-produced book. I will give you some exercises here to help you deduce this list.

Your personal sweet spot will be defined by geographic location, size, industry, structure, and your personal knowledge of the company. It will be further refined by your product's sweet spot as defined by the target market identified by your marketing department.

Let's do a quick example. Perhaps your product marketing team has identified your product will be excellent for banks but not very appropriate for manufacturers. Obviously, you would want not spend time prospecting to manufacturers in your territory but instead would focus your attention on banks. You may want to include insurance companies in your territory, though, since there may be some overlap of need with insurance companies. In this way, the focus of your product will dramatically influence your sweet spot analysis.

Your sweet spot also has a lot to do with your honesty regarding your specific skills and network. This is not a time for wishful thinking. You need to prioritize your opportunities, and you cannot prioritize if you are not truthful about your skills and capabilities.

Your sweet spot is an honest appraisal of where you are personally the most effective. If you answer the following questions with the general answer that you are good at everything, you simply are not being honest. You cannot be equally good at all things. Even if it is personal preference, you are best at something, and you need to focus on your strongest traits.

Answer the following questions with a range of 1-5 where 5 is the highest confidence and 1 is the lowest confidence. Don't cheat; this assessment will help you focus on your best prospects based on your personal capability.

Geography

Every territory is different. If your territory is only one city or part of a city, then all accounts will score a 5. However, if you have a larger geographical territory, you need to score each account, with the farthest being a three and the closest being a five. Geography should never be given a one or a two simply because if your territory is so large that it is inconvenient to call on a prospect, you should probably take that prospect off your territory list.

Size

Where are you most successful selling? Have the majority of your historic deals been smaller companies with fewer decision makers or larger companies with more decision makers and bigger budgets? Be honest here. Just because you sold one thing last year to the largest company in the city doesn't make you a big company guy. You will want to rate smaller or larger companies higher or lower based on your personal success history. It is possible that you do better with medium sized companies and don't do well with larger companies and smaller companies - it is fine to score medium companies as a 5 but have small and large companies getting a 1 or 2.

Industry

Assuming your product can be sold to multiple industries, this will be an important consideration. Your territory is likely to be heavy in a couple of industries. Also, your understanding of those industries will affect your weighting.

It is important that you do not let your industry knowledge affect your success in your territory. You must go the extra mile to learn the most important industries in your territory. One of the ways to do this is to join industry groups that meet within your geography. Typically, there are associations and meet-ups that people will attend to talk about similar interests. You need to attend these on a regular basis to network.

Similarly, there are newsletters and discussion groups online that are very beneficial for you to grow your network and learn industry information. An excellent example of these is the various groups on LinkedIn. You should join 10 to 15 industry groups on LinkedIn so that you are familiar with the issues and terminology of the industries that are in your territory.

Ultimately, you need to have industry knowledge as part of your sweet spot evaluation. For each industry create an evaluation that matches the product's ability to solve problems in that industry with your territorial knowledge of the industry. This will allow you to focus on the industries that are most relevant for selling that particular product.

Structure

The structure is often aligned with the size of the company. You may be more comfortable selling to the owner of a small company than to a director in a large company. You may be more comfortable dealing with buyers in purchasing than with people in the marketing department. While this is uncomfortable to discuss since it identifies your weaknesses, it is important that you are truthful with yourself to assess your best fit.

Identify your strengths based on your ability to sell to the structure of the company and how that relates to the product you are selling. Are you more comfortable with small companies where you have access to the owner? Or should you be looking at large multinational companies where you will have to influence people who aren't even within driving distance of your office? This truthful self-evaluation will make you more successful since you will be targeting companies where your comfort level is higher.

Score Your Sweet Spot

You should take the target industries that your product marketing has identified and create a list of every company in your territory in those sectors. To the side of every business, create a column and put your scores for geographic location, size, industry, and structure.

On this score, you probably cannot change much. The companies aren't going to move, and they aren't going to change their structure to make life easier for you. The one thing that you can change is your ability to have a personal relationship with individuals within the company.

Personal Relationship

You now have to improve and capitalize on your personal relationships with the companies in your territory. You should probably focus on the top five to ten companies based on the total score that you just built above. If you do not know someone at one of your top 10 accounts, that is not a reason to skip them. You must build that relationship.

The balance of this chapter will focus on how to build that personal relationship and the building of your personal brand.

You will create these relationships by leveraging:

- Your best clients.
- Your former employers and former co-workers.
- People that your prospect respects.

The best way to make a connection to your unknown prospects is via the social platform LinkedIn. The site is arguably the most important social platform for business and especially for salespeople. According to HubSpot, 65% of B2B companies report that they have acquired a customer through LinkedIn.

According to Jim Keenan, the social sales specialist in the "The Impact of Social Media on Sales Quota and Corporate Revenue" report, 78.6% of salespeople using social media to sell outperformed those who weren't using social media. Also, social media users were 23% more successful at exceeding their quota by at least 10% than their non-social media peers. In 2012 non-social media users missed quota (by more than 10% or more) 15% more often than social media users.

LinkedIn is often identified as the place to go to look for your next job. Certainly, it is used extensively by recruitment consultants the world over to find and approach candidates. But to simply look at it this way is to do the network a significant disservice.

LinkedIn is a great way for you to build your personal brand. As I have explained elsewhere, customers buy from you based on three criteria - your product, your company and you. LinkedIn is an excellent way to build that third component of your value portfolio.

You should be using LinkedIn as a source of new leads and tangible revenue. In fact, for business to business, LinkedIn is a critical tool that can make your prospecting faster, smoother and, ultimately, more profitable.

Contacts are the power of LinkedIn. If your contacts are predominantly family, friends and old school pals, you've got some work to do. Your first level contacts open up a route to a full range of second and third level connections. This is how you scale your network. Strike while the iron's hot – whenever you meet anyone (online or off), always follow up quickly with a connection request while you are still fresh in his or her mind.

You need to use LinkedIn to map out the decision makers within your target prospects. In a complex sale, there are numerous people involved in making and influencing a purchase.

When you meet an individual, you can learn a great deal about that person. Many people are quite open on their LinkedIn profiles. You can frequently discover which team they're on, which office they work out of, and what projects they're focusing on. With a little detective work, you can quickly build up a picture of who you should be talking to, what they're like, and what they've done before. Make sure you read the recommendations that they have written and that are written about them, as this gives you an idea of who influences them.

With LinkedIn, you can almost always learn enough about someone to make your call more relevant and useful to them. And it's not simply a case of digital stalking.

You should pay particular attention to changes in profile, status updates, connections in common and anything they've posted to a group (which can be reason enough to call them in the first place).

One of the easiest ways to become known to a prospect is to like or comment on anything that the prospect has posted. This won't propel the prospect to reach out to you, but at least you will not be a stranger. After a couple of appropriate comments, the prospect will likely be much more interested in having a conversation with you.

Commenting on your prospect's activity is also important within the forums or groups. You should join the groups that your top prospects frequent. When you are viewing your prospect within the group, you can follow their activity. Following a prospect allows you to have their updates and conversations in your LinkedIn feed.

If you are not connected to the prospect, then use InMail to make that first introduction. InMail is LinkedIn's internal email system and allows you to send an email to any LinkedIn user. It ensures your email gets through to their inbox. LinkedIn claims that an InMail is 30 times more likely to get a response than a cold call.

LinkedIn has a fabulous search function. With their advanced search, you can find people by title, company, location or keyword. By intelligently mixing the different filters you can get deep and identify key individuals quickly and easily.

You can also save your search criteria and get a weekly report listing anyone new who matches the criteria. For example, you could save a search for Database Administrators in the retail industry within 50 miles of Atlanta. Then, each week, you will get an email with anyone new who matches the search criteria.

Information is king. This statement is particularly the case when it is account news. With information, you can make appropriate decisions. As any salesperson will know, change creates opportunity. People join, people leave, companies make important announcements – any change can present a good reason to get in touch and offer to help. More than that, information on your prospect allows you to:

- Respond to the events affecting your customers and prospects.
- Have background talking material during your sales calls.
- Find opportunities.
- Establish financial justification for your opportunities.

There is a lot of information to gather about your accounts. You need a quick and convenient way to review the highlights of your account news so that it doesn't overwhelm you.

LinkedIn makes discovering these changes easy. You can follow any company that has a LinkedIn page. That way you'll see anything that changes directly in your updates. It's an easy way to stay up to date and spot new opportunities.

Keep Track Of Important Events At Your Prospect

Business changes at your prospects are so important that you need a better tool than just LinkedIn. LinkedIn will primarily give you information that is "volunteered" by other individuals. Tracking changes is so important that you need the power of the most popular search engine in the world to help you succeed.

You should program Google Alerts to send you information. Google Alerts is a part of Google's search engine. You are going to automatically have Google search for a particular set of information and send it to you on a regular basis.

Google Alerts can be a bit overwhelming if you just set it up with brute force tactics. You will want to filter out the noise in Google Alerts by getting rid of stock analysts commenting on the company. Type in the company name (put quotes around it if it has a space in the name), the stock symbol, and "-trading -resistance -upgrade -downgrade -upgraded -downgraded" to eliminate some of the noise.

If you want all of the recent information about General Motors, you will type:

> "General Motors" GM -trading -resistance -upgrade -downgrade -upgraded -downgraded

This will give you all of the Google News for General Motors or GM (the quotes makes the two words General and Motors into one string). If the article has both GM and General Motors, then it will score higher.

If the article contains any of the following words, score it lower:

- trading
- resistance
- upgrade
- downgrade
- upgraded
- downgraded

Dave Trapper was able to get notified of the changes at GlueWorks by using Google Alerts. It allows you to stay informed of important developments without having to spend hours per day reading various news sources.

Learn To Think Like Your Prospect

You should also subscribe to the groups where your buyers tend to congregate. They can give you the perfect reason for making contact with a prospect.

I assume you are already connected to some people who are your ideal target audience. For the purpose of this exercise, let's say that perfect target is named Joseph Brown. Go to Joseph's profile and scroll down to the groups he belongs to in LinkedIn. There will likely be some school groups and maybe some philanthropic organizations. There will also be some trade groups. You should join those trade groups.

By joining the LinkedIn trade groups that your prospects subscribe to, you will begin to hear from their peers. You will be able to participate in the discussion of ideas, concerns, and goals that are relevant to your prospects. By educating that trade group, your reputation and your brand with your prospect will be enhanced.

Develop A Plan To Meet Your Prospects

Any good wilderness Trapper knows that he must be patient and place his Traps where the animals are likely to pass. The Trap will not necessarily be successful the first day that it is in place, but rather a long-term strategy is required. The same is true for sales; you must develop a long-term plan that will allow you to find your prospects and have them trust you. Let's look at some statistics that help confirm this statement:

- GE Capital Retail Bank's second annual Major Purchase Shopper Study has found that a growing number of consumers extensively research and compare prices and financing offers before making major purchases. According to the study, 81% of consumers go online before buying.
- Gleanster Research estimates that 50% of leads are qualified but not yet ready to buy.
- According to Forrester Research, companies that excel at lead nurturing will generate 50% more sales-ready leads at 33% lower cost.
- The Annuitas Group notes that nurtured leads make 47% larger purchases than non-nurtured leads.

Social selling allows us to meet our prospects where they're doing their research. Our prospects are doing their research online. With the amount of vendor variety today, being an old school pushy salesmen is no longer an option. If buyers get the wrong vibes from us, they will just move on.

If we go out of our way to help the prospect in their journey from research to vendor selection, we have presented our companies and ourselves as a valuable partner. Therefore, we must make sure that we are always providing value to our prospects.

Providing value is sharing useful information on an area of interest, industry trend or competitor strategy. Introducing someone to a person that they can form a mutually beneficial business relationship with. Notifying someone of an event that would be beneficial for them to attend. These are all examples of how we can provide value.

The people who are the best at providing value all have two things in common: research and creativity. As an example, If you see "karate" in the Interests section of your prospect's LinkedIn profile, try sending them an awesome martial arts video to break the ice. At the very least you will have made a lasting first impression.

Develop A Content Strategy

Content is your most powerful sales tool. But to deliver content that's relevant and helpful to prospects, you have to identify the specific audience you're targeting and understand the information they need. You need:

- Attributes of your prospects.
- An in-depth industry analysis.
- Goals your potential customers might have.

Then, you craft educational articles that speak to the right audience and are unique from your competitors' content. The information you provide should teach prospects about your company and industry, your product, and you.

Set Up An Email Marketing Campaign

Once you have your content, your email marketing campaign will deliver it to the right people at the right time.

In the traditional sales process, salespeople check in with prospects every couple of weeks, usually to find that not much has changed. With an email campaign, you are reaching out to prospects to provide relevant information.

Your prospects will read the content you send through your email marketing campaign, download one of your whitepapers, or even subscribe to your blog. The result is new customers who choose you because they understand what they need and what you offer. They trust you and your company because you have guided them through the buying process with engaging educational content.

Once you put the processes in place, all the gears can work together to qualify prospects naturally, leaving you with loyal customers in the long run.

You are trying to find Discoverers as well as people who are already in process. Discoverers do not self-identify themselves. You need to identify titles and job functions within your sweet spot accounts that should be interested in your types of products. For those people, you want to slowly show them that you are a valuable resource. Once they learn that you add value to their lives, they will be more than happy to spend time discussing their goals with you.

You want must make this a personal win for the Discoverer. Obviously, individuals will occasionally do things altruistically but, more often than not, they need some real personal benefit to be motivated to action. You will do best to have several things that will give them a personal win so that you can have many chances of success.

This personal win must be in keeping with a Vision Goal that you will define later in this chapter. While it is true that pain avoidance is a prime influencer in behavior manipulation, a person will be far more motivated to work toward achieving a Vision Goal. A Vision Goal is one that motivates the individual or the organization.

An effective technique to help you promote this new problem is to show it relative to individual needs of influential people in the organization. Show the Discoverer that each of these individuals will receive a personal win with the solution. By his solving the problem, they would be indebted to the Discoverer and increase his status. This is exactly what Dave Trapper did in Chapter 2 when he worked with the director before the project was even announced. This effort helped him rapidly move GlueWorks to a significant and profitable order.

Once you have itemized and validated these potential wins to key individuals, you must continuously evangelize the problem to them. You must show them how a solution to the problem will be a personal win for them. Your ultimate plan is to help them develop their Vision Goal that includes your solution. You will then need to regularly communicate with them on the status of the solution.

Find Coaches

Some of the first people that you meet at the prospect will turn into Coaches. Coaches are often the first to become intimate with the problem, and they will draw certain conclusions as to the correct solution very early. If they conclude that you have an appealing product, then they will help you succeed. One or more of these people will start to confide in you and coach you in how to win this opportunity.

Find Champions

You will find your Champions from among your Coaches. The Champion may not originally be a Coach, but it will be someone that the Coach respects and trusts. You should identify this leader as soon as possible and recruit him as your first Champion. Your Champions will help you drive the decision to purchase your product. This person will likely be the Decision Owner for the Discovery Decision Triangle.

6-3-1 Program

The key element in your territory building is to establish credibility and trust within your prospects. It may seem confusing that you need trust from a person you wish to influence, but that is the reality. To properly influence someone, that person must think you have that person's best interest at the forefront of your actions. Once someone thinks you have their best interest in mind, they will trust the advice you give them and heed that advice. When a person takes your advice, you can control the decision process.

The vast majority of people in the corporate world want to improve their situation in their job. They want more prestige, more power, more money or more standing within the corporate community. As a salesperson, you have little influence on these wins for the prospect, except to make the prospect smarter.

Let's explore this issue a bit more. When was the last time that the CEO or President at one of your customers asked your opinion on whom to promote to an open position? This request has probably never happened (or at least very rarely). The lack of influence means that you cannot offer a low-level person the favor of a promotion. You can assume that your opinion on the promotion means absolutely nothing simply because no one is asking your opinion. Similarly, you cannot give the low-level person a raise in pay. You also cannot make the low-level person more respected among his or her peers. In essence, you offer almost nothing to the most frequent personal ambitions of the low-level person.

If you offer nothing to the low-level person, why should s/he listen to you? No one will pay attention to you unless they are getting value from the discussion. The key value that you provide is knowledge. You can make the low-level person much smarter. In today's economy and corporate world, knowledge is king. Aside from a personally returned favor, the best way to get ahead in the corporate world is achieving success toward objectives and knowledge. It is easily argued that these are the same: the reason for success in attaining objectives is because the person is knowledgeable.

You are most effective as a Trapper when you are giving information to a prospect before the prospect truly understands that he needs it. This is your Bait (as we will explore in Chapter 6). When a prospect first starts to explore a new project, technology or product, the first learning in that area is the comparison standard for every similar offering. You want to be that comparison standard.

A technique to develop respect and trust with a prospect is the 6-3-1 program. This program is designed for you to find people who are slightly interested in a subject and develop credibility with them. I have never found a process that is better at cultivating relationships and credibility.

I must advise you that the 6-3-1 program requires perseverance and patience. It is typically more effective than standard marketing or sales letters simply because it takes the long-term view of the process rather than seeking a quick hit. Remember, being a Trapper means you are planning and setting yourself up for long-term success rather than the quick kill of the Hunter, the reliance on others of a Gatherer, or the reliance on luck that is the foundation of a Farmer.

The 6-3-1 program is a series of seven pieces of correspondence that offer more information than actual requests for action items. The first five pieces are designed to get the prospect to respond to you. The sixth correspondence has a specific time-bound action item that drives three phone calls by you (hence the three in the middle). The seventh communication is the transition to a long-term "nursing" program.

Before the program can be implemented, you need to have a list of likely individuals. This list is gathered earlier in this chapter. You will divide the list into discrete groups that you can cover each week.

Many salespeople will be far too aggressive on the size of work covered each week. While the initial work on the small list is only a few minutes per week, by the end of the second month that you have been working with this system, you will find the weekly effort explodes. You need to make up to three phone calls to every name on your list in the time span of five working days.

To estimate the size of your weekly list, you need to honestly budget your time and the time you can afford to do new prospecting. The middle stage of the program (the middle "3" of 6-3-1) can be considerably time intensive. If you underestimate the time you have to dedicate, the program will fail dramatically.

I suggest you work through the following analysis to arrive at your perfect weekly working list. Please keep in mind that you are doing this work in addition to your standard workload. Many people say that they can dedicate one or two hours a day for three days of the week.

    A. How many phone calls can you make in one day and leave a one-minute voice mail?

    B. How many phone calls can you make in one day and have a ten-minute conversation?

We will assume that you can only afford to prospect for two hours a day for three days per week. You can adjust this based on your schedule, and it should be easy for you to understand how to scale this number up or down appropriately.

Let's assume that your answer to A is 30. This is reasonable since you are talking for 1 minute, dialing for 10-20 seconds, and waiting for the voicemail system to pick up for another 20-30 seconds.

Let's assume that your answer to B is five. This is reasonable since you are talking for 10 minutes plus you have the overhead of dialing the phone and recording any notes about the conversation.

As you make your calls, you will find that even though the prospect knows when you are calling (more on that later), you will still not reach the prospect 80-90% of the time. Don't get discouraged about this: it is a fact of life, so just deal with it. If you make 50 calls, you will only have five to ten conversations.

Some simple math shows us that you can, therefore, call 40 people in two hours. This will mean you will leave 36 two-minute voicemails (or 90%) and have four ten-minute conversations with notes.

You can scale this number up or down as needed. If you can only afford to spend one hour per day three times per week, then you can only call 20 people. If you have more time dedicated to prospecting and can call for three hours per day three times per week, then you can call 60 people.

The next step is to understand that you will lose about 25% of your list as you work through the first five letters. This will primarily come from people who have changed jobs within the organization or left the organization. You will also have some people tell you that they simply are not interested in hearing from you. This means if you want to end up with 40 people, you will need to start the program every week with 50 new names. For 20 people to call, start each week with 25 names. To have 60 people to call, you will need to have a list of 75 every week.

Finding Names For Your List

It is a bit difficult for me to advise you on how to develop a list of raw names within your sweet spot. Each reader will be in a different situation and therefore will need to proceed differently. I suggest that you immediately compile a list of 500 people you do not know within the sweet spot of your territory.

There are many sources to build this list of 500 names:

- Internal database of old leads
- Internal database of old customers
- Purchased list from a third-party data source such as RainKing, Data.com, Avention, LeanData, InsideView, Discover.org, or similar services
- Networks from friends and associates

You can also use LinkedIn to generate names, but it is more laborious. I suggest you view this as a secondary source or a means of verifying names.

Many companies will have a license for one of these services or a similar service. If your employer doesn't see the value in this, you cannot let that get in the way of your success! The pricing will vary for each service and will likely change from the time of this writing to when you read this. However, at the time of this writing, individuals can get access to hundreds or even thousands of names for less than $1 per name. This is somewhat inexpensive, and you should personally consider joining a service if your company doesn't provide the capability. The cost is tax deductible if your employer doesn't reimburse you. Also, the commission value of closing a deal surely exceeds the cost of personally buying a few leads.

The Letters Of The 6-3-1 Program

Many marketers will call the 6-3-1 program a drip program. This is partially correct, but many marketers will not like some of the advice in the content of the letters.

Marketers tend to be rewarded and graded based on the response to the mailings that they send out. As a salesperson, you are rewarded by the money that person gives you. The response to an individual letter means nothing to you since you are paid on revenue, not activity.

▼▼▼▼▼▼▼▼▼▼▼▼▼▼▼
Do not confuse activity with commissionable revenue!
▲▲▲▲▲▲▲▲▲▲▲▲▲▲▲

Because making a decision is a long and slow process, your treatment of the prospect needs to be long and slow. I understand that you are an impatient salesperson with a quota to achieve and a boss breathing down your neck. If you are only concerned about killing what you can eat today, be a Hunter. If you want to make sure that you will eat well for the rest of your career, be a Trapper.

Your first email to the unknown prospect will not have any action item or maybe have an easy action item. I suggest that the first letter only include the action item to have them visit your profile on LinkedIn. I don't even think you should invite them to link to you.

As the emails continue on a weekly basis, you will give them more information. You will make them smarter. Also, your requested action will be increasingly more deliberate.

Finally, you will ask them for a meeting. This request will come after a month of them receiving information from you! You will give them lots of information before you ask for the one thing that you want. You want a meeting with them so that you can create a dialog.

Occasionally, you will strike gold early in the program. Don't be surprised if someone you send information to responds early and says they want to talk to you about your products. This is unusual and unexpected. Don't plan on it, but rejoice when it happens.

Use a casual tone and let the prospect know that you are available to them should they desire guidance in your particular area of expertise. Your only goal here is to maximize your chances of converting the prospect into a meeting and an opportunity. Doing so will make it easier for you to nurture them through their decision-making process and stay top-of-mind.

The First Letter Of 6-3-1

The first letter is more of an introduction than anything else. It introduces you and your company. It establishes that you will be communicating with the person and covering a set of topics.

Here is a sample that Dave Trapper (from Chapter 2) uses for Premium Software.

> Subject template: An introduction to {your technology or service} by {your company}
>
> Dave's subject: An introduction to understanding personnel skills using artificial intelligence by Premium Software
>
> {First_Name} -
>
> [First paragraph is a short statement about your industry]
>
> Over the last five years, artificial intelligence has been developed specifically to address many challenges. The

biggest result of these successes is the amazing reduction in productivity.

[Second paragraph is how your company fits into this industry]

Premium Software is known for helping companies understand the unique and powerful skills of the workforce. We're known for our easy scalability, consistently high performance, 24x365 availability, and a flexible data model.

[Third paragraph establishes some credibility.]

Companies like Apple, Cisco, LinkedIn, Orbitz, Midwest Products and hundreds of others around the world use Premium Software to empower their employees and maximize their individual contributions.

[Fourth paragraph explains what is going to happen.]

In the coming weeks, I will show how Premium Software can help you:

- o Improve business processes.
- o Reduce enterprise costs.
- o Attract and retain new customers.
- o Create new products.
- o Target customers and markets more effectively.
- o Consolidate business operations.
- o Maximize employee productivity.

[Fifth and sixth paragraphs offer a very soft action item and a way to get out of the email campaign.]

If you have a free minute, please go to LinkedIn and review my personal profile at https://www.linkedin.com/in/dTrappermadeupprofile. If you already know that you have some of these challenges, please give me a call at 911.555.9999.

If you think that I am wasting your time with this information, drop me a note, and I will stop sharing information.

Sincerely,

Dave Trapper

Make sure that you include your company-approved signature. If your company doesn't have a preferred template, at a minimum it should include your office phone, your mobile phone, and a link to your LinkedIn profile.

The Second Through Fifth Letters Of 6-3-1

The second through fifth letters are more difficult for me to give you a strict template for. Many types of salespeople with many types of offerings are reading this book. Some general guidelines are below.

The second letter is primarily about your most common value proposition to your typical customer. It should mimic the major themes of your company website. You should limit this email to 3-5 paragraphs with no more than 350 words in the entire email.

The final paragraph in the main body of the second letter should invite the prospect to visit your company website to view a customer success story or a product overview. At this point, you probably want to avoid any page that will take longer than a few minutes to read and probably doesn't require the prospect to register. Here are the last two paragraphs from Dave Trapper's second letter:

I invite you to read more about Premium Software and specifically, Midwest Product's implementation. Please follow this link: http://www.theTrapper.com.

If you would like me to explain how you can maximize employee profitability, drop me a reply or give me a call at 911.555.9999. You can also check out my LinkedIn profile at https://www.linkedin.com/in/dTrappermadeupprofile.

If you think that I am wasting your time with this information, drop me a note, and I will stop sharing information.

Sincerely,

Dave Trapper

The third letter starts to build a goal around a specific value offering. It may not be the most common value proposition but instead a niche offering.

The action item for the third letter needs to be a bit more time intensive than the second letter. The best content is to have the prospect watch a marketing video or a training video or to download a whitepaper. You still would prefer to point the prospect to a place where registration is not required. You want to make it seem like you are educating the prospect and not trying to capture contact information.

If your company has content on YouTube that is freely available to all, that is the best request for the third letter. The content will likely take multiple minutes to view but will not require the prospect feel like his movements are being tracked.

The end of the third letter can drop the paragraph "If you think that I am wasting your time with this information, drop me a note, and I will stop sharing information." You should always invite them to view your LinkedIn profile though.

The fourth letter needs to be a bit more brazen than the first three. At this point, you want some positive reinforcement. You will again build a niche use case (hopefully a different use case than the third letter), but your action request needs to be firmer.

For the fourth letter, I suggest that you point the prospect to some content that requires registration. Hopefully, this content has something to do with the niche use case that you explain in your email text. Perhaps a whitepaper or a webinar would be appropriate at this point. Anything that is a bit longer than the standard website page but requires the prospect to fill out a form is a good possible choice.

The fifth letter needs to return to your most popular use case. This is the use case deployed by the highest percentage of your existing customers. You also are going to ask for two action responses in this letter. The first action is going to be to download or view some content that is behind a form that captures the contact information (this is similar to the fourth letter). The second request, though, is for them to specifically contact you. I suggest a paragraph similar to the following:

> Over the past few weeks, I have been trying to educate you on {your product}. I hope that the information has been valuable for you. Can you please give me a call at 911.555.9999 and let me know your thoughts?

Your sixth letter is very short and to the point. You want a meeting, and it is now time to ask for the meeting. There are few variations to this email regardless of your industry.

In this email, you are going to ask for a phone conversation during a two-hour window three or four days in the future.

> Subject: May I call you on {day of week}?

> {First Name} -

> Over the past several weeks, I have shared with you some information to improve your knowledge of {your industry}.

In particular, I have focused on {three two-word features of your product} of {your product's name}.

May I call you on {day of week, date and month such as Thursday, August 21}, to discuss this?

I promise to not take more than 10 minutes of your time. I will try to call you between {two-hour time span such as 1 PM and 3 PM}. If there is a better time on {day of the week} to call you, please let me know, and I will try to accommodate you.

Now It Is Time For Three Calls For The 6-3-1 Program

Congratulations! You have now completed your first set of six for the 6-3-1 program!

It is important that you confine this first group of recipients to a group that you can reasonably call in a given day. That is why I suggested above that you limit the group to maybe 25-50 people. By the time you get to the end of the first six weeks, you will have lost 20-30% of them, which means you still have 15-35 phone calls to make. Each of those phone calls is going to be quite "warm" because you have been educating them and warned them that you were calling at a specific time.

Do not be surprised that your largest response rate is from the sixth email. People who were ignoring you suddenly will take notice when you tell them you are calling at a specific time. Many of them will tell you they are not interested and this is fine because you can qualify them out or suggest another step for them.

Some people will see that specific requested time and ask for a different time slot. You should accommodate that request, if possible. This is an excellent signal that the prospect is interested in your product.

Even though you have requested a time to call, you will not reach everyone at that time. If the prospect doesn't answer, simply leave a quick message similar to the following:

> "Good afternoon, John, this is Dave Trapper from Premium Software. I had sent you a note that I was going to call you at this time. I am sorry that I missed you. Please call me back at 911.555.9999. I will also try you again in a few days when my calendar opens up again."

The reason for the middle 3 of the 6-3-1 is that you cannot give up after one call. You need to call that prospect two more times. You do not need to warn them with an email, just call them every few days.

Your voice mail for the second no-answer should be something like:

> "Good morning, John, this is Dave Trapper from Premium Software. I had sent you a note that I was going to call you a few days ago, but I missed you for that call. Please do me a favor and call me back at 911.555.9999."

Your third phone call may also not connect. If it doesn't, you need to explain what is going to happen next.

> "Good morning, John, this is Dave Trapper from Premium Software. I have been trying to reach you for a few days, but keep missing you. Please do me a favor and call me back at 911.555.9999. I am not going to bother you anymore as I assume you are busy and do not need to talk to me right now. I put out a newsletter every month (or quarter), and I am going to put you on that list. Hopefully, you will get value out of my personalized newsletter."

You now simply put this person on your newsletter list. Trying to beat your head against the wall to reach this person is a waste of time. The prospect knows you want to talk and by not acknowledging you, they are simply saying they do not see value in the conversation. The newsletter will bring more value to your relationship.

Your Personal Newsletter

Your newsletter is the best tool for maintaining a relationship with existing customers and qualified prospects that are uninterested at this time. I suggest that you send out your newsletter at least every quarter, but it would be more effective if you send it every month to your mailing list. I also suggest that you post your newsletter to LinkedIn using their blogging capability.

Your customers should all receive your newsletter. Your customers need to be constantly cultivated for new business. Also, your customers may change jobs, and you want them to call you immediately. They will only do this if you have been consistently adding value to their working lives. Remember, the only way that you add value to a prospect is by making that prospect smarter. You can help an existing customer a few more ways by offering good customer service, but the most proactive method is to make them smarter.

It is not practical for me to put a template of a newsletter into these pages and have it be useful for every reader but below are some suggested sections:

- Title/Subject: Make sure your title clearly states that this is a newsletter. Your title will be in your subject line of your email, and it will be at the top of your blog post on LinkedIn. You want your email recipients to know that this is an email to many people.
- First section: A personal note of about 100-200 words on your industry or the local situation. Don't be afraid to congratulate the local college for a great sports season. It should be personal and, if your prospects are local, it should be relevant to your geography.
- Second section: News from your company. This literally could be a copy of a relevant or important press release. If someone in your product-marketing group puts out a blog, that can be great content. Just make sure you include a URL link to the original content.

- Third section: Links with a short description to download some new company content. Perhaps a new whitepaper was published, or a new video on YouTube.
- Fourth section: This section contains selected paragraphs from a published article. This article should not mention your company but rather be about your industry. You don't want this article to be a sales pitch, but rather it is included only to make your prospect smarter.

Power Matrix

As you meet people and develop the opportunity within the organization, you need a tool to help you make sure you develop relationships with the correct people with the appropriate power and influence to help you.

The Power Matrix is a great tool to understand the organization. I promise you, if you can successfully fill out the Power Matrix in every account, you will be phenomenally successful.

There are two different versions of the Power Matrix. The Small Power Matrix is for deals that are relatively smaller. I advise salespeople that the cutoff for a smaller deal is one that is smaller than approximately 5-10% of your annual quota. This should be varied depending on the product that you sell and your industry in general, but it is unreasonable to use the Large Power Matrix more than 20 times in a fiscal year.

The Small Power Matrix encourages you to map out nine different people at your prospect. These nine people are in three levels of the organization and three different departments. Graphically, the Small Power Matrix looks like Figure 5-3.

	Dept. 1	Dept. 2	Dept. 3
Upper mgmt			
Coach level			
End users			

Figure 5-3 – Small Power Matrix. All figures are also available at http://www.thetrapper.com/book_figures

The people in this matrix are people who are in the Decision Group that we learned about in other chapters. They may not be all of the people, but they will be the most influential. If you think that your Decision Group is smaller than nine people, then I encourage you to do more investigation. There are very few decisions made by organizations that have fewer than nine people that are affected by the decision and therefore do not have an influence on that decision.

It is important to understand that the Power Matrix is not an organization chart. Rather, it is an influence chart. These are the nine people most likely to influence the decision. Therefore, the end user in Department 3 doesn't have to specifically report to the coach's level of Department 3. Rather, the end user should respect the opinion of the coach and vice versa.

Similarly, the upper management of Department 3 may not necessarily have the Department Coach as a direct report. However, the upper management person must respect the opinion of the Coach in the Department.

The easiest way to understand the three levels is that people on the same horizontal row have virtually the same organizational power. One person may be a Director, and the other column may contain a Vice President, but that may not be a reflection of power. Often, titles are a reflection of employment tenure and not true power in the organization. It is not unusual for a very bright Director to have as much influence in an organization as a Vice President. This can be especially true between different Departments that may have larger or smaller communities. Don't let titles sway your analysis; rather, observe the reactions and respect of others to make sure you have the correct person.

I like to put my primary Coach's name in the center of the chart in the Department 2 column. The Department that the Coach belongs to will be the part of the organization that will most benefit from the final decision. Therefore the upper management person directly above the Coach should be your best possible Champion.

It is possible that your primary Coach is not in the department that will most benefit from the decision. If that is the case, you must consider that you need another Coach. A Coach is most effective when there is a direct personal gain from the decision. Since you can have multiple Coaches in any one selling campaign, you should consider finding another Coach who is in the department with the most to gain.

In fact, everyone at the Coach level of the Power Matrix should be considered a Coach. One of the goals of the Power Matrix is to try to force you to develop three Coaches. The primary Coach will be the one who has the most to gain, but you should find and develop Coaches in other departments. You can never have enough Coaches to help you win your deal.

I encourage you to label each person in the Power Matrix with the Roles and Strengths found in Appendix A. You need to be able to look at the matrix and see who is helping you and who is hurting you. You need to understand your Coaches, your Champions, the Sailboats, and the Daddy Warbucks.

The Large Power Matrix is very similar to the Small Power Matrix. The Large Power Matrix is used for sales opportunities that are forecasted to be more than 10% of your annual quota. In other words, these are decisions that, if guided correctly, could significantly enhance your earnings. With a reasonable win rate, it is doubtful that you would have to do more than 10 of the Large Power Matrix analyses in any given year.

The Small Power Matrix is a 3x3 matrix. It is asking you to have in-depth conversations with three people in three different departments. The Large Power Matrix is more of an investment in time; it is asking you to identify five people in five different departments. It is a 5x5 matrix and is shown in Figure 5-4.

Similar to the Small Power Matrix, the Coach with the most to gain should go in the center of the Power Matrix. I encourage you to put Departments that have less to gain on the outside (columns 1 and 5) and those with more to gain next to the middle column.

In the Large Power Matrix, it is even more likely that it will not line up with an organizational chart. It is not uncommon to have several Vice Presidents and several Directors in any given department. The virtual influence on this one decision may be larger with one Director than another even though both are at the same organizational level. The more powerful person would be higher on the Power Matrix. Also, other Departments may not be devoting as many people to the effort, and therefore the rankings on any given column are different.

Below the Coach level are the end users. In a larger decision, some end users will be more affected than others. Also, one end user may be asked to be involved in all aspects of the decision, but another will only be asked to occasionally help. The occasional user would be listed on the lowest row of the Power Matrix while the more active user would be listed closer to the Coach.

	Dept. 1	Dept. 2	Dept. 3	Dept. 4	Dept. 5
Upper mgmt					
Mgmt					
Coach level					
End users					
Casual users					

Figure 5-4 – Large Power Matrix. All figures are also available at http://www.thetrapper.com/book_figures

You should begin to use the Power Matrix to keep track of whom you know and how well you know them. You will need to put a plan together to meet and understand the people who are openings in your Power Matrix.

Personal Vision Goals For The Power Matrix

Each person in the large or small Power Matrix needs five personal reasons to purchase your product. That is simply a fact. If you cannot identify the five reasons for that person to buy your product, then you need to be concerned.

Note that I am saying they need five personal reasons to buy YOUR product. I am not saying they need five reasons to buy any product. The reasons have to be personal to that individual, and they need to be specific to the outcome that you want: the organization decides to buy your product.

With less than five personal reasons to buy your product, the individual is not properly motivated to overcome obstacles. There are always obstacles to every purchase decision. The very act of making a decision to buy means that you are going to change the status quo of the prospect. There are many reasons why changing the status quo can be painful, so you need multiple reasons to overcome that inertia to not make a change.

By making the reasons a personal win, you allow the individual to emotionally commit to the decision. It is by this emotional commitment that you will ultimately overcome your competition. In fact, if you have confirmed five personal wins to buy your product from nine or twenty-five people in the organization, you will eliminate your competition from the opportunity.

Lifestyle-Changing Deals

Occasionally, you will find a deal that could be 50% or more of your annual quota. These are lifestyle-changing deals. These deals are so large that you are virtually guaranteed to blow away your annual quota and perhaps win the coveted "Salesperson of the Year" award at your company's annual sales meeting.

For lifestyle-changing deals, you need to think of the 5x5 large Power Matrix as a minimum. In this case, you need to consider having a relationship with 50-100 people in your prospect. That will mean that you may expand the horizontal or vertical dimensions of the matrix even more.

For those extremely large deals, you may also need to know three to ten people who effectively fill the same square in the matrix. This is okay. For a massive deal that could be lifestyle altering, the amount of work that you need to put in needs to be commensurate with the amount of quota that you will retire.

The good news is that everything else is still the same. You still need to understand how those 50-100 people relate to each other and whom they trust. You still need to document five personal reasons why they will choose your solution.

Lifestyle-changing deals are exactly that - a lifestyle-changing opportunity. You cannot put enough work into these deals. You have to win. They are worth the extra effort to follow the same process as you would for a deal that is 10% of your quota. Don't scrimp by only doing the minimum amount of work and you will be rewarded.

Finding prospects and managing the relationship throughout the buying decision process is a lot of work. The most successful salespeople are diligent about understanding who is buying, why they are buying, and working to control that decision process. This is your job - do it well, and you will be financially compensated.

Chapter 6 – The Bait - Enticing Your Prospect To Come To You

"Jack, you need to learn to see reality through the eyes of your adversary."

Admiral Greer to Jack Ryan in Tom Clancy's "Red Rabbit"

To be an effective Trapper, you must learn to create and use Bait. Bait is information prepared to encourage the prospect to think in a certain way. Bait allows the Trapper to create a Trap that influences and controls a prospect.

For some, creating Bait will be very easy and quick because their company has adopted Trapper techniques. Others may struggle because their company has not realized how to do many of the background steps of Bait development. Regardless of the tools provided by your employer, the development and deployment of Bait is ultimately the individual salesperson's responsibility.

This chapter has three main sections. These sections follow logically with the steps in creating and presenting Bait to the prospect.

- Understand the prospect.
- Decide which distinctive benefits are critical.
- Explain the Bait to the prospect in a way that they can understand and use.

This first section is critical. If the salesperson does not understand the true driving reasons behind the prospect's actions, the salesperson will fail. Without this knowledge, the salesperson will only be delivering a canned message to the prospect and only win a small percentage of his or her sales campaigns.

With the knowledge of the true reasons for the prospect's interest, the salesperson can then decide the unique benefits to explain to the customer. To do this, the salesperson must evaluate the competition and deduce which benefits have an advantage for and are of interest to the prospect.

Once the salesperson understands the prospect's reasons and has identified the unique benefits of what she is selling, she must deliver this information to the prospect in a way that is memorable, convincing, and powerful. This will set up the prospect for a Trap that should help eliminate the competition.

You need to learn to create and use Bait to be an effective Trapper. At its core, Bait is information that increases the knowledge of the prospect. Bait is information designed to appeal to a prospect. Bait allows you to create a Trap that influences and controls a prospect.

An often-quoted line by Tom Hanks' character in the movie "A League of Their Own" is: "There's no crying in baseball!" Similarly, there is no crying in sales. You, ultimately, are responsible for your success or failure. Do not blame your company or marketing department because they have not adopted these principles; take it on yourself to be successful. If your company has not realized the benefits of adopting the Trapper Methodology then you will quickly rise to the top of your peers. You will be the top revenue winner on your team and will be seen as a pillar of success throughout your management.

The first step is to learn the goals, issues, and needs of the prospect organization and the Decision Group involved in the decision. After you know this list, you must decide how your product excels. Then whittle down this list to what matters most to the prospect. Compare the list to your competitors' offerings to find those things that are unique to your company's offering. Finally, turn this information into Bait so that the prospect can understand your offering and its advantages over the competition.

When first exposed to the process of Bait creation, many people complain that this is what marketing should be doing. This is not true! Your marketing department can assist you by providing you with data about your product, company, and competitors. It is your job to practice "Applied Marketing" by using this wealth of data in your individual sales campaign. You are responsible for defeating your competitors. In a broad sense, this is what 'sales' is all about. When you do it well, it is Trapping.

Goal, Issues And Needs List

For outdoorsmen, it is impossible to create Bait without knowing what kind of quarry they are trying to attract. Similarly, it is impossible for you to create Bait in sales without a thorough understanding of your prospect. Even a company that has fully adopted the Trapper methodology must rely on you, the salesperson, to develop this knowledge of the prospect. Your marketing department cannot accomplish these items, although they can give you guidelines and suggestions that will accelerate the implementation.

There is interdependence between goals, issues, and needs. Goals highlight issues, which raise needs that must be satisfied. This dependence chain is important to understand. Every capability you discuss must solve a need that is ultimately dependent on an issue and goal. If you fail to make these connections, you will waste your time and not control the decision-making process.

The Prospect's Goals

The first step in understanding the prospect is to develop a list of the prospect organization's goals. These goals drive budgets, corporate behavior, and the actions of individuals. Well-written goals are bound to organizational metrics or other verifiable information. If your prospect has not developed metrics or verifiable information, you should consider not pursuing this organization. It will be very difficult to generate enough desire in the organization to result in a successful sales campaign.

Goals help for your sales campaign because they tend to be rallying points for the entire prospect organization. Many salespeople who do not follow the Trapper methodology may try to align themselves with the organization's stated pains, needs, or issues. By not understanding how these items relate to a goal of the prospect organization, these competitors will leave themselves vulnerable to your attacks.

Organization Goals

The top management of your prospect creates high-level organizational goals. They communicate most of these goals to the entire company in a formal or informal way. Many times, these goals are published on the organization's website, newsletter, marketing collateral, or in public statements (e.g., annual report or SEC filings). Departments, divisions, and teams within the organization may have goals as well. You can find these posted on bulletin boards or in speeches or office fliers. Watch for these postings so that you are prepared to take advantage of them.

By stating an organizational goal, an employee is acknowledging that this item is extremely important. This importance may overshadow most other concerns of the organization. It is possible that achieving the goal will make other pains or needs immaterial by comparison. This is why it is so important to focus on the goals of the organization rather than the pain or need of a particular person.

In Chapter 2, GlueWorks had a goal for their organization to expand and realign their company by market segment. The CEO stated this goal in a company-wide speech as: "We want to organize the company to be more market focused. To do this, we will reorganize the company along four major verticals plus General Purpose. We will accomplish this realignment by the end of the fiscal year and it will result in $5,000,000 in additional revenue and cost savings." This is a great goal because it is direct, measurable, and has a specific timetable.

Presumably, the organization is actively communicating this goal to their employees. Several key employees will actively monitor the progress toward attaining this goal, and many people will have specific tasks associated with ensuring that the organization attains the goal. Ultimately, the top executive of the organization has a significant amount of visibility into this goal. S/he regularly monitors its progress and has specific action items to accomplish the goal.

As a successful Trapper, you need to find other goals that are not publicly stated. You need to find goals that you can use to justify the purchase of your product. For instance, you may offer tools that help organizations manage their health benefits. While the chief executive of the organization may not state this goal to his board members, you may be able to link your benefit to the stated goal of reducing costs, decreasing turnover, increasing employee happiness or some other relevant goal. If you are trying to sell a product that is not important to the organization's goals, you are in danger of not having your purchase funded when it comes time to make the sale!

▼▼▼▼▼▼▼▼▼▼▼▼▼▼
Organizations will purchase products that are critical to their success. You need to understand how the organization measures its success and position your product appropriately.
▲▲▲▲▲▲▲▲▲▲▲▲▲▲

Personal Goals

Goals that the players in the organization create for themselves can be excellent leverage points. These personal goals are just as important for your success as an organization goal since they more closely affect the behavior of the individual. People will work harder and be more motivated if they feel their actions will help them. They will usually work harder to satisfy organizational goals if they perceive a direct or indirect benefit to themselves.

The easiest personal goals to find directly relate to an organizational goal. In the GlueWorks example in Chapter 2, the person slated to manage the reorganization may benefit from this increased responsibility. It should be simple to deduce the personal goals that he will realize when achieving this organizational goal.

Indirectly, every employee at GlueWorks may benefit from the reorganization. Many people will alter their behavior or efforts to support the organizational goal and have a personal goal to help the organization be successful. Their motivation can be as simple as trying to be a good member of the organization or can be much more complicated.

Some individuals may have a personal goal to undermine the organizational goal. They see this organizational goal as a bad thing for them. They may try to sabotage its success through action or inaction. You need to deduce the personal agenda of every person in the organization to decide how you can use them in your strategy.

Most professionals have a set of goals they aspire to attain. A myriad of authors, including most notably Steven Covey, have espoused the value of goal setting. These goals may include business goals, family goals, spiritual goals, etc. Understanding these personal goals is crucial to controlling the behavior of that person. You can then tailor your discussions much more precisely. You can also understand which individuals may be your friends or enemies. If you align your product to the attainment of someone's personal goal, you have a high likelihood of controlling his or her behavior.

If there is an individual in the organization who is an expert in a particular vertical industry, you can use this potential personal win to help them drive the success of this initiative. In this case, you are using the organizational goal to find the appropriate individual who will benefit from its attainment. Riding the coattails of this rising star employee will assist you in your sales campaign.

Side Effects

With every goal, there are side effects or repercussions. These side effects are due to compromises when another goal receives resources, priority, or attention. It is important to understand these possible side effects. You must discover if a goal adversely affects your sale and who within the organization is affected.

The first step in assessing a side effect is to deduce if the goal adversely affects you. A possible ramification in the GlueWorks example is a change in management structure in the organization. This may change the decision-making process within the organization and decrease the ability to purchase your product. This is a major problem since you need to align with the goals of the organization to win.

Being the victim of a side effect is almost as bad as trying to work with a prospect who does not have a goal that you can use. Your chances of success, in either case, are very low. Once you realize that you are on the wrong side of a goal, address the issue quickly. Your basic options are:

- Identify this as a new decision-making process.
- Try to change the goal to include your offering.
- Align yourself as a complementary solution that is not at odds with the goal.
- Stop working on this initiative to allow time for other opportunities.

New Decision-Making Opportunity

Your first step, in this instance, is to talk with the Decision Group. They may not be aware that this goal may preclude their purchase of your product. They also may have a strategy that you are not aware of to address this issue.

If you still see support for your solution, then you can start this as a new decision-making opportunity. You will be starting at step 1 of the decision-making process of Chapter 4. This is a very effective strategy, but it may delay your successful sale.

Change The Goal

It is possible that the goal will have enemies within the organization. These people prefer that the goal is changed. You may want to align yourself with these Influencers and try to get the overall goal modified. This can be a dangerous strategy if it fails since you are fighting an organizational directive, but it may be your only choice.

Make Yourself Complementary

Usually, the best option is to change your offering so that it is complementary to the goal. With imagination, this is usually possible. This allows you to move the process forward, align with the goal, and position yourself against your competition that does not react similarly.

When you make yourself complementary, you are often combining both of the above strategies of changing the goal and creating a new initiative. This dual effort further reduces your chance of losing the order and may eliminate your competition as well.

Stop Working On This Initiative

In the worst case, you need to cut your losses with this prospect. Keep them on your prospecting campaign list, however. By continuing to prospect to this organization, you will eventually find a chance to sell your product to them. Do not be ashamed to move on to easier opportunities. This will ensure that your sales pipeline is full.

Goals Drive Issues

Now that you understand the basic organization and individual goals, you can identify the issues that these goals create. Issues are broken into two main areas: challenges and results. Challenges must be overcome to realize the goal. Results are the positive or negative effects that occur upon the completion of the goal.

Challenges

Challenges are incredibly important to understand. They are the reasons that a goal fails. Even if the prospect organization is truly committed to its goals, they may fail due to unsolved challenges. For this reason, if you can align your product with a goal's challenge then you have a justification for the prospect to purchase your product. Organizational goals are so critical that most expenditures are easily cost-justified to ensure the goal's attainment.

It can be difficult to fully understand the challenges that an organization faces to attain its goals. To help you internalize this, think of the organizations with which you are personally associated, e.g., your employer, church or synagogue, local school systems, as well as local, state, and federal governments. Each of these organizations has goals, and as a result, challenges, that it is confronting.

Since hindsight is 20/20, you can analyze the past goals of these organizations and quickly find challenges that were confronted. It is not surprising that the organization did not anticipate or underestimated these challenges. This lack of ability to anticipate all of the challenges is not a lack of character or intelligence; rather, it is merely the result of too many factors to analyze in advance.

Since you are not a member of the organization and do not have all of the information, you may have a more difficult time discerning your prospect's challenges. In other cases, you will be able to easily see obstacles that are not obvious to the prospect since you have the advantage of an outside perspective. You also have the advantage of experience working with similar organizations and their similar experiences. You must develop a strong relationship with a wide group of people to deduce their challenges and verify your observations.

Since you can anticipate certain challenges that the Decision Group cannot, you can give them your insight and build your credibility. This guidance to the Decision Group may build enough value that you will quickly outshine your competition and be seen as a trusted advisor.

▼▼▼▼▼▼▼▼▼▼▼▼▼▼

Your personal perceived value to the Decision Group may overcome product and/or company disadvantages and allow you to win the opportunity.

▲▲▲▲▲▲▲▲▲▲▲▲▲▲

In the GlueWorks example, Dave Trapper often gave advice on the challenges that they were going to experience. The Decision Group appreciated the advice and acted upon it. Dave built a tremendous amount of loyalty due to the professional nature of his advice. By the end of the decision-making process, his guidance made him integral to GlueWorks' goal attainment.

Regardless of the product you sell, you are much more important to the Decision Group if you align your product with the challenges that threaten a goal. Your experience with other customers will make it easy to identify these issues. Do not underestimate your importance to the Decision Group.

Results

Results are the effects of the completion of a goal. These can positively or negatively affect the organization. It is very common for the result of a goal to have both negative and positive components, and the overall impact may be in doubt. Typically, it is easier to identify positive results since many of these are present at a basic level in a well-written goal statement. Negative results may be more difficult to ascertain, but often these are larger motivators for the actions of the members of the organization.

Positive Results Are Rewards

Nearly everyone in the organization will have some idea of the rewards for accomplishing an organizational goal. Many professionals will align their personal goals with these goals as well.

You should align your product with rewards. In the GlueWorks example, the result of achieving this goal was $5,000,000 in additional revenue and cost savings. You may not be able to help with the GlueWorks' reorganization, but you can deduce that they want to understand their customers and perhaps you can help in that area.

You are in an extremely strong position if your product is a key factor in the accomplishment of the reward.

Negative Results Are Pains

Avoiding failure is very important for organizational goals. Most organizations will mobilize a similar number of resources to avoiding failures as they do to achieving goals. One of the most common quotes by Arthur Conan Doyle's literary sleuth Sherlock Holmes is "When you have eliminated the impossible, whatever remains, however improbable, must be the truth." The most successful way to achieve a goal is to eliminate the chance of not attaining the goal.

Certain people within the organization will be more receptive to a failure avoidance discussion. This affinity will be due to a variety of factors including personality, job description, or past failures. You must understand your prospect organization well enough to identify the needs of each of the Influencers and tailor your Bait to fit their profiles.

Practice aligning your product to reduce or eliminate failure. This packaging appeals to the prospect's base desires and is an extremely old sales tactic. By using Fear, Uncertainty, and Doubt (FUD), you compel the prospect to value your product.

In the GlueWorks example, Dave Trapper preyed upon GlueWorks' fears of failing to effectively realign the company. He packaged his product as a safety net for them and made his competition appear to be the unsafe choice. This perception was a key factor in his ability to win the sales campaign.

Regardless of what you sell, your offering is much more effective if you create Bait that aligns with the goal and its issues. When you build the issues Alignment chart later in this chapter, be attuned to how the prospect can fail and how you can help them succeed.

Issues Create Needs

Needs are at the most basic level of human existence. They are 'things to be satisfied.' Needs are created by the issues that a person or the organization confronts. Target your conversations and correspondence with the members of the Decision Group to needs rather than goals or issues. Needs are much more personally motivating for the individual than goals or issues. Needs tend to be short-term and immediate.

Needs are broken into two segments: Organizational and Personal. Organizational needs are addressed by the organization. Similarly, personal needs are an individual's issues based on his or her individual goals or organization goals.

Personal Needs are always more individually compelling than Organizational Needs. The key thing to remember in every conversation with the Decision Group is WIFM: "What's in It For Me." In every situation, you can achieve control over someone's actions if you can anticipate how s/he will prosper or be hurt. By understanding how each goal and issue affects every individual, you can tailor your Bait to his or her specific temperament and need.

Create Needs

Needs can create new goals. In the GlueWorks example, the customer quickly learned that they needed to enhance their product development process. This opened further sales opportunities to be explored as this new need developed into a goal.

In your sales campaigns, build strategies that allow you to add goals, issues, and needs that feature your product. Remember that you have sold your product dozens, if not hundreds, of times. Your prospect may have never bought something like what you sell. You are the expert; help them develop their needs. This advice becomes more important as you try to distinguish your products from your competition.

▼▼▼▼▼▼▼▼▼▼▼▼▼▼

Be confident! You are the expert on your product and its repercussions. The prospect is not an expert. Guide the prospect through the process of buying your product.

▲▲▲▲▲▲▲▲▲▲▲▲▲▲

Keep It Current

It is important that you constantly confirm these goals, issues, and needs with each member of the Decision Group and each Influencer. Also, each piece of correspondence, other than simple "Thank you" cards, should reference back to one of these three items. Your call planning should include the particular needs, issues, or goals that you are going to address in the call. The official Trapper website, www.TheTrapper.com, contains examples of call planning and correspondence that you can download to help you accelerate your learning and adoption of this methodology.

These needs will change and evolve. You do not want to be in a situation where you are working with an old need. By constantly refreshing and reconfirming this list, you will be applying your time more efficiently. Remember, a Trapper works very hard at being successful but also works very efficiently.

Everyone Has Needs

As discussed in Chapter 5, every person in the Decision Group has needs to satisfy. For every person on your Power Matrix, list five needs that concern that individual. If an individual cannot identify five needs that are personal or organizational, you have a problem. Organizations only buy to satisfy needs, if the members of the Decision Group can identify multiple needs that are satisfied with the product. If there are less than five needs for each person, the organization may not invest in your product due to a higher value return in some area of the business.

In those cases where the individual cannot itemize five needs, you must help. Start by discussing the identified goals for the organization. This discussion will naturally lead to the challenges and the results from the goal. As you explore these challenges and results, inquire how they will affect the individual's personal goals. Also, explore the areas of the organization that the individual works in for the possibility of conflict or improvement. This discussion should result in multiple needs that the individual did not consider.

If you are unsuccessful in developing five needs for an individual, you must replace them on your Power Matrix. Do not belittle the importance of that open spot in the Power Matrix. You must have nine to twenty-five people in your Power Matrix to ensure a successful sales campaign. Doing less will only undermine your ability to secure an order.

Prioritize Needs

As part of your confirmation process, prioritize the needs of the organization and the individuals. This prioritization is very straightforward and is divided into:

- Must have this need addressed.
- Should have this need addressed.
- Would like to have this need addressed.

It is possible that you will not be able to solve every need with your product. It is okay to solve most of the needs. The prospect rarely understands all of their needs. Part of the decision-making process is to convince the customer that a 'Must Have' need is only a 'Should Have' or perhaps a 'Like to Have' need. Conversely, there may be benefits that your product offers that are unique. In this case, you need to elevate the importance of the needs related to these benefits.

You must cross-verify that the prioritization is correct with the other members of your Power Matrix from Chapter 5. By doing this, you will learn an immense amount about what is important and relative to each Decision Group member. You will find that some people do not feel that a need is critical. You will also understand how each person regards other people in the Power Matrix, which can be incredibly valuable as you set Traps.

You should be concerned with how you are going to cover all of the players each time a new Need is developed.

Must Have Needs

The 'Must Have' needs are the most important to the Decision Group. They will not buy a product that does not include a solution to these needs. These needs are marked with an 'A' priority.

Should Have Needs

The 'Should Haves' are marked with a 'B' priority. The Decision Group prefers that your product addresses all of these needs but will not disqualify a product that does not include some 'B' items. The Decision Group will compromise on a few of the items on this list; however, the successful product will address many of these needs.

Sometimes the Decision Group needs to be educated that 'B' Needs are in conflict with each other or conflict with an 'A' item. This is usually due to the inexperience of the Decision Group in buying this type of product. This technique will allow you to re-prioritize the list to your benefit.

Would Like To Have Needs

Rank the Decision Group's 'Would Like to Have' needs with a 'C.' These needs may tip the purchase to one vendor but are not critical. The more 'C' needs you satisfy, the better you will be, but they will not take the place of any "Should Have" or "Must Have" need.

Build Needs Into The Decision Timeline

Typically, needs have milestone dates. These dates will drive the behavior of your prospect, which will allow you to forecast your resources more accurately. In the earlier GlueWorks example, the goal has a deadline; therefore, the issues and needs raised due to this goal will have deadlines.

Once you have established that a need is critical to the organization, build it into your Decision Timeline. Your desire is to create an atmosphere within the Decision Group to purchase your product after investigating their needs. By accomplishing this, you will:

- Drive decisions to particular dates.

- Bring in different Influencers into the decision making process.
- Develop activities within the prospect to explore these issues.
- Develop metrics for justification.
- Develop coaches and champions who are more powerful.

Chapter 7 covers these tools in more detail. Chapter 7 will also teach you how to confirm the ability of your competition to complete these items.

Close When The Need Is Solved

It is important that you check off needs after they are covered. This will allow you to move on to other activities and move the prospect through the Decision Timeline. By verifying the prospect's satisfaction with their ability to solve this need with your product, you will effectively remove this 'excuse' from your negotiations later in the sales process. Chapter 7 explains this in much more detail.

Itemize Your Strengths And Weaknesses

You will satisfy the needs of the Decision Group through personal, product, and company strengths. To create a plan that addresses the prospect's needs, you must understand those strengths.

You must also understand the weaknesses. This can be very difficult since your understanding of these items can be one-sided. Quite often, you must not believe your marketing department and your own sales pitch when you create this list. The most difficult task is understanding your shortcomings.

You are selling a mixture of product and company benefits. You are combining that with your personal abilities and characteristics. The Decision Group must evaluate, prioritize, and understand each component to make an effective decision.

You should not minimize your importance to this package, as there may be situations when your product and company are inferior but the Decision Group has a high level of respect for you. Your sales campaign will dictate what percentage these components play for your Decision Group.

Your marketing department probably inundates you with information detailing how great your company and products are. While this is important, it is equally important to understand that your company has made trade-offs to achieve these features. These trade-offs imply there are some things your company and product cannot do as well as some competitors. For instance, typically the more power and features an automobile has, the higher its price will be. The trade-off is that the automobile may be considered a luxury vehicle and not available for bargain prices or to be sold only on cost.

Making trade-offs is not bad; rather, it is typical for all companies and products. Do not be upset or worried that you have identified weaknesses in your offering. Every product has weaknesses and shortcomings. The goal is to understand them and to deal with them effectively.

The challenge in finding these internal weaknesses is usually due to your familiarity with and acceptance of them. Sales trainer Nick Miller of Clarity Advantage describes being snow blind. When driving your car in a snowstorm, your headlights reflect off the snow coming at you and may eliminate your ability to see what is happening in front of you. When you turn off your lights, the snow becomes virtually invisible, and you can see. When exploring your weaknesses, turn off the 'headlights' you use every day to help you see your way and look at the information from a different perspective.

It is often helpful to undergo this exercise by thinking of competing with yourself. Ask yourself the following question: "What would I tell my prospect if I was my competitor selling against my product?" This is a wonderful exercise for sales team meetings. Have one of the sales people give a mock sales campaign against your product and company, in favor of another. The ensuing discussion is quite revealing.

It may be more difficult to itemize your personal strengths and weaknesses. You must look into a virtual mirror and decide what you personally offer a prospect. You must also determine what things you are not capable of doing. Perhaps your skills lie in handling minutiae, so they rarely have any problems with customer service. Conversely, you may have a weakness in looking at the big picture and understanding how to guide the prospect to their intended goals. Whatever your self-appraisal reveals, you are only hurting yourself if you do not itemize these weaknesses.

When you analyze your personal skills and weaknesses, make sure to include items such as:

- Education
- Friendship
- Honesty
- Integrity
- Market expertise
- Reputation
- Responsiveness
- Vision
- Wisdom

Figure 6-1 is an example Strengths and Weaknesses chart. Note that it is a standard "T" chart with Strengths on the left side and Weaknesses on the right. There may not be a relationship between the two sides, i.e., not every strength has a corresponding weakness. Also, note that after each entry, there is a 'P' for Product, 'C' for Company, and 'M' for Me. While much of this chart will be identical for each prospect organization, many of your individual strengths and weaknesses may not be a factor for some organizations. You should create a custom chart for each new prospect organization. An electronic version of this chart is available on the official Trapper website, www.TheTrapper.com.

▼▼▼▼▼▼▼▼▼▼▼▼▼
A feature that has no benefit is not a feature.
▲▲▲▲▲▲▲▲▲▲▲▲▲

Write all strength statements in benefit format. A feature that does not have a benefit for the organization or an individual is not truly a feature because they will not use it. For example, it does not matter to you, the consumer, if light bulbs are made of glass or some other material. What may matter, though, is the color of the material, its ability to withstand shock, or its ability to transmit light. If you sell light bulbs, your prospect organization does not care about the material (which is a feature); instead, they care what that material can do for them (which is a benefit). If you can convince your marketing department to develop the initial version of these charts, you will accelerate your implementation of the Trapper methodology.

Strengths	Weaknesses
22% market share provides stability for the customer. (C)	Higher list price than most competitors (P)
Free 24x7 customer hotline allows customer to ensure minimal downtime with little long term cost. (C)	Overseas-based company (C)
On-site customer support means that the customer can have experts diagnose problems. (C)	Bigger than other widgets on the market (P)
Able to perform 'What If' analysis on decisions means that the customer will have security. (P)	Never sold to this customer (M,C)
15 years of industry experience ensures that the customer will always have appropriate advice. (M)	No personal relationship with Decision Maker (M)
Accredited by industry allows the customer to trust advice. (M)	Poor interface with prospect's other gadgets (P)

Figure 6-1: Strengths and Weaknesses. All figures are also available at http://www.thetrapper.com/book_figures

Create Selling Differentiators

Now that you have developed this chart for your company and yourself, you need to do the same for your competition. Avoid the personal weaknesses of individual salespeople, since these may change and the practice hints at you being unethical. It is very appropriate to chart their personal strengths since you are going to have to deal with these in your campaign.

Initially, you may not see the value of comparing your strengths to your competitor's strengths. While these features and benefits may be standard fare in your market, do not be lazy in this area since more than one sale has been lost because the customer perceived that one company was superior to its competitors in a certain area. This superiority was not true, but the customer's perception swung the sale. As discussed in Chapter 4, you want your competition to educate the Decision Group on standard capabilities, but you want to confirm with the Group that you also have these abilities.

▼▼▼▼▼▼▼▼▼▼▼▼▼▼

Perception is 100% of reality. It is your job to change that perception and create a correct reality.

▲▲▲▲▲▲▲▲▲▲▲▲▲▲

You now need to compare your company, product, and personal attributes to your competition. Figure 6-2 shows an Issues Alignment chart of how to do this for the GlueWorks example and the various competitors that Dave Trapper encountered. It is simply a listing in the first column of all of the identified needs, in the order of their relative importance. The next columns denote how the competitor can satisfy this need. Mark an advantage with an up arrow (↑) and a disadvantage with a down arrow (↓). If both offerings satisfy the need, note it with an equals sign (=).

You should be careful that you compare these with some reality in mind. If your company has a 22% market share and your competitor's market share is 20%, this may not be enough of a factor to conclude you have an advantage. Finally, a buying decision like this would include more needs at both the organizational level as well as the individual level than shown in this simple example.

Be mindful that there is often more than one way to 'skin a catfish.' If the Decision Group expresses a need to work with a vendor who has been in business for 15+ years, they may be concerned with stability. There may be several ways to prove stability (such as the number of customers), resulting in confidence for the prospect. If the prospect specifies a feature and not the benefit, you can usually conclude that it is a Trap placed by your competitor. Refer to Chapter 7 and the discussion on escaping Traps for techniques to turn this Trap against your competitor. For example, if GlueWorks was concerned about stability and they accept the number of customers as the measure, Dave Trapper would win against Amy Gatherer.

Need	Importance	Dave Trapper	Amy Gatherer	Ben Farmer	Carla Hunter
Market stability	A	= In business for 10 years	= In business for 15 years	= In business for 22 years	= In business for 12 years
Market stability	A	= 550 customers	↓ 200 customers	= 625 customers	↓ 150 customers
Presence in Ivytown	A	= Yes	= Yes	= within 50 miles	↓ No
Multidepartment capability	A	↑ Yes – multiple examples	↓ Poor – few examples	↓ Poor – few examples	↓ No
Number of consultants	B	↓ 100	↑ 1,000	↑ 4,000	↓ 450
Flexible licensing	B	↑ Named user or server (on premises only)	= Named user only (on premises or cloud)	↓ Named user only (on premises only)	↓ Named user only (cloud only)
Size on hard drive	C	↑ 100M if server-based	↓ 228M	↓ 900M	↓ NA
US based support staff	A	↑ Yes	↓ Not really	= Yes	= Yes
Strong product development expertise	A	↑ Yes	↓ No	↓ No	↓ No

Figure 6-2: Issues Alignment Chart. All figures are also available at http://www.thetrapper.com/book_figures

You should spend very little time talking about virtually equal areas. Instead, you should confirm that the Decision Group understands that you offer this benefit and then allow your competitors to spend their time teaching the prospect about this standard fare in your market. This is one of the ways that you can conserve your time, make sure that the prospect needs that benefit, explain that everyone has this capability, and refer him to some industry source or maybe even your competitor for further information.

▼▼▼▼▼▼▼▼▼▼▼▼▼▼

You should not spend time teaching your prospect on things that do not differentiate you from your competition.

▲▲▲▲▲▲▲▲▲▲▲▲▲▲

You will build an Issues Alignment chart for each prospect in your Power Matrix that you created in Chapter 5. This is important since not all of the players will feel all of these needs. They will also have different priorities on these needs and different beliefs in your ability to satisfy these needs. Remember, people buy from people, and every member of the Decision Group has a voice in the final decision.

Build The Bait

All of the answers to the prospect's needs will have well–thought-out Bait. In some cases, you will develop multiple pieces of Bait for each need to help the customer understand your advantage. You will need to develop more Bait for needs where you have an advantage and fewer for those where you are equal. You will also need to have a considerable amount of Bait that defends your capabilities for needs where your product is lagging. You will use these Baits extensively in the next chapter, which discusses how to escape Traps.

You must make your Bait easy to understand and remember! Too often, marketing literature has a confusing message that is lost on the prospect and therefore may not propel you to your goal of winning the sale. You must package the information you have about yourself, your company, and your product in a way that the customer can understand and remember after you leave the meeting.

When packaging your Bait, you should keep in mind the "Memory Law of Five." You should create Bait that has only five to seven main points in it. You should also only discuss five to seven things at any meeting. Many researchers have documented that the human brain has difficulty remembering more than seven items at one time. George Miller wrote in the Psychological Review in 1956 that the 'magical number' was seven plus or minus two. Herbert A. Simon and A.D. deGroot concluded that the optimum number of items that a person can effectively act on without extreme study is only six. Be a safe Trapper – keep your Bait to less than seven points.

▼▼▼▼▼▼▼▼▼▼▼▼▼▼

The Memory Law of Five should guide all of your conversations and correspondence with your prospects.

▲▲▲▲▲▲▲▲▲▲▲▲▲▲

One of the 'B' needs from above is the need for the prospect to have flexible licensing arrangements. In this case, the Bait could be set up as follows:

1. Growth - the reduced risk if the need for the software grows substantially.
2. Anticipation - the difficulty in anticipating a company's needs.
3. Management – It is easier to manage one server than many separate implementations.
4. Expense - The expense advantage in server-based pricing versus individual user pricing.
5. Example - An example of a satisfied customer who used server pricing to mitigate one of these concerns.

These five points will be easy for the prospect to remember and, when used with the Trapping techniques in Chapter 7, will be very effective in communicating your message.

It is important to plan your sales conversations with the prospect so that you are only covering five to seven separate points in one conversation. In our simplistic T-chart example above, there are only six needs. In your daily sales campaigns, though, you probably have lists that are much more extensive. Limit the topics that you introduce to only five so that the prospect can understand all of your points.

Move It Into The Brain

In addition to making the Bait the right size for the prospect to understand, you need to help them remember it. You must effectively package and deliver your Bait.

The United States' Central Intelligence Agency has conducted extensive research on memory. In their book "Psychology of Intelligence Analysis" they conclude that information starts with sensory information storage (which lasts for several tenths of a second), moves to short-term memory (lasting a few seconds or minutes), and then to long-term memory (no limit to how long it lasts).

During this process, the brain filters and categorizes the information uniquely for each individual. This causes the listener to 'perceive' the information in a particular manner. Since you cannot deduce the perception of your information, repeat the message multiple times and in multiple ways. Repetition is key to many aspects of learning. This ensures the Decision Group member perceives the information the way you desire. There are not enough nickels in the US Treasury to cover the number of times salespeople have said, "I told the prospect about that capability, but he did not understand it."

▼▼▼▼▼▼▼▼▼▼▼▼▼▼▼▼

Perception is 100% of reality. It does not matter if something is true or false — only that the prospect believes it. This is a positive or negative depending on what the prospect 'perceives.'

▲▲▲▲▲▲▲▲▲▲▲▲▲▲▲▲

It is crucial that you put your information into your prospect's long-term memory, the third stage. The key factor in doing this is to develop associations with the new information and what the prospect already knows or understands.

There are three primary methods to commit information to memory.

1. Rote
2. Assimilation

3. Acrostic Device

Rote

This is the least efficient way of remembering information, but you are probably very familiar with it. It involves constant repetition of the information, which builds its pattern into long-term memory. This is similar to the technique of a primary school student who constantly repeats the spelling of a certain word before the spelling test. The student's goal is that the repetition will allow him to pass the test. Unfortunately, often the student will pass the test but then not remember how to spell that difficult word the next day. This emphasizes the inefficiency of only using rote learning to commit something to memory.

Rote learning is accomplished by repeating your message multiple times. To assist in making your points memorable, structure your communications in three sections: opening comments, the main point, and then a confirmation comment. This is what most speech consultants will coach – tell them what you are going to tell them, tell them, and then tell them what you told them.

You will also use multiple media and times to convey your message, such as:

- Phone conversation – setting up the meeting and telling the Decision Group member what you would like to discuss.
- Personal conversation – a dialogue on the subject with the Decision Group member using active listening skills.
- Written – confirmation letter covering the points that you made and possibly the Decision Group's responses.
- Printed material – that covers the same points made in your conversation.

Assimilation

Assimilation relates the new information to something we already know. The ancient Greek senators reportedly gave speeches that lasted hours without the aid of notes. They remembered the salient points of their presentation by associating it with a room or piece of furniture in their house. They then walked around their home in their mind and discussed the topic related to that room. Many memory experts teach their students to use similar tricks to enhance memory such as remembering the name 'Bill' by picturing a hundred dollar bill attached to Bill's forehead.

An excellent way to use this technique is to make an example or story that conveys the information that you need. You should choose stories or examples that are very similar to your prospect's business. This allows the prospect to associate your benefit to your story, which is easier to remember.

Acrostic Device

Acrostic devices are little tricks that help us to develop patterns in our brain. School-age children often use these tricks to learn a particular topic. A couple of familiar examples:

- The Great Lakes - HOMES: Huron, Ontario, Michigan, Erie, and Superior
- Directions of a compass – Never Eat Soggy Waffles: North, East, South, West

Even the memorization of the English alphabet is taught with the very popular ABC song. Ask a 6-year-old child if she knows her ABC's and she will sing the song for you. If you then ask her what letter precedes the letter P, she will likely slowly sing the song to herself to find the answer. Eventually, after years of repetition of singing the song, teenagers and adults remember that the letter O precedes P in the English alphabet.

List the top four to seven features of your product that nearly all prospects are interested in understanding. Take this list, create an acrostic device, and use that device in your personalized brochures, correspondence, and discussions. Earlier, we used an example of Bait that had five points. The last point was an example of a customer, so if we discard this item we have:

- Growth - the reduced risk if the need for the software grows substantially.
- Anticipation - the difficulty in anticipating a company's needs.
- Management – It is easier to manage one server than many separate implementations.
- Expense - The expense advantage in server-based pricing versus individual user pricing.

This develops into the acrostic device GAME. Dave Trapper, when he was selling to GlueWorks, constantly referred to GAME in his correspondence and discussions.

Build acrostics for the combination of approximately five very important benefits that appropriately position your product to the prospect and against your competition. This can be broken into five for your product, five for your company, five for you. Personalize this message for each Influencer in the decision-making process. Your personalization should target the Vision Goal that you established with the prospect using the techniques of Chapter 5.

Deliver It Effectively

The more complicated the concept, the more important it is to internalize the information. The most common technique is to write down the information. You should encourage your listener to take notes. If you are giving a slide presentation, give them small copies of the slides with a place to take notes on the side. You may even want to prompt them to write something down with statements similar to: "You will note that…" or "We will refer to this point later so you may want to write this down."

Provide an outline of your discussion in a pre-printed format. Highlight the major points that you will be discussing in your conversation and put bullets for each of them. If you have an acrostic device for your product, put the first letters of the device in the document for the prospect to fill in the rest.

Creating personalized collateral helps to emphasize these points. Your marketing department may be able to package this information for you, but you will need to customize the message for your prospects. Today's personal computer tools make this very easy to accomplish.

Turn It Into A Trap

You have developed your Bait. It is time to use it! You have designed your Bait to pull your quarry into your Trap. The next chapter will show you how to create a Trap with your Bait so that you can control and influence the Decision Group's decision-making process and eliminate your competition. After reading the next chapter, you may find it beneficial to review the steps in creating Bait.

It is now time to develop your sales campaign that includes all of the Bait for the prospective organization. The first step is to develop a Vision Goal for the organization. Then each need that is important to the prospect is listed with the features and benefits of your product that solve this need. We then plan how we are going to communicate this information to the prospect and how the prospect has acknowledged that we have satisfied this need.

Build The Vision Goal

The first part of the sales campaign is the creation of the Vision Goal for the prospect organization. The Power Matrix that you developed in Chapter 4 follows this effort. Each person in the Power Matrix should have a personal Vision Goal.

The Vision Goal is a far-reaching statement that satisfies the vast majority of the prospect's desires and needs. It is probably not easy to attain this goal, and it is a combination of the major benefits of a successful project. It is personalized to the wins of the individual. It is usually several sentences long.

It is a compilation of the list of issues that affect the individual (not the organization) and that the individual wants to achieve:

- It has a personal win component to it.
- This win can be more than financial in nature.

- It can include department wins that affect the individual.
- It can include organizational wins that can affect the individual.

To be an effective Trapper, you must learn to create information prepared to encourage the prospect to think in a certain way. This information allows you to create a Trap that influences and controls a prospect. This packaged information is Bait.

It may be easy for you to create Bait because your employer has adopted Trapper techniques. Most readers will find this exercise challenging because their company has not realized how to do many of the background steps of Bait development. Regardless of the tools provided by your company, the development and deployment of Bait is ultimately the salesperson's responsibility. It is your commission that gets paid when you win, and therefore it is your responsibility to create the Bait that lands that deal.

Chapter 7 – Setting The Trap (And Escaping It)

"Most of the things we decide are not what we know to be the best. We say yes, merely because we are driven into a corner and must say something."

- Frank Crane

The essence of being a Trapper is setting and escaping Traps. There are few skills that differentiate a true competitor more than the ability to control the sale by asking intelligent questions and avoiding difficult situations. This skill requires practice and forethought in dealing with your competitors.

Competitors are typically good for you so do not worry about their involvement. Competitors will help you teach the prospect about the market, your industry, and your overall technology. This will save you valuable time and money since much of what they discuss will be relevant to your offering.

For example, GlueWorks had to learn many of the industry-related issues. These issues were nearly identical for all competitors; therefore, it was effective for Dave Trapper to suggest his competitors for a source of that knowledge. This allowed Dave to spend time discussing the features that made his offering different. Dave did not need to discuss common features that all the vendors offer and will not win the order.

Features that you have that are the same as your competitors are not Traps. Essentially, these are non-issues. You should never try to set a Trap based on features that are essentially standardized in your market.

Types Of Traps

There are three types of Traps that are explained and explored in this chapter:

1. Accidental Traps
2. Unintentional Traps
3. Collaborative Traps

Each of these types of Traps can destroy your ability to turn a prospect into a customer. They can be used by you to eliminate your competition, or they can be used by your competitor to eliminate you. In this chapter, we will explore each type of Trap. We will also describe how to set the Traps against your competition. Finally, we will explore how to escape a Trap that has been sprung on you.

Accidental Traps

Accidental Traps are honest information gathering by the prospect but leave you open to making a mistake with your answer by making your product look less than optimal. It is an opportunity to lose the sale, and it is also an opportunity to Trap the competition.

In the process of learning about your product, the prospect will ask questions. This is a normal and required part of you educating the prospect. Without questions, you simply will not be able to effectively make the prospect smarter about your product.

Most of these questions are simply clarification questions. The customer heard something and wants to understand the information more fully. These questions usually are restatements of information that has already been presented.

Some questions will not be clarification questions, though, but instead will be product fit questions. Product fit questions can quickly become an accidental Trap. These questions take some of the information that has already been shared and apply it to the prospect's situation. The prospect is not trying to clarify what he heard but rather is trying to apply that new knowledge to an existing issue.

Product fit questions should be recognized as a potential danger signal. When a prospect is trying to mentally apply a product to a new problem, the answer received can often cause the prospect to eliminate the product. Every product fit question should be fully understood before it is ever answered. You do not want your product to be eliminated simply because the prospect came to a quick conclusion that the product couldn't solve a need.

The benefit of a product fit question is that it will allow you to dig into a need and ultimately the goal behind that need. When a prospect asks you a product fit question, you now have a clue as to a new need. Even if it is an existing need, you now have the opportunity to explore the importance of the need and explore the applicability of your product to solve the need. As we will see later in this chapter, escaping the Trap, even an Accidental Trap, allows you develop value for your product.

Unintentional Traps

Unintentional Traps are when the prospect doesn't know he is being used by the competition. This is the most frequent type of Trap. In this case, the prospect has been educated by the competition to inquire about your specific weakness or the general weakness of your industry. This can be very troubling, as you know that you are against a tough competitor.

An Unintentional Trap will start out as an Accidental Trap. It will be couched into a product fit question. As above, you will be tempted to answer the question directly, even if it is a capability that you don't directly have, but you think you can explain the issue. You have probably heard this question before and think that you can effectively "spin" against it. Don't take this Bait!

Instead of answering the question, you need to understand the reason behind the question. You need to understand whether the prospect has the appropriate needs or goals to understand the question. If the prospect cannot explain why the issue is important, you can assume that you have found a skilled competitor.

Unfortunately, some Traps work. There are almost definitely deficiencies in your product or company that are not advantageous to the prospect. This Unintentional Trap is going to hurt, but by asking the prospect the underlying reason before you answer the question, you can immediately minimize the pain. You will need to answer the question, but you will now be armed with the knowledge that the prospect doesn't truly need the feature so you can minimize the issue. As you will learn later in this chapter, you will also learn how to escape the Trap and attack your competitor in return.

Collaborative Traps

Collaborative Traps are the most dangerous Traps. In this case, the prospect is knowingly working with the competitor to ask the question. This is relatively rare in most sales campaigns, but it is the most dangerous if misdiagnosed.

A Collaborative Trap occurs when the prospect needs the feature in question, and you don't completely cover the need. The competitor knows this deficiency and tells the prospect to ask you about it and that your answer isn't going to be favorable.

As I said above, some Traps work and are effective against you. That is our life in sales. We must understand what is going on in this situation and effectively work against it.

We can deduce that it is a collaborative Trap by our questions before answering their question. The first clue will be that the prospect will have a very good reason for asking the question. The prospect will also have some idea of how your product doesn't satisfy the need or that other competitors do satisfy the need. He may say that Competitor X told him that you didn't have the feature but that is the goal.

Luckily, most prospects are not truly trying to trip you up. They will usually tell you that Competitor X has the feature and you do not. They will usually point out at this time that Competitor X suggested the question. This gives you a clue that Competitor X is a tough competitor, and you are going to have to spend time building a strategy to eliminate this competitor. You also need to answer the question, but that is later in this chapter, where I discuss escaping Traps.

Setting A Trap To Differentiate From A Competitor

Setting a Trap is much easier to understand and implement than escaping a Trap. You will gather the knowledge that you have developed in previous chapters about the prospect, the driving reasons, and the differentiators. You will use this knowledge to convince the prospect of your superiority over the competition. This knowledge is used in every conversation with the prospect and in developing the Decision Timeline.

The four steps in Trap setting that are explained in this chapter are:

1. Develop the need with the Bait from the previous chapter.
2. Confirm that we meet the need by confirming the relevance that we deduced in the previous chapter.
3. Question whether competition meets the need to instill doubt in the individual's mind.
4. Request feedback on how the competition responds so that we know that the Trap was sprung and we know if the Trap worked.

Trap setting is not obvious to most people, so you should also practice it with your manager and fellow salespeople.

Developing the need is relatively straightforward once you have developed the Bait from the previous chapter. Review those steps again if you are not clear as to how this works. The most important thing to remember is that your Bait must be relative to this particular prospect and the specific individual that you are working with at the prospect.

You should not use Bait that is not important. The Bait chosen for any Trap must be important to the prospect, or you will not be successful. If you know that payment terms are important and you have an advantage in payment terms, then you can use that feature as Bait. However, if payment terms are not important to the specific individual at the prospect, then using payment terms will not be effective even if you have an advantage.

Remember that to set a Trap, your Bait must have an advantage over the competition and must be desired by the specific individual at the prospect. In other words, the feature must offer a benefit to the individual and the individual must fully understand and agree to the benefit. A feature that has no benefit is simply not a feature worth discussing.

The next step in setting the Trap is to confirm that benefit to the individual. If you are having a conversation, you will bring up the feature that you wish to focus on and remind the prospect of the benefit. You can be so blunt as to ask the simple question, "Am I correct that if the payment terms were 60 days, it would be good for your company and help you make your budget limitations and ultimately help you achieve the goals for your department?"

This confirmation is critical. You need to bring this to the front and center in the mind of the individual. You need the individual to believe that only by having this feature can he attain his goal.

The third step is the most precarious. The third step is to question the competition. You can do this directly by naming Competitor X, or you can do this against all competitors. It is often less confrontational to make it far reaching, but I will try to help you with both.

For all competitors, you need to say something similar to the following: "I don't have great information on my competition, but I am told by my marketing team that we are unique in offering this kind of feature. How are you going to evaluate the other companies in this area to make sure they satisfy your goal?"

When you have to directly attack a specific competitor, you have to be even more subtle. Something like this may work, "I don't know a lot about Competitor X, but I have heard that they do not have that feature. I may wrong, though. Have you asked them about the feature?"

The first three steps set the Trap, but now you must make sure it closes and that it worked. You won't be present when the Trap closes, so you need to get confirmation. The easiest way to do this is with a simple question. Try something like this: "As I have said, I really do not know much about my competition. I would hate to be talking about them with information that is not correct. Can you do me a big favor and tell me what was said when you confirm the presence of this important feature? If they do have it, then my ethics require that I don't repeat the statement. Your feedback allows me to be a more honest salesperson and my integrity is very important to me."

It is important to note that when you receive confirmation, you start to turn the individual into a champion. You have challenged the individual to do something for you. Perhaps it isn't a big request, but it is a request. When they tell you the result of the question, you have started to build a level of trust and collaboration with the prospect. After a couple of Traps, you will not only eliminate or weaken your competition, but you will also strengthen your relationship with the individual, and that is the first step in creating a champion.

While I tried to give you a few things to say to set Traps, the easiest way to set a Trap is to do it in a letter or email. You may want to verbally set a Trap but then follow it up with a well-crafted email. Let's review Dave Trapper's email from Chapter 2, which I have recreated here so you don't need to jump back and forth.

You will see in the middle of the email that Dave Trapper mentions that he thought a feature was unique in the marketplace but asked for confirmation of that uniqueness. Dave has now set a Trap that allows him to come back to Greg in the future to ask about that uniqueness. Also, note that Dave had earlier confirmed the value of that feature's benefit to Greg.

Dear Greg -

Thank you for your time discussing your optimization project. I have put my notes into this email in the hopes of confirming what I heard and our next action items. Please let me know if I have missed anything. I would like to get your feedback.

You have made it clear that the new solution must:

- Assess the skills of each employee.
- Identify the skills that need to be developed for each employee.
- Allow a manager to create specific requirements for each headcount in his/her department.
- Allow a manager to create a specific skills analysis for each project and recurring activity in his/her department.
- Compare departmental needs to skills within departments and the entire organization.
- Create detailed reports on human skills available and skills needed on personal, departmental, and organizational levels.
- Analyze learning paths to identify best candidates for enhanced training for any skills detriment.
- You mentioned that it was important that the software be flexible enough that it can be applied to other use cases within GlueWorks.

- You mentioned that other people on the committee might have other specific needs, but these were the most important needs to you.

Do I have these needs itemized correctly?

I am confident that we will be able to show you how we accomplish all of these points. Please let me know if you have any concerns as we work together over the next few months.

We are very proud of our Intelligent Assessment Advisor (IAA), which can rate every employee in an automated peer-review 360-degree view. We think that we are the only company to offer this technology to the marketplace. I would be curious to hear your feedback if you see anything like this in your research.

I am specifically curious about the last bullet item of applying artificial intelligence across multiple divisional problems. To the best of my knowledge, no other product that can match us in Human Resources issues can also be applied in areas such as Product Development, Manufacturing, and Logistics. If you find that I am wrong, can you help expand my knowledge of the industry by letting me know of your research?

Can we put the review of IAA on the agenda for our meeting next Wednesday? I would enjoy hearing your comments on how we approach this problem compared to other potential solutions.

I am also attaching an electronic version of the Decision Timeline that we discussed.

I look forward to seeing you at 10A next Wednesday to review the Decision Timeline and the IAA.

Sincerely,

Dave

P.S. Don't forget to sign up for our webinar on improving efficiency on Friday. You can register at http://www.thetrapper.com.

This is probably not a big change from a confirmation letter you have sent to prospects in the past. You may have intuitively put a Trap into that letter, but I would like you to do use this technique for the majority of your prospect communication. Your goal should be to use these communications to create separation between you and your competitors.

Escaping A Trap That Could Make You Look Poorly

Escaping a Trap is much more critical and difficult to accomplish. The successful Trapper understands that a sales campaign will be lost if Traps are not effectively escaped. As noted above, some Traps are innocent questions by a prospect and not purposely set by competition. This means that every sales campaign has Traps to avoid and therefore opportunities to use Traps.

The four primary steps in escaping a Trap are:

1. Clarify the meaning of the question so that the salesperson answers the true question rather than a perceived one.
2. Acknowledge the business importance of the request to truly understand the driving reason and its relationship to this opportunity.
3. Respond to the request with a well-thought-out answer.
4. Using the tools above, set a Trap that is similar to the request since the salesperson understands that this issue is important to the prospect.

Let's explore these various steps in more detail. Escaping a Trap is not obvious to most people, so you should also practice it with your manager and fellow salespeople.

The first step in escaping a Trap is to make sure you understand the meaning of the question. Too often, a salesperson will almost answer the question before the prospect has taken a breath after the question. Please remember to take your time and think before you talk. The only effective way to escape a Trap is to think through your response.

Your initial answer almost needs to be, "I don't understand your question." You should almost always ask a prospect to clarify the meaning of the question. Just like in a spelling bee, the student has the right to ask for the word to be used in a sentence as well as the definition, you have the right to truly understand the question.

When you ask for clarification, you will almost always get more information. This is what you want - more information. This increased information allows you to make sure you are answering the true question but it also gives you time to think of an effective answer.

Even this clarification should not be enough, though. You want to know the business goal that this question covers. Perhaps the prospect has given you the business goal, but typically it is still not verbalized. You must get the business reason that the question is important. So after you have asked for clarification, you need to ask for another clarification, but now it is about business.

A good business clarification question needs to be appropriately modest but also needs to be leading. Here is a good example: "I am sorry that I am confused but do you need feature X because you are trying to accomplish business goal Y?"

You now have asked two clarification questions. You may think this is abusive, but it is not. Instead, it has allowed you to make sure you understand the question and the reason behind the question. It has also given you a few minutes to think of your response!

This still is not enough. Now you must restate the feature question and the business goal back to the prospect. Something similar to this will probably suffice: "Let me confirm that I understand. You are concerned about Feature X and how it will allow you to accomplish Business Goal Y. Do I understand your question correctly?" Silence is golden at this point, and you should allow the prospect to reply. In fact, you may want to pause after the reply to see if the prospect will give you even more information.

You now need to give the best answer that you possibly can give to the question. I like to say that most questions are repeated from prospect to prospect, so you have probably heard the question before this conversation. In fact, this is why you may have rushed the answer in the first place. Now it is time to talk, and you need to give the best answer that you possibly can give to the question.

All of this clarification has allowed you to build a bit of understanding about the business needs of the prospect. The original question would not have been asked if there wasn't a business issue. You must now set a Trap for your competitors. You must set a Trap on the same business issue as was just asked of you.

Setting a Trap in response allows you to minimize the damage that the original question caused to your efforts. If the Trap from your competitor was effective or even if it was an Accidental Trap, you now want to hurt your competition. You know the business issue was important enough for your prospect to ask a question; therefore, it is important enough to spring a new Trap.

The last step in escaping a Trap is to set a Trap in return. Use the business issue that was just presented to ask a question using the techniques of setting a Trap that we explored above. This will allow you to hurt your competitors more than you were hurt by the original question.

Competitive Knowledge

It is probably obvious to you that to effectively set Traps and escape Traps you will need to understand your competition. While it is possible that your marketing group will create much of this information for you, do not leave this to chance. You need to build files on each of your competitors, and you need review this information on a regular basis.

You need to capture this knowledge into a competitive database. You will use this database of competitors and their particular advantages extensively. This database may be as complex as a shared electronic database for use by your entire sales organization, or as simple as paper files in your file drawer. Regardless of the mechanism that works best for you, this information will be very useful for your career.

Many prospect organizations will compile a list of likely vendors. This list usually has less than a dozen vendors and may be as short as three companies. You should assist your prospect in compiling this list and make sure it has plenty of 'C' vendors. A good mix will be six 'C' vendors that are not fringe competitors, four 'B' vendors, one 'A' and you. This will allow you to quickly dispatch the six 'C' vendors and most of the 'B' vendors while laying long-term Traps for the stronger 'B' vendors and the 'A' vendors.

As discussed in Chapter 3, the Decision Group is not going to select the best solution but will settle for a product that satisfies the majority of their perceived needs. Chapter 6 builds on this concept and helps you prioritize your resources.

Multiple Traps In A Row

Deploying multiple Traps is a skill that takes practice. You primarily use the technique against a specific competitor. Traps are most effective if there are multiple Traps laid out for the competitor to trip over. You also want to increase the nuisance factor to your competitors by making them constantly respond to your questions, thereby eliminating their own agendas.

Multiple Traps need a well-developed understanding of the competitor. You will need to understand the weaknesses of the company or product far more than just reading their website. In fact, you may need to know as much about the competition as you do about your own product and company.

Multiple Traps also mean that you need a long-term strategy for the competitor. It is not practical that you would lay all of the Traps in one meeting. Rather, you need to have a strategy that lays out a series of conversations with your prospect over several sales calls.

Since a multiple Trap strategy takes a great deal of planning, you will want to do it for only your top competitors. These A-list competitors are the ones that you see most often, and they are the competitors that offer a nearly identical value to your own offering.

A typical multiple Trap strategy should end with the toughest Trap that you understand about your competitor. The strategy is to grow the complexity with each successive question. The first question that is asked is typically not the most critical. In fact, you would probably be surprised if the first couple of Traps trips up the competitor.

Dave used multiple Traps to raise concerns about Amy Gatherer's support model in Chapter 2. He did this when he was helping the prospect understand the extra value that his company could offer in access to top-level architects, support, and product planning. He was also able to get GlueWorks to see that Amy Gatherer's company was not strong in the United States even though it was doing well in a part of Europe.

When Dave sprang this multiple Trap strategy, he could have gone straight to the end Trap. He could have done an immediate compare and contrast to his support offering locations and his competition's locations. However, this confrontation could have seemed too aggressive. Also, it would show a level of insider knowledge about his competitor that may have been perceived as unseemly.

Instead, Dave asked questions where he already knew the answers, but he needed the prospect to gain more knowledge for the last Trap to work. In reality, the first two meetings and Traps were quite easy to get through, but the answers to those questions set up the final Trap.

In the end, a multiple Trap strategy is much more effective than a single Trap. As shown with Dave Trapper, it takes patience and planning to pull it off. Don't be surprised if it takes you several sales cycles to refine your questions to achieve your end goal.

The Wrong Competitors Are Involved

Analysts in your industry may group several fringe companies as relating to your company. However, you know that those fringe companies simply do not address the same market as you do. In fact, if a prospect has you and Competitor X as finalists in the same evaluation then the prospect is probably very confused. In this case, you need to get Competitor X off of the list.

Leaving a fringe competitor in the evaluation may cause the prospect to change the requirements to take advantage of the unique capabilities of Competitor X. This is bad for you and you will lose if the requirements are expanded. In this case, if you do not have Competitor X removed you will essentially lose the sale.

To remove a competitor, convince the Decision Group that they are straying from their originally-intended direction and therefore make them re-think their direction. This result is possible when the Decision Group has mentally connected your products with their problem.

There are times that you may offer to withdraw from the prospect's process as a way of eliminating a C or a B vendor that offers a significant number of features that you do not offer. If you withdraw stating that you do not feel there is a fit, they may re-evaluate their situation. This strategy is very effective if you want to realign the prospect's goals and all other efforts have failed. This is a 'doomsday' gambit, though, since if you do not get the prospect to change, you are permanently out of the running for the order.

If you decide to withdraw, then you must admit to yourself that you failed to create a qualified opportunity. The prospect may eventually purchase something, but you could not capitalize on it.

Intercepting The Hail Mary

It is important that you control the exceptions to the process in chapter 4. Invariably, anyone who is eliminated will try to get back in by doing something exceptional to gain attraction.

You must understand that this Hail Mary is a Trap that is being set for you. You must escape from this Trap, or you run the very real chance of losing the opportunity at this re-inclusion. It is reasonable to review the steps of how to escape a Trap before we talk about intercepting a Hail Mary.

1. Clarify the meaning of the Hail Mary so that you answer the true question rather than a perceived one. This is even more important for a Hail Mary, as it is often an unusual question that you may not have heard in previous sales campaigns.
2. Acknowledge the business importance of the request to truly understand the driving reason and its relationship to this opportunity.
3. Respond to the request with a well-thought-out answer.
4. Set a Trap that is similar to the request since you now understand that this issue is important to the prospect.

The best way to prevent this re-inclusion is to understand when the company is going to eliminate vendors. Chapter 4 does a good job of explaining these decision points, and you need to map them to your selling. Several days or weeks ahead of this event, you should start laying Traps for the losers. These Traps are to reaffirm the validity of the prospect's process and make sure the Decision Owner holds firm.

Sometimes the Hail Mary works, though. Sometimes the eliminated vendor can influence someone with the power to put the vendor back into the process. This will obviously show the strength of that vendor, the vendor's Champion, and the strength of your own Champion. It also shows the strength of the Decision Owner.

At this point, you need to turn this into a positive for you. You need your Champion to challenge the integrity of the process and justify to you that you should continue. If the previously excluded vendor is being put back into the pool, then do you really have a chance to win? What happens when you beat that vendor again? Will the outside influence allow their favorite vendor to ultimately lose again? If so, then why re-include them now and waste everyone's time?

The re-inclusion will show everyone's hand. You will find out who your true Enemies are and who your true Friends are in the organization.

Competing With A Gatherer

If you are competing with a Gatherer then you have another critical decision to make: Can you beat her?

Regardless of your skill or the advantages of your product, the Gatherer will always have the upper hand if she can stay a close second. Part of the Gatherer's strength is the prospect's desire to standardize on solutions from one company. She will play that desire against you if you are ahead. This can be an extremely strong Trap that you may not be able to survive!

As with many Traps, this one may backfire. To counter the Gatherer's Trap, you must risk everything by confronting the Decision Owner on this issue. You must ask him if you prove your product to be better than the Gatherer's product if you will be awarded the sale. This conversation will have three possible outcomes:

1. The Decision Owner will commit to you that the best product will win the sale. Further, the Decision Owner will explain the decision-making process. This letter will explain to you the decision-making criteria. You will then send him a letter documenting the conversation and the commitment or preferably, he will document the commitment to you in writing. This will aid you later in the process if the Administrator tells you that they cannot award the sale to you because they already have a relationship with the Gatherer.

2. The Decision Owner will confide in you that they really are not happy with the Gatherer's products and not interested in growing the relationship. You must use this against the Gatherer. You will need to use this Trap repeatedly in the evaluation process. You must follow this information with more questions regarding your ability to displace the Gatherer in her other implementations. This will have the added benefit of putting the Gatherer on the defensive as she tries to strengthen her existing implementation.

3. The Decision Owner will tell you that you need to be significantly ahead of the Gatherer to offset her advantage. If this is the case, then you will need to evaluate if this is possible. You will then need to go through the same thought process described above and decide if you should conserve your resources and withdraw from the evaluation process.

Finally, you must understand that the Decision Owner is not personally invested in your company and therefore may not tell you the complete truth regarding the Gatherer. This could be due to blatant lying or it could be from lack of authority.

While I never condone a salesperson lying to a prospect, I do acknowledge that a prospect may lie to a salesperson. It is not a perfect world and as successful salespeople, we must always worry that we are being lied to. This lie may be blatant, or it could be innocent, and the Decision Owner doesn't really have the power and influence to make the assertion.

It is advisable to not completely trust a Decision Owner on any conversation regarding a Gatherer. You must assume that the Gatherer has influence beyond the immediate Decision Owner. Therefore, a higher authority may politically override the Decision Owner. This is a prime example of why you need your Power Matrix covered earlier in the book. You need to understand how others influence your Decision Owner in the organization so that you can neutralize those threats or at least understand your risks.

The Enemy Of My Enemy May Be My Friend

If you are competing with a Gatherer, then you need to encourage as many B or C competitors to become involved as possible. This may seem like a strange tactic, but it is very effective. Having a large number of competitors will disrupt the Gatherer's strength on the account and cause her to deal with more competition than she is used to fighting. The Gatherer will likely be your most difficult competitor so using the strategy of 'the enemy of my enemy is my friend' can be quite effective.

It is fairly easy to introduce more competition. As you engage with the prospect, the articles that you share should have lists of competitors or perhaps be industry review articles. Even articles that include quotes from multiple competitor executives will drop the hint that the prospect should engage with more potential vendors.

Adding more competitors also increases the likelihood of delaying the decision. This is potentially a valid strategy when up against a Gatherer. A longer sales cycle can give you more time to include others in the decision who are not necessarily aligned to your embedded competitor.

Competing With A Hunter

The most effective technique for a Hunter to use is a delay. She will intentionally try to add events or activities that not only delay a decision but also give her opportunities to make relationships.

Hunters, in particular, often do not have the time management skills needed to work many different accounts in different stages. You may consider having one of your existing friendly prospects ask the Hunter to come to them to give them an update on their product, services, or company. This may distract the Hunter and cause them to not pay attention to the real opportunity that you are competing with them for. If they do a poor job with your friendly prospect as well then you may have further solidified your relationship with that prospect also.

▼▼▼▼▼▼▼▼▼▼▼▼▼▼

An effective way of competing with Hunters is to keep them doing busy work. This prevents them from being proactive and ties them up on this account to prevent them from attacking another account.

▲▲▲▲▲▲▲▲▲▲▲▲▲▲

Stress All Of The Education Done In Advance Of The Deal

You will need to outwork a Hunter to beat her. A Hunter is trying to steal your deal by coming in late and showing a last-minute equality or competence. The easiest way to do this is to be "high and wide" in the account. Use the Power Matrix to create differentiation.

With the Power Matrix, you should have been educating the prospect on the benefits of your product and company. This multi-person education process will allow you to differentiate against a newly added Hunter. As soon as you see new competitors being added to the mix, you need to reach back out to each and every person that you previously talked to earlier in the sales campaign. Your longer-term relationship with these decision influencers will benefit you against a new competitor.

Stress Your Company Knowledge

During your renewed conversations with the Power Matrix, you must reinforce your understanding of the prospect's business and its goals. You have talked to nine or twenty-five other people (depending on the size of the deal), and you must use those conversations to show that you understand how to help the prospect achieve its goals.

Your knowledge of the prospect and the organization's goals will differentiate you from a Hunter. A Hunter is trying to short-circuit the process and only speak to a few influential players. You must expand the importance of a large number of people to counteract this strategy.

Finally, the Hunter will often deploy a delaying strategy. She will suggest visits by executives and product line leaders. She will immediately try to renegotiate the deliverable timetables. Your prospect will be tempted to accommodate these requests in the goal of being complete. However, this delay strategy means the Hunter is behind. This means that you are ahead and you must close. It is now time to put deadlines on your actions. It is time to show that the customer is wasting precious time in waiting and it is time to start implementations.

Competing With A Farmer

A Farmer has great relationships with a few people at your prospect. In fact, the Farmer will often have better relationships than you have with those few people. You need to assume that a Farmer is the best friend of everyone he knows at the prospect. It is futile to try to be a better friend with those people.

The Farmer tries to win the entire deal with those great relationships. His strategy is to count on his friends to shepherd him through the decision process. He hopes that his strong relationships will allow him to position his product competitively.

The strategy to be a Farmer is to be valuable to more people rather than trying just to be more valuable to a few people. The Power Matrix will serve you well in this effort. The Farmer will tend to be aligned in one vertical of the Matrix, so you need to be wider than him.

Essentially, you can assume that the Farmer has eliminated one of your departments in your Power Matrix. If you are working on a small deal and have covered a 3x3 matrix of influencers, you can assume that the Farmer has dominated one of those departments. The Farmer is an expert at getting someone to trust him, as that is his skill. Therefore assume that if the Farmer is regularly meeting with one of the departments (or columns in your Power Matrix) that you have probably lost that department.

In fact, if you feel that a Farmer is competing effectively with you, you may want to widen the Matrix. In Chapter 5, I explained that you should have a 3x3 matrix in small deals or a 5x5 matrix in larger deals. If you see competition from a Farmer, you may want to expand this a column or two. In the event of a small deal, you may want to make your Power Matrix a 4x3 or a 5x3. In other words, you may want to know more vertically-aligned influencers. This can effectively strengthen your position.

For larger deals, you may want to expand beyond the five verticals. You may want to expand out to six or seven departments. I grant that this can be a large amount of work, but it may be necessary, and you don't get a commission check for a lost sale.

Chapter 8 – Negotiating And Closing

"You are what you repeatedly do. Excellence, then, is not an act, but a habit."

- Aristotle

Negotiating the final terms of the sale and closing for the order becomes anti-climactic for a Trapper. By the time the opportunity gets to this stage, it is almost a foregone conclusion that the order will be awarded to the Trapper.

This chapter focuses on the continuation of earlier Traps into the closing process. This prevents any difficulty in closing the order. It also encourages the salesperson to be prepared to 'walk away' from an opportunity that suddenly ignores the entire decision process to date so that the buyer can extract more concessions.

While closing is the final step of a successful sales campaign, it is the step that you have been setting up the entire time. Everything that you have done before now leads to this step. As you understand how you are going to close and negotiate the deal, you establish appropriate Traps to assist you.

The best way to have Traps help you is to constantly develop metrics that position your solution as beneficial to the organization. If you have metrics that show cost savings or an income generation, it is much easier to win the negotiation.

The metrics that you develop have to tie back to the potential buyer's goals. This is the only way to have Win-Win negotiations and not: "I win, and I don't care if you do or do not win."

Taking the time and forethought to prepare for the "I win and you must also win" negotiation enables the very best outcome. Even in those circumstances where there will be no ongoing relationship, a win-win is required. Remember that one of the three values that you sell is you. Your credibility and professionalism are at stake with each deal you negotiate. You don't want a situation where you ruin your ability to leverage this organization to enhance your reputation.

Before you get to the negotiation stage, outline your goals for a good outcome as well as the goals that the other party wants to achieve. Understanding these and/or attempting to determine the other parties' expectations will help you think more deeply about important considerations.

Do You Want This Order?

It is important that you understand your limits during the negotiation. Your limits are the lines in the sand that you will not cross. Ultimately, when will you walk away from the negotiation table? When is it a better deal for you to not win than to win?

What are the financials and implications of getting a deal versus not? Clarifying how the deal will help your financial goals will help you better understand the pricing position. Remember that your final price may have more implications than just this one transaction. Do you want to set the price level for all future transactions? If you do not win the order, will you have over-capacity elsewhere?

What are you willing to give up during the discussion? Always remember, though, if you give something away, you should always ask for a tangible something in return. This is commonly called "quid pro quo" (a Latin phrase meaning "something for something") in the industry. Quid pro quo is the general term for any transactions that exchange goods or services for money, but in this case, it is for non-financial agreements that may affect the health of the relationship.

Have you analyzed the people you are dealing with? Do you understand the role they play in the decision process? Only when these items have been listed can you prepare your approach and your responses. Remember, if they have played games before they WILL do it again.

Thinking about not getting the deal done may be painful, but this part of the preparation is critical. It forces you to look into the real circumstances of why you are at the negotiation table. If this deal MUST be closed, how are you going to recover if you get derailed?

Your positional power in this sales/buyer deal is also important to understand. If you are one of many sellers and the buyer is large and can offer substantial business levels, then you are likely going to negotiate at your cost. If the tables are turned, and you are one of a few sellers, and the buyer has little leverage, it will be a price-based negotiation.

Finally, if this is an existing client and you are trying to do some extra work with them, maybe a simple price increase, then list out the historical events and key metrics if appropriate. Be sure that both parties view your metrics as the same before you try and discuss new items. Without this agreement, the new discussion will be derailed and overtaken by history.

Discounting To Win The Deal

In some organizations, it is required to discount to get to street pricing. Those companies will have a "list" price that is significantly higher than the market or street price. There are many logical reasons for this, and I am not going to condemn the practice. Usually, this strategy is sound and often is tied to legal standards or previous contracts.

In all cases, there is a street price or market price for your product. This is the price that most of your transactions will use. It is also the price at which the majority of your A competitors sell their product. In some cases, this will be the list price, but many times it will be at a discount, depending on the practice of your company.

Think of street pricing as similar to buying a new car - few people pay the price on the sticker. Instead, they get a slight discount in the form of a negotiation or by receiving a rebate. In the selling of new cars, an entire online community has sprung up to give you insight into the street pricing of any given car based on its options and its location.

The goal of any salesperson should be to at least hold your street price. In fact, you need to sell your products at a premium. You are worth a premium. You have controlled the selling process and eliminated your competition. This elimination process was for cause, and therefore you should be rewarded for that effort.

Your price will be higher and should be higher simply because you have established a premium for your product over the competition. Because they were eliminated, their product is less valuable than your product. The entire selling process was establishing your premium over the competition.

The Inevitable Discount Request

Even though you have effectively eliminated all competition, do not be surprised if you are asked for a discount. This isn't your buyer being mean or inconsiderate. It is simply the reality that asking for a discount is painless. If the buyer doesn't ask for a discount, then you will never have to give a discount.

It may be necessary that you have to give a gratuitous discount. There are many reasons to give a small discount, and most of them are tied to industry practices. Even in an industry that demands a small discount, you need to position this discount for maximum value.

The most crucial part of discounting is not to call it a discount. You need to position your discount as paying for a favor or service. Never position your discount as a discount. Instead, all discounts should be in exchange for services given by the customer to the vendor.

It is also possible that you will have to offset a built-in product deficiency with a larger discount. Remember earlier we discussed that some Traps hurt because they are real. It is possible that your product is missing some benefits in a particular area. There are times when you will need to have an honest and frank discussion about this deficiency with your Champion and Coach. In those cases where your deficiency is relatively minor but still important, you may need to discount your product more to offset the lack of benefit to the prospect. The interesting thing about doing this is that you can frequently limit your entire discount to just this one area and often you will be able to sell your product at a price that is reasonably close to street level pricing.

Fighting No Decision

In sales, we are constantly faced with the dreaded No Decision. We all hear delay tactics and brush-offs. We keep asking for the order and trying to get our prospects to make a decision, yet they give us no answer other than

- "I have to think it over."
- "We have to wait for the new budget cycle."
- "Our new manager has to get settled into her new position before we can proceed with this."

This can be very frustrating. It is often the most frustrating part of selling. It is likely more frustrating than prospecting for new business.

It is much better to get an answer of "No" than to receive no answer at all. When someone says "No," then we know where we stand with that relationship. We can either walk away or counter with methods that attempt to reverse the decision.

So what are we supposed to do when we get no answer from a prospect? There's a fine line between walking away too soon and hanging in there too long. If we walk away too soon, we could be missing out on an opportunity. If we stay too long, we could be wasting valuable time and resources.

There are several ways to handle a prospect's objections and stall tactics. Assuming you've addressed objections but are still faced with indecision, you need to decide how credible the delay is.

Ask yourself the following questions:

- Have you already built a relationship with the prospect where you can trust him?
- Have you covered everyone in your Power Matrix? If you have only done a Small Power Matrix, do you need to expand it to a Large Power Matrix?
- How comfortable are you with the eventuality that the prospect will ever make a final decision of yes or no?
- Have you laid out an effective Vision Goal and does the prospect agree it is correct?
- Have you created an Issues Alignment chart for each person on the Power Matrix?

Many times you are getting a non-answer only because you simply haven't built your case. Your non-answer isn't indecision but instead is a lack of urgency by the prospect. Usually, that lack of urgency is because the prospect doesn't agree with your Vision Goal or there is someone else in the organization who remains unconvinced.

A non-answer on the offer usually means there was no opportunity. Whenever the prospect defaults to a No Decision, you need to examine whether you have effectively followed the Trapper Sales Methodology. It is tempting to skip steps and take shortcuts. There are no shortcuts in sales.

Collecting The Reward

Winning the deal is important. You will receive more financial security in the form of loyalty from your employer as well as increased commissions. However, you need to put an internal incentive into your mind to help you through the tough times of the next sale.

▼▼▼▼▼▼▼▼▼▼▼▼▼▼
Celebrate any victory over 5% of your annual quota.
▲▲▲▲▲▲▲▲▲▲▲▲▲▲

We all know that there are times in the selling process that are just plain frustrating for the sales team. The prospect may be asking questions that are very basic. Or the prospect may be making it difficult to create a positive relationship. Whatever the frustration, it is helpful to have a little extra incentive to motivate you through the tough times.

Think of a sprinter in a track and field event. The sprinter wants to win so that her team will get more points and win the event, but that is not the sprinter's only motivation. The sprinter is also motivated to beat her personal best time. The sprinter is also motivated to beat her arch-rival in the lane beside her. The sprinter is motivated to hear the cheers of the crowd and the accolades of her teammates, friends, and family.

This personal motivation is used by the sprinter to fight through challenging practices. She visualizes winning the race when she is trying to do that last painful lift in the weight room. She visualizes the first place award when she practices her first three steps over and over for hours. She doesn't visualize the team winning; she visualizes her personal win. It is the personal win that inspires the extra effort and sacrifice.

The sprinter's job is to score more points for the team. That is why she is on the team. While she wants the team to do well, she also wants to do well and needs her own motivation. You are like the sprinter, and it is your job to sell your product. Selling the product keeps your company afloat and helps to employ all of the people in the company. Just selling the product and having your company do well may not be enough to fight through those challenging sales calls.

You should develop your personal win award. You may think that your manager should do this for you, but if there is anything that you should have learned in this book, it is that you cannot depend on others for your success. You need to create the personal win that will motivate you to push through those tough sales calls.

I suggest that the personal win is something that you greatly enjoy, but you can live without it on a daily basis. Set aside one activity that you will only do when you have won a deal of 5% or 10% of your annual quota. Once you have identified that win, never do it without closing a deal. It is your trophy activity.

It is not possible for me to select your trophy activity. I can give you suggestions based on what others have selected. None of the following list may be personally motivating for you, but hopefully, it will give you some ideas.

- Massage (or if you get massages frequently, a stone massage)
- Dinner at a specific restaurant that you only go to when you win a big deal
- A trip to the casino
- Tickets to the local sporting event (or maybe better tickets than normal if you regularly attend)
- A specific bottle of wine (or other favorite beverage)
- A round of golf at a specific course (make sure it is not your regular course - you want this to be a special treat)
- A new handbag or pair of shoes
- Tickets to a show

It is worth repeating the one rule regarding deal trophies. Whatever activity you select as your trophy, make it an activity or purchase that you never do unless you win a deal. So if you chose to purchase a pair of shoes, a handbag, or attend a show, perhaps it is a certain style of shoes or handbag, or it is shows that are only at a specific venue.

After a couple of wins and the resulting reward, you will be able to visualize yourself doing this activity again when the sales process is challenging. You will be able to fight through the tough times because you know that there is a trophy at the end.

Hopefully, you are in sales because you have the drive to provide for yourself and your family with the wealth that few other careers offer. Successful salespeople are among the highest paid people in the community. While doctors and lawyers may get all the accolades and envious discussions, a successful salesperson can often generate more personal wealth than nearly every other profession.

While salespeople can be highly paid, it is not unusual that salespeople have very uneven paychecks. Even with the skills that I teach in this book, you will not close massive deals every two weeks. In fact, if we define a large deal as being at least 10% of your annual quota, you will probably only close five to ten large deals per year. This requires a bit of wealth planning for the successful salesperson.

I could probably write an entire book on managing your finances (in fact, I have: *The Confident Investor*), so I am not going to spend more than a few sentences here. It is important that your closing strategy includes your strategy on the commission. I have said multiple times in the preceding chapters that you are one of the three things that the customer is buying, specifically:

- Your product
- Your company
- You

We know the rewards for everyone else in the sale, but you need to identify your reward.

My first suggestion before you do anything with the commission (after paying any applicable taxes) is to donate a portion of the commission. Do it immediately, before you get other priorities. Taking care of your fellow man is one of the most important charters of well-to-do professionals. Many people do not have the blessings and capabilities that you enjoy, and it is your responsibility to make their life easier.

While everyone has different targets for sharing their wealth with others, I strongly suggest that you set 10% as your goal. Giving 10% of your income to charity has been a template for caring for others since words were written. It is a time-honored tradition and has proven to be completely within the capability of anyone who has been given great gifts in life.

The next thing that you should do with your big commission check is to pay yourself. Regardless of your effort, you will hit a dry patch of revenue. Maybe the industry or locality that you are in will suffer a recession. Maybe your company will fall behind the competition, forcing you to find new employment. As with everyone, eventually, you may want to not sell every day and may want to sit on a beach, visit family, climb mountains, or tend a vineyard. No matter how much you love your job, someday you will want to do something more enjoyable.

To save for that rainy day or even that day when you don't want to work, you need a plan. That plan is well described in my book *The Confident Investor*, but it starts with paying yourself first. It starts with taking 10% of that commission check and putting it into an account where that money will work for you and grow. My book *The Confident Investor* can help you make that money grow more quickly than most methods, but the first step is to set the money aside.

▼▼▼▼▼▼▼▼▼▼▼▼▼
Immediately invest 10% and immediately donate 10%.
▲▲▲▲▲▲▲▲▲▲▲▲▲

So right now, before you get that check for the big deal you are working on, prepare for the commission. Find two or three charities that you can support. Find out how to efficiently donate to them. You don't need to set up a trust or anything fancy - just find out where to send the check. If you don't have a specific charity, consider a donation to your neighborhood church or The United Way.

After the charity has been found, open up an investment account. There are multiple brokerage companies that you can consider and my book *The Confident Investor* will help you find them. If you don't want to buy my book, consider opening an account with Fidelity, TD Waterhouse, Schwab, or Scottrade.

Develop Momentum

After winning a big deal, you may experience a massive emotional high. You have worked hard and achieved success, so this is a normal feeling. You may feel so excited about your recent achievement that you almost feel like you could sell anything to anyone.

This feeling of emotional invincibility is normal. You need to take advantage of it and use it to your benefit. Your optimism and confidence have been pushed to new heights, so you need to use that feeling to achieve more success.

When you have won a new big order and you are filled with massive confidence, you need to use that confidence to move your other opportunities closer to a successful conclusion. The best way to take advantage of this is to ask for a reference story and for introductions to others.

Reference Stories

You should leverage your customer's success with your product to influence other prospects. While your new customer probably hasn't been overly successful immediately after the order, they probably have a great feeling about their decision to buy your product. You need to lay the groundwork for them to be a reference customer now, before the ink is dry on the contract.

At some point in the future, they believe that they will be successful and achieve many of their goals. This is why they acquired your product. This is the time to leverage that good feeling for a reference commitment at some point in the future.

Obviously, if the implementation in the future is not optimal, you won't use them as a reference. However, that is the assurance that you need to give to the new customer - your future use of them as a reference is tied to their future success with your product. By asking them to be a reference, you are tying your future to theirs.

Tying the future success of both parties together is the pitch that you should be making right now. You need to explain to them that if they agree to be a reference story to others in the future, you will be obligated to work extra hard to make sure they are happy in the future. This is a win-win situation.

It is important to tie down this commitment early after the purchase simply because it allows both you and your customer to work toward a common goal. Perhaps you should even target a future annual user meeting or convention for the customer to present their success.

Introductions

Your customer knows people in other companies in their industry. Those companies are likely in your Sweet Spot for prospecting. Now is the time to request an introduction.

By now, you are LinkedIn to the various Decision Makers within your new customer. Even if they didn't accept a LinkedIn invitation from you when they were a prospect, they will likely do so now. You should refresh this relationship and make sure every person on your Power Matrix is in your LinkedIn network.

Once you have a LinkedIn network relationship with a person, you can peruse their LinkedIn network connections. It will only take you a few minutes to find all of the connections at other Sweet Spot companies. You should then ask these connections for an introduction.

Obviously, not every person you ask for an introduction will respond positively. However, there is no better way to network into companies that you have targeted than an introduction. Taking the few minutes necessary to request these introductions could be extremely profitable for you.

Develop More Metrics

Your reference requests will be more powerful if you can develop strong success metrics. It is very easy to capture metrics if you follow a very simple process that I call PONI (pronounced "pony"). PONI is an acronym that stands for:

- Project
- Old
- New
- Impact

Project: A good reference should have a name associated with it. You want this reference to have significance in casual conversations, so you should tie it to a named project within the organization. Names such as "Project MARS" or "SCMP - Supply Chain Modernization Program" give the metric a way to relate to the organization. For each metric, confirm if it was part of a project or program name and then never refer to the metric without that name.

Old: You need to compare the new success metric to a baseline. That baseline is the old way of performing the task. Every good metric has a quick explanation of how the organization used to perform the task or at least the amount of effort that was required to perform the task.

New: The new way of accomplishing the goal is enhanced by using your product. As part of the metric discussion, explain how the new method works for the organization and how it saves them more time or money.

It is possible that the new method is a success due to something other than time or money; however, you should try to relate it to one or both of those standards. For instance, the new method may be best described as allowing higher precision, greater repeatability, or faster speed. If that is how the customer thinks of success, that is fine, but you should dig in a little deeper to find a time or money correlation.

Impact: Any good metric has an impact on the business. This impact may not be the difference between profitability and loss, but that is not the point. Businesspeople understand that much of the daily effort in life is simply to make constant and small improvements in the business.

Account Management

The most powerful salesperson is a combination of a Trapper and a Gatherer; in other words, a Trapper who is still working with an existing customer and is tasked with growing that relationship for further revenue opportunities.

When I first described the types of salespeople back in the first chapter, I said that a Gatherer naturally has the trait of another salesperson but acts differently due to the relationship with the account. When that natural trait is a Farmer or Hunter, the Gatherer has some severe innate weaknesses. However, a Trapper who becomes a Gatherer can be incredibly powerful.

Your new customer now has a special relationship with you. They bought from you. At least some portion of the customer has a good feeling about all three aspects of your relationship: your product, your company, and you. You need to capitalize on that good relationship and make it stronger and more profitable.

We just finished discussing gaining metrics and references to impact your business at other companies. These same references and metrics are even stronger within the new customer. It is time to cultivate these references and document the metrics so that you can become a trusted adviser to a larger portion of the customer.

Use the new relationship to get higher and wider for your next deal. Now is the time to set yourself up to sell more. You need to challenge yourself to think of another goal you can accomplish within the new customer. Do you have other products that you can sell them? Can you sell them training and consulting? Can you apply your existing product to a different use case that has applicability to other goals that the customer is trying to achieve?

Congratulations on closing the deal. Your phone is ringing. It is your management asking you about the next opportunity on your forecast. They know you are successful and need you to continuously deliver. It is time to apply your Trapper techniques to deliver more revenue at this customer and every other customer in your territory.

Appendix A – Roles In Decision Cycle

In every buying process, each of these roles exists and needs to be identified. If you do not identify these people, then you can assume that you are missing a portion of the decision-making process and therefore you are putting yourself at risk of losing the order. Each role also has their strength in the organization. As a Trapper, your goal is to add people to the buying process who are friendly to you and reduce the influence of your enemies.

Roles

Discoverer - This person first understands that there is a problem. This person may fade into the background later in the decision-making process or may continue to be a factor. The Discoverer will rarely be a Sailboat as they are the type of person that looks for problems to solve.

Competitor - This should be obvious, but eventually a Farmer (rarely a Hunter) will forecast an opportunity and state that there is no competition. This declaration is never accurate. The competition may be very weak or way behind, but it is always present at the time of the purchase. No organization will decide without weighing options, and therefore it is foolish to think that there is no competition. At the very least the problem has competition from other issues receiving the attention and resources of the organization. Organizations always have the option of choosing the most dominant competitor around: 'No Decision.' Trappers measure our effectiveness with competition in two ways: what is the likelihood of the purchase and what is the chance that we will win the purchase decision.

Decision Owner - This person is the champion for solving the problem for the organization. This person may or may not be involved in many of the steps but usually has the power to veto any sub-decision from the group. This person can also dramatically influence the outcome of the decision by stacking the deck against or for a particular solution. Just because the Decision Owner is the champion for the problem, do not think that he is your champion.

Decision Group - This is an entity containing one or more Players. They discuss, evaluate, and make a particular decision. There are two logical Decision Groups in each Decision Triangle - the Primary and the Confirming.

Influencer - this is a person that is not an acknowledged member of a Decision Group, but by desire, design, or proximity they can affect the thinking of Players in Decision Groups. Quite often, you can have Influencers act upon a Decision Group if you have little control of that group or you think that they are going to make a decision that is not in your best interest. Often, Administrative Assistants are some of the most powerful Influencers in an organization.

Daddy Warbucks - This person will have to make the ultimate choice that your solution is worth the cost to the organization. Quite often, this person is the core of the Confirming Decision Group. This person must be acknowledged and understood early in the process, or the purchase will be lost to 'No Decision.

Gatekeeper - The Decision Owner uses this person to make sure that the available solutions will satisfy the minimum requirements of the group as well as to ensure that the solution does not create more problems for the organization than it solves. This Player can be an effective Champion but can be quite weak if the competitor has a Champion that does not play the role of Gatekeeper. More than likely, the Gatekeeper is a solid Coach since he may see your solution as causing fewer problems in the organization and therefore has a personal reason for you to win.

Player - the generic name for someone in the decision-making process. It is more appropriate to call the members of the various decision groups Players since they may not all be members of the organization but could be outside influences on the organization.

▼▼▼▼▼▼▼▼▼▼▼▼▼▼
Not all Players in the decision making process will be members of the organization. You should look for outside Influencers to affect the outcome.
▲▲▲▲▲▲▲▲▲▲▲▲▲▲

Strengths

Sailboat - This designation is someone that acts much like a sailboat. This person is always checking to see where the politically correct decision is likely to be and follows along with that decision. Occasionally, the person will put their 'rudder' down, tack into the wind, and be a leader but this is rare. By finding the Sailboats in the organization, you can often find the Leaders of the organization because the Sailboats are taking their cue from the leaders. You should track Sailboats and make sure that you know those Players that are blowing them around.

Friend - This person thinks you have the best available solution for their problem. You will not win the opportunity without this person (and it is preferable to have several).

Enemy - This person thinks you do not have the best solution for their problem. Typically, the Enemy thinks another solution is better and has aligned with that solution, although this is not always the case. The Enemy may also be against the importance of, or perhaps the existence of, the problem and therefore is against all solutions to the problem

Neutral - This person may be mistaken for a Sailboat, but differs in that they will not take any side at all. They do not care about which solution solves the problem, and they may not even care if there is a solution to the problem. Many times a salesperson will spend a great deal of time with Neutrals and not realize that there is a buying process taking place because the Neutral will not think it is important enough to mention.

Coach - A Coach is someone that will tell you how to position yourself, what is going on in a private meeting, or what the competition is doing. It is essential that you have at least one Coach for every opportunity, and it is desirable to have more than one. A mistake that many people make is to confuse a Friend with a Coach. The litmus test must be 'Did this person give me information that was not widely known and did that information give me a competitive advantage.' Many times the Friend will say, "I think that you have a great product and I hope that you win." This type of statement doesn't qualify as a Coach unless it is followed with something like: "If you did X then I think that your competition would not be able to match that and that would be very important to our decision-making process."

Champion - You need at least one of these to ensure victory. This is often the single most common reason for a loss - the lack of an identified Champion. As with the Coach, it is imperative that the Champion undergoes a litmus test. The best standard to use is: Will this person stand up in a meeting and say that the organization must choose your solution and, if not, the Champion will resign from the organization or at least appeal the decision to the highest level of the organization, effectively putting his career at risk.

You will find that there is a relative strength to this person compared to the Champion for your competitor. It is possible for you to have a Champion that is not as powerful as the Champion of your competitor. This "mine is bigger than yours" battle can be critical in the final stages of the process. In this case, you must ask yourself an additional question to the one above: provided that my Champion and my competitor's Champion put their careers at risk, which person would the organization rather lose as a result of this decision. Also, the Champion of your competitor is your Enemy.

Appendix B – Decision Process Action List

A successful Trapper will plan a strategy for the entire buying and selling process. The following checklist will assist you in creating this strategy. Many times an action item will be preceded several steps earlier with a planning action item so that you are effectively prepared by the time the prospect arrives at that step. You will note that many of the earlier action items repeat for the entire process, this simply underscores their importance. It also makes it easier in the final stages since all you have to do is to make sure that nothing is changed. This is why the Trapper Methodology tends to make the closing process easier – you have done most of the hard work in the early stages, then the wins come much more often, and soon they will start to get bigger.

New items are bulleted with an arrow and items that appeared on a previous step are marked with a checkbox.

Discovery Stage

1. Discover - Individual at the prospect realizes that there is a potential problem or missed goal.

- ➤ Understand organization goals and how this project relates to those goals.
- ➤ Identify Discoverer's friends and confidants.
- ➤ Develop Friendship Traps with Discoverer.
- ➤ Develop Power Matrix and communications plan.

- ➢ Identify potential competitors.
- ➢ Search for any Gatherers in the organization.
- ➢ Build justification defense plan.
- ➢ Find candidates for first initial Decision Group.
- ➢ Develop candidate for Decision Owner.
- ➢ Create a Vision Goal for the Discoverer.
- ➢ Develop a Vision Goal for the critical people in the organization.
- ➢ Build a Vision Goal for potential Decision Group members.
- ➢ List reasons why you will win.
- ➢ List reasons why you will lose.

2. Individual Clarification - Prospect clarifies in his or her own mind the meaning of the problem or missed goal.

- ➢ Document potential problems if project does not proceed.
- ➢ Help Discoverer rationalize and justify problem.
- ➢ Find and develop potential Influencers.
- ➢ Select competitors to nominate for consideration to Decision Group.
- ❏ Understand organization goals and how this project relates to those goals.
- ❏ Identify Discoverer's friends and confidants.
- ❏ Develop Friendship Traps with Discoverer.
- ❏ Refine Power Matrix and develop communication plan.
- ❏ Identify potential competitors.
- ❏ Search for any Gatherers in the organization.
- ❏ Build justification defense plan.
- ❏ Develop candidates for the first Decision Group.
- ❏ Develop candidate for Decision Owner.
- ❏ Create a Vision Goal for the Discoverer.
- ❏ Develop a Vision Goal for the critical people in the organization.
- ❏ Build a Vision Goal for potential Decision Group members.
- ❏ List reasons why you will win.
- ❏ List reasons why you will lose.

3. Initial Communication - Individual communicates to small group other people in the organization about the missed goal.

- ➤ Influence Decision Owner that project aligns with organization goals.
- ➤ Develop strong relationship with first Decision Group.
- ➤ Develop strong relationship with Decision Owner.
- ➤ Develop Coaches and Champions.
- ❑ Understand organization goals and how this project relates to those goals.
- ❑ Identify Discoverer's friends and confidants.
- ❑ Develop Friendship Traps with Discoverer.
- ❑ Refine Power Matrix and develop communication plan.
- ❑ Identify potential competitors and build Competitive Benefits chart.
- ❑ Search for any Gatherers in the organization.
- ❑ Build justification defense plan.
- ❑ Develop candidates for the first Decision Group.
- ❑ Develop candidate for Decision Owner.
- ❑ Create a Vision Goal for the Discoverer / Decision Owner.
- ❑ Reaffirm Vision Goal with key members of the organization.
- ❑ Build a Vision Goal for existing and potential Decision Group members.
- ❑ List reasons why you will win.
- ❑ List reasons why you will lose.
- ❑ Document potential problems if project does not proceed.
- ❑ Help Discoverer rationalize and justify problem.
- ❑ Find and develop potential Influencers.
- ❑ Refine competitors to nominate for consideration.

4. Initial Impact - Small group of people does an initial impact of the problem or missed goal.

- ➤ Develop Decision Timeline with milestones.
- ➤ Predict the A, B, and C competitors.
- ❑ Understand organization goals and how this project relates to those goals.
- ❑ Identify Discoverer's friends and confidants.
- ❑ Develop Friendship Traps with Discoverer.

- ❏ Refine Power Matrix and develop communication plan.
- ❏ Identify potential competitors; build Competitive Benefits chart and strategy to beat each competitor.
- ❏ Search for any Gatherers in the organization.
- ❏ Build justification defense plan.
- ❏ Develop candidates for the first Decision Group.
- ❏ Develop candidate for Decision Owner.
- ❏ Refine a Vision Goal for the Discoverer / Decision Owner.
- ❏ Reaffirm Vision Goal with key members of the organization.
- ❏ Build a Vision Goal for existing and potential Decision Group members.
- ❏ List reasons why you will win.
- ❏ List reasons why you will lose.
- ❏ Document potential problems if project does not proceed.
- ❏ Help Discoverer, Decision Group and Decision Owner rationalize and justify problem.
- ❏ Find and develop potential Influencers.
- ❏ Refine competitors to nominate for consideration.
- ❏ Influence Decision Owner that project aligns with organization goals.
- ❏ Reaffirm strong relationship with first Decision Group.
- ❏ Develop strong relationship with Decision Owner.
- ❏ Develop Coaches and Champions.

5. Initial Prioritization - Small group prioritizes this problem of known organization issues.

- ➢ Anticipate which areas of the organization will be involved in the final decision and include them in the Decision Timeline.
- ➢ Warn Decision Owner about Gatherer's efforts to eliminate competition.
- ➢ Communicate to executives the status of small group.
- ❏ Understand organization goals and how this project relates to those goals.
- ❏ Develop Friendship Traps with Decision Owner.
- ❏ Refine Power Matrix and develop communication plan.
- ❏ Identify potential competitors; build Competitive Benefits chart and strategy to beat each competitor.
- ❏ Search for any Gatherers in the organization.

- ❏ Build justification defense plan.
- ❏ Refine a Vision Goal for the Discoverer / Decision Owner.
- ❏ Reaffirm Vision Goal with key members of the organization.
- ❏ Build a Vision Goal for existing and potential Decision Group members.
- ❏ List reasons why you will win.
- ❏ List reasons why you will lose.
- ❏ Document potential problems if project does not proceed.
- ❏ Help Discoverer, Decision Group and Decision Owner rationalize and justify problem.
- ❏ Find and develop potential Influencers.
- ❏ Refine competitors to nominate for consideration.
- ❏ Influence Decision Owner that project aligns with organization goals.
- ❏ Reaffirm strong relationship with first Decision Group.
- ❏ Develop strong relationship with Decision Owner.
- ❏ Develop Coaches and Champions.
- ❏ Develop Decision Timeline with milestones.
- ❏ Predict the A, B, and C competitors.

6. Promotion of Problem - Small group promotes this problem or missed goal to a wider audience.

- ➢ Assist prospect in writing requests to possible vendors.
- ➢ Develop understanding of other areas of organization that can or may be impacted by the purchasing from you, your competitor(s) or not purchasing at all.
- ➢ Map out all traps for prospect, competitors, and potential competitors. Include when you will use them and who will receive them.
- ➢ Should you proceed analysis.
- ❏ Understand organization goals and how this project relates to those goals.
- ❏ Develop Friendship Traps with Decision Owner.
- ❏ Refine Power Matrix and develop communication plan.
- ❏ Identify potential competitors; build Competitive Benefits chart and strategy to beat each competitor.
- ❏ Search for any Gatherers in the organization
- ❏ Build justification defense plan.

- Refine a Vision Goal for the Decision Owner.
- Reaffirm Vision Goal with key members of the organization.
- Build a Vision Goal for existing and potential Decision Group members.
- List reasons why you will win.
- List reasons why you will lose.
- Help Decision Group and Decision Owner rationalize and justify problem.
- Find and develop potential Influencers.
- Refine competitors to nominate for consideration.
- Influence Decision Owner that project aligns with organization goals.
- Reaffirm strong relationship with first Decision Group.
- Develop strong relationship with Decision Owner.
- Develop Coaches and Champions.
- Refine Decision Timeline with milestones.
- Predict the A, B, and C competitors.
- Anticipate which areas of the organization will be involved in the final decision and include them in the Decision Timeline.
- Warn Decision Owner about Gatherer's efforts to eliminate competition.

Unification Stage.

7. Initial Assignment - Initial assignment of duties to fix the problem or missed goal.

- Develop a plan to minimize the negative side effects of your solution.
- Develop, refine, and educate Decision Group members on the best evaluation process for your product.
- Include all functional areas in Decision Timeline to accelerate step 10.
- Meet potential Influencers that may effect decision. Encourage friends to join and suggest that enemies are not needed.
- Understand organization goals and how this project relates to those goals.
- Develop Friendship Traps with new Decision Owner.
- Refine Power Matrix and develop communication plan.

- ❏ Identify potential competitors; build Competitive Benefits chart and strategy to beat each competitor.
- ❏ Search for any Gatherers in the organization.
- ❏ Build justification defense plan.
- ❏ Create a Vision Goal for the new Decision Owner.
- ❏ Reaffirm Vision Goal with key members of the organization.
- ❏ Build a Vision Goal for existing and potential Decision Group members.
- ❏ List reasons why you will win.
- ❏ List reasons why you will lose.
- ❏ Help Decision Group and Decision Owner rationalize and justify problem.
- ❏ Refine competitors to nominate for consideration.
- ❏ Influence Decision Owner that project aligns with organization goals.
- ❏ Reaffirm strong relationship with Decision Group.
- ❏ Develop strong relationship with Decision Owner.
- ❏ Develop Coaches and Champions.
- ❏ Refine Decision Timeline with milestones.
- ❏ Predict the A, B, and C competitors.
- ❏ Anticipate which areas of the organization will be involved in the final decision and include them in the Decision Timeline.
- ❏ Warn Decision Owner about Gatherer's efforts to eliminate competition.
- ❏ Assist prospect in writing requests to possible vendors.
- ❏ Develop understanding of other areas of organization that can or may be impacted by the purchasing from you, your competitor(s) or not purchasing at all.
- ❏ Map out all traps for prospect, competitors, and potential competitors. Include when you will use them and who will receive them.
- ❏ Should you proceed analysis.

8. Initial Evaluation - Find possible solutions.

- ❏ Understand organization goals and how this project relates to those goals.
- ❏ Develop Friendship Traps with Decision Owner.
- ❏ Refine Power Matrix and develop communication plan.

- Identify competitors; build Competitive Benefits chart and strategy to beat each competitor.
- Build justification defense plan.
- Refine a Vision Goal for the Decision Owner.
- Reaffirm Vision Goal with key members of the organization.
- Build a Vision Goal for existing and potential Decision Group members.
- List reasons why you will win.
- List reasons why you will lose.
- Help Decision Group and Decision Owner rationalize and justify problem.
- Influence Decision Owner that project aligns with organization goals.
- Reaffirm strong relationship with Decision Group.
- Develop strong relationship with Decision Owner.
- Develop Coaches and Champions.
- Refine Decision Timeline with milestones.
- Predict the A, B, and C competitors.
- Anticipate which areas of the organization will be involved in the final decision and include them in the Decision Timeline.
- Develop understanding of other areas of organization that can or may be impacted by the purchasing from you, your competitor(s) or not purchasing at all.
- Map out all traps for prospect, competitors, and potential competitors. Include when you will use them and who will receive them.
- Assist prospect in writing requests to possible vendors.
- Develop a plan to minimize the negative side effects of your solution.
- Develop, refine, and educate Decision Group members on the best evaluation process for your product.
- Include all functional areas in Decision Timeline to accelerate step 10.
- Meet potential Influencers that may effect decision. Encourage friends to join and suggest that enemies are not needed.

9. Initial ramification - Evaluate if solutions have major side effects.

- ➤ Discourage an unstructured evaluation process.
- ➤ Educate prospect on potential implications in the organization if they do not buy from you.
- ➤ Warn prospect about potential impact on the organization if they buy from your competitor.
- ❑ Understand organization goals and how this project relates to those goals.
- ❑ Develop Friendship Traps with Decision Owner.
- ❑ Refine Power Matrix and develop communication plan.
- ❑ Identify competitors; build Competitive Benefits chart and strategy to beat each competitor.
- ❑ Build justification defense plan.
- ❑ Refine a Vision Goal for the Decision Owner.
- ❑ Reaffirm Vision Goal with key members of the organization.
- ❑ Build a Vision Goal for existing and potential Decision Group members.
- ❑ List reasons why you will win.
- ❑ List reasons why you will lose.
- ❑ Help Decision Group and Decision Owner rationalize and justify problem.
- ❑ Influence Decision Owner that project aligns with organization goals.
- ❑ Reaffirm strong relationship with Decision Group.
- ❑ Develop strong relationship with Decision Owner.
- ❑ Develop Coaches and Champions.
- ❑ Refine Decision Timeline with milestones.
- ❑ Predict the A, B, and C competitors.
- ❑ Anticipate which areas of the organization will be involved in the final decision and include them in the Decision Timeline.
- ❑ Develop understanding of other areas of organization that can or may be impacted by the purchasing from you, your competitor(s) or not purchasing at all.
- ❑ Map out all traps for prospect, competitors, and potential competitors. Include when you will use them and who will receive them.
- ❑ Assist prospect in writing requests to possible vendors.
- ❑ Minimize the negative side effects of your solution in other areas of the organization.

- ❏ Develop, refine, and educate Decision Group members on the best evaluation process for your product.
- ❏ Include all functional areas in Decision Timeline to accelerate step 10.
- ❏ Meet potential Influencers that may effect decision. Encourage friends to join and suggest that enemies are not needed.

10. Re-evaluation of duties - Add more appropriate team members.

- ➢ Add new team members to Power Matrix.
- ➢ Identify Gatekeepers and befriend them.
- ➢ Lay groundwork to eliminate No Decision.
- ❏ Understand organization goals and how this project relates to those goals.
- ❏ Develop Friendship Traps with Decision Owner.
- ❏ Refine Power Matrix and develop communication plan.
- ❏ Identify competitors; build Competitive Benefits chart and strategy to beat each competitor.
- ❏ Build justification defense plan.
- ❏ Refine a Vision Goal for the Decision Owner.
- ❏ Reaffirm Vision Goal with key members of the organization.
- ❏ Build a Vision Goal for existing and new Decision Group members.
- ❏ List reasons why you will win.
- ❏ List reasons why you will lose.
- ❏ Help Decision Group and Decision Owner rationalize and justify problem.
- ❏ Influence Decision Owner that project aligns with organization goals.
- ❏ Reaffirm strong relationship with Decision Group.
- ❏ Develop strong relationship with Decision Owner.
- ❏ Develop Coaches and Champions.
- ❏ Refine Decision Timeline with milestones.
- ❏ Predict the A, B, and C competitors.
- ❏ Anticipate which areas of the organization will be involved in the final decision and include them in the Decision Timeline.

- ❑ Develop understanding of other areas of organization that can or may be impacted by the purchasing from you, your competitor(s) or not purchasing at all.
- ❑ Map out all traps for prospect, competitors, and potential competitors. Include when you will use them and who will receive them.
- ❑ Assist prospect in writing requests to possible vendors.
- ❑ Minimize the negative side effects of your solution in other areas of the organization.
- ❑ Develop, refine, and educate Decision Group members on the best evaluation process for your product.
- ❑ Meet potential Influencers that may effect decision. Encourage friends to join and suggest that enemies are not needed.
- ❑ Discourage an unstructured evaluation process.
- ❑ Educate prospect on potential implications in the organization if they do not buy from you.
- ❑ Warn prospect about potential impact on the organization if they buy from your competitor.

11. Formal evaluation - Find the best few solutions.

- ➢ WIN THE EVALUATION!
- ❑ Understand organization goals and how this project relates to those goals.
- ❑ Refine Power Matrix and develop communication plan.
- ❑ Identify competitors; build Competitive Benefits chart and strategy to beat each competitor.
- ❑ Build justification defense plan.
- ❑ Refine a Vision Goal for the Decision Owner.
- ❑ Reaffirm Vision Goal with key members of the organization.
- ❑ Build a Vision Goal for existing and new Decision Group members.
- ❑ List reasons why you will win.
- ❑ List reasons why you will lose.
- ❑ Help Decision Group and Decision Owner rationalize and justify problem.
- ❑ Influence Decision Owner that project aligns with organization goals.

- ❏ Reaffirm strong relationship with Decision Group.
- ❏ Develop strong relationship with Decision Owner.
- ❏ Develop Coaches and Champions.
- ❏ Refine Decision Timeline with milestones.
- ❏ Predict the A, B, and C competitors.
- ❏ Anticipate which areas of the organization will be involved in the final decision and include them in the Decision Timeline.
- ❏ Develop understanding of other areas of organization that can or may be impacted by the purchasing from you, your competitor(s) or not purchasing at all.
- ❏ Map out all traps for prospect, competitors, and potential competitors. Include when you will use them and who will receive them.
- ❏ Minimize the negative side effects of your solution in other areas of the organization.
- ❏ Develop, refine, and educate Decision Group members on the best evaluation process for your product.
- ❏ Meet potential Influencers that may effect decision.
- ❏ Educate prospect on potential implications in the organization if they do not buy from you.
- ❏ Warn prospect about potential impact on the organization if they buy from your competitor.
- ❏ Identify Gatekeepers and befriend them.
- ❏ Lay groundwork to eliminate No Decision.

12. Short list - Focus on the best few solutions.

- ❏ WIN THE EVALUATION!
- ➢ Understand Administrator.
- ❏ Understand organization goals and how this project relates to those goals.
- ❏ Refine Power Matrix and develop communication plan.
- ❏ Identify competitors; build Competitive Benefits chart and strategy to beat each competitor.
- ❏ Build justification defense plan.
- ❏ Refine a Vision Goal for the Decision Owner.
- ❏ Reaffirm Vision Goal with key members of the organization.
- ❏ Build a Vision Goal for existing and new Decision Group members.

- List reasons why you will win.
- List reasons why you will lose.
- Help Decision Group and Decision Owner rationalize and justify problem.
- Influence Decision Owner that project aligns with organization goals.
- Reaffirm strong relationship with Decision Group.
- Develop strong relationship with Decision Owner.
- Develop Coaches and Champions.
- Refine Decision Timeline with milestones.
- Predict the A, B, and C competitors.
- Anticipate which areas of the organization will be involved in the final decision and include them in the Decision Timeline.
- Develop understanding of other areas of organization that can or may be impacted by the purchasing from you, your competitor(s) or not purchasing at all.
- Map out all traps for prospect, competitors, and potential competitors. Include when you will use them and who will receive them.
- Minimize the negative side effects of your solution in other areas of the organization.
- Develop, refine, and educate Decision Group members on the best evaluation process for your product.
- Meet potential Influencers that may effect decision.
- Educate prospect on potential implications in the organization if they do not buy from you.
- Warn prospect about potential impact on the organization if they buy from your competitor.
- Identify Gatekeepers and befriend them.
- Lay groundwork to eliminate No Decision.

13. Final Ramifications - Find the best solution.

- WIN THE EVALUATION!
- ➢ All traps should be set by now.
- Understand organization goals and how this project relates to those goals.
- Refine Power Matrix and develop communication plan.

- Identify competitors; build Competitive Benefits chart and strategy to beat each competitor.
- Build justification defense plan.
- Refine a Vision Goal for the Decision Owner.
- Reaffirm Vision Goal with key members of the organization.
- Build a Vision Goal for Decision Group members.
- List reasons why you will win.
- List reasons why you will lose.
- Help Decision Group and Decision Owner rationalize and justify problem.
- Influence Decision Owner that project aligns with organization goals.
- Reaffirm strong relationship with Decision Group.
- Develop strong relationship with Decision Owner.
- Develop Coaches and Champions.
- Refine Decision Timeline with milestones.
- Predict the A, B, and C competitors.
- Anticipate which areas of the organization will be involved in the final decision and include them in the Decision Timeline.
- Develop understanding of other areas of organization that can or may be impacted by the purchasing from you, your competitor(s) or not purchasing at all.
- Minimize the negative side effects of your solution in other areas of the organization.
- Develop, refine, and educate Decision Group members on the best evaluation process for your product.
- Meet potential Influencers that may effect decision.
- Educate prospect on potential implications in the organization if they do not buy from you.
- Warn prospect about potential impact on the organization if they buy from your competitor.
- Identify Gatekeepers and befriend them.
- Lay groundwork to eliminate No Decision.
- Understand Administrator.

14. Negotiation - Deciding what will be purchased.

 ➤ Negotiate from power.

- ❑ Understand organization goals and how this project relates to those goals.
- ❑ Refine Power Matrix and develop communication plan.
- ❑ Identify competitors; build Competitive Benefits chart and strategy to beat each competitor.
- ❑ Build justification defense plan.
- ❑ Refine a Vision Goal for the Decision Owner.
- ❑ Reaffirm Vision Goal with key members of the organization.
- ❑ Build a Vision Goal for Decision Group members.
- ❑ List reasons why you will win.
- ❑ List reasons why you will lose.
- ❑ Help Decision Group and Decision Owner rationalize and justify problem.
- ❑ Influence Decision Owner that project aligns with organization goals.
- ❑ Reaffirm strong relationship with Decision Group.
- ❑ Develop strong relationship with Decision Owner.
- ❑ Develop Coaches and Champions.
- ❑ Refine Decision Timeline with milestones.
- ❑ Predict the A, B, and C competitors.
- ❑ Minimize the negative side effects of your solution in other areas of the organization.
- ❑ Educate prospect on potential implications in the organization if they do not buy from you.
- ❑ Warn prospect about potential impact on the organization if they buy from your competitor.
- ❑ Lay groundwork to eliminate No Decision.
- ❑ Understand Administrator.

15. Decision - Purchase product or service for the solution to the problem.

- ➤ Where will you get your next order? .
- ❑ Understand organization goals and how this project relates to those goals.
- ❑ Refine Power Matrix and develop communication plan.
- ❑ List reasons why you will win.
- ❑ List reasons why you will lose.

- Help Decision Group and Decision Owner rationalize and justify problem.
- Reaffirm strong relationship with Decision Group.
- Develop strong relationship with Decision Owner.
- Develop Coaches and Champions.
- Refine Decision Timeline with milestones.
- Educate prospect on potential implications in the organization if they do not buy from you.
- Understand Administrator.
- Negotiate from power.

Appendix C – Decision Timeline

You, the salesperson, present a decision timeline to the customer. It is designed to have an agreement of the high-level activities between the sales organization and the prospect. It does not need to be any more complete or specific than Figure C-1 below.

There are a couple of high-level goals for a decision timeline:

- Have the prospect understand that your goal is to arrive at a decision resulting in an order. You will remember in Chapter 2 that Dave Trapper tried this and the prospect pushed back on this requirement. That is acceptable. You only want to have the conversation with a prospect that this is your goal.
- Discuss with the prospect that there will be several times you and the prospect should sit down and agree that everything is going well and both companies want to continue to invest the time and resources required to proceed to the next step. If for some reason either company feels that it didn't make sense to continue, you will shake hands and wish each other well.

The goal of the timeline is not that there will be no changes to the evaluation effort or that everything needs to be planned upfront. In fact, that also happened to Dave as he did not plan on there being an RFP in the GlueWorks sales process and he had to add it to the Timeline. Don't use the timeline to make a rigid process but use it to negotiate new items and to place proceed checkpoints before and after each of these unplanned activities.

Date Start	Date due	Event	Owner
15-Jan	4-Feb	GlueWorks needs discussion	Both Dave Trapper and GlueWorks
5-Feb	5-Feb	Decide to proceed	Both Dave Trapper and GlueWorks
7-Feb	8-Apr	Technical discussions	Both Dave Trapper and GlueWorks
9-Apr	9-Apr	Decide to proceed	Both Dave Trapper and GlueWorks
11-Apr	30-Apr	RFP response preparation	Dave Trapper
1-May	1-May	RFP due	Dave Trapper
4-May	11-May	RFP review	GlueWorks
14-May	14-May	Decide to proceed	Both Dave Trapper and GlueWorks
18-May	25-May	Review proposal	Dave Trapper
27-May	27-May	Decide to proceed	Both Dave Trapper and GlueWorks
1-Jun	15-Jun	Negotiate legal contract	Both Dave Trapper and GlueWorks
17-Jun	17-Jun	Decide to proceed	Both Dave Trapper and GlueWorks
22-Jun	22-Jun	Place order	GlueWorks

Figure C-1 Decision Timeline. All figures are also available at http://www.thetrapper.com/book_figures

About the author

Sean O'Shaughnessey has been in sales for over thirty years and has achieved or exceeded quota more than twenty-five times (so far). He has produced more than 250% of quota several times. While he has been formally trained in multiple sales process philosophies, he has always found them to be lacking. This book was started over fifteen years ago in frustration after returning from yet another lackluster sales training class by a sales trainer that could only sell sales training. Unfortunately, Sean was forbidden from publishing the book for many years due to his various employers refusing to allow him to publish the secrets to his success.

Recently, Sean joined one of the most exceptional software companies in the world, and they enthusiastically supported the finishing of the project. Of course, after so many years, this required a near re-write of the book to accommodate modern tools of the trade. Sean finished the project while still exceeding quota every year.

Sean lives in a suburb of Cincinnati, Ohio with his high school sweetheart and wife of over thirty years. They are the proud parents of three adult children.